INDIAN THOUGHT PAST AND PRESENT

R. W. FRAZER, LL.B., C. E., I. C. S. (RET.)

GYAN

Published by

GYAN

Gyan Publishing House
5, Ansari Road
Daryaganj, New Delhi-110002
Phone: 011-47034999, 9811692060
E-mail: books@gyanbooks.com

Distribution Network
gyanbooks.com
India, USA, Canada, UK, Australia, France

ISBN: 978-81-212-8668-8 (PB)
First Published, 1915

2nd Impression 2023

Printed at: Gyan Press, Delhi.

INDIAN THOUGHT PAST AND PRESENT
Author: R. W. Frazer

SEATED BUDDHA.

Frontispiece.

INDIAN THOUGHT
PAST AND PRESENT

By R. W. FRAZER, LL.B., C.E., I.C.S. (RET.)

LATE PRINCIPAL LIBRARIAN AND SECRETARY TO THE LONDON INSTITUTION, LECTURER IN TAMIL AND TELEGU, UNIVERSITY COLLEGE, LONDON
AUTHOR OF "A LITERARY HISTORY OF INDIA"
"BRITISH INDIA," ETC.

ILLUSTRATED

T. FISHER UNWIN, LTD.
LONDON: ADELPHI TERRACE

PREFACE

One result of the present War, which has aroused all India to manifest her oneness with the Empire in the defence of right and justice, will be to create in the West an increasing desire to know more, than in the past, of the underlying Thought of India, and of how she has striven through the ages to solve the problem of the Universe and of the relation of man thereto. That the indigenous Thought of India has much that is worthy of study and of preservation is evidenced by the fact that there is now before the Legislative Council in India a Bill to establish a Hindu University at Benares with Faculties in Oriental Studies and in Hindu Theology. Further, within the past few years, efforts have been made to establish in London an endowed and fully-equipped School of Oriental Studies.

I have therefore endeavoured to set forth, in as simple a manner as possible, a history of Indian Thought in so far as that Thought has influenced the aspirations, religious beliefs and social life of all thinking and Orthodox Hindus. On subjects which are still problems for future research I have given the opinions of recognized authorities. Among these problems are included the influence of Christianity on early Indian Thought, the historical connexion, if any, between Christ and the child-Krishṇa, as well as the origin of the hero, or deity, Krishṇa-Vāsudeva. I have in most cases verified quotations by reference to the original Sanskrit and Tamil texts. As this book is intended for the general reader I have not in all cases adhered strictly to scientific transliteration, especially as regards lingual and guttural nasals, when such transliteration would afford little or no aid to correct pronunciation.

I beg to acknowledge with many thanks the permission given by the Secretary of State for India and the Royal Asiatic Society to reproduce plates and photographs from official publications. My sincere thanks are also due to Dr. Ananda K. Coomaraswamy for his cordial permission to use illustrations from his Art collections and for much appreciated information. I trust that my many Indian friends, Christian, Buddhist, Brāhman and S'aivite alike, with whom I have often discussed questions of Indian philosophy, will ascribe anything in this work they consider not fully representing their views as due to *avidyā* and not to a desire to judge between the merits of conflicting modes of Thought or Belief.

R. W. FRAZER.

September 1, 1915.

CONTENTS

Contents

ILLUSTRATIONS

Illustrations

CHAPTER I

INTRODUCTION

INDIA for the past thirty centuries has brooded over the problem of the Universe. She has ceaselessly striven for some satisfactory answer to the question of the How and Whence and Wherefore of it all. Is the solution to be sought in Kantian and Gothic individualism, in which each man is a law unto himself? Or, on the other hand, can it be asserted "as a biological fact that the moral law is as real and external to man as the starry vault. It has no secure seat in any single man or in any single nation. It is the work of the blood and tears of long generations of men. It is not in man, inborn or innate, but is enshrined in his traditions, in his customs, in his literature and his religion."[1] If this be true, as an ascertained fact of science, then is it any wonder that India should cling to the heritage of her own past traditions, and seek to retain the birthright won for her by the intellectual labours and ascetic penances of past generations?

[1] "Evolution and the War," P. Chalmers Mitchell, 1915, p. 107.

Indian Thought

It has been pointed out that: "A system of belief or practice which is not indigenous—even though it is the outcome of a higher civilization developing itself elsewhere—if transplanted to a foreign soil is doomed to failure *ab initio.* If it seems to succeed for a time, its success is always more apparent than real; and in a vast number of instances the reactions are stupendous. The reason is that the old currents of belief and practice, which were hereditary race elements, continue to operate silently under the new stream of tendencies."[1] Indian thought has outwardly adapted itself to Western modes of thought, and this grafting of the new on the old has resulted in a modification, sometimes in mere semblance of modification, of much of the old which was found to be incompatible with the fundamental ideas of Western civilization. As the pressure of Western thought increased, the fear arose that it might swamp and overcome the whole of the indigenous racial and climatic elements. The fear nourished unrest, which has found outward activity in strengthening the defences of traditional customs and beliefs and in a sullen defiance of the belligerent forces of Western civilization. If the reaction is not stupendous it is at least pronounced, and when fomented has often led to political disaffection and to deplorable and senseless outrage. The war that has convulsed Western civilization brings to India a message of peace. No longer can aspiring ambitions seek to plunge India into a chaos of deso-

[1] Knight, *Mind*, 1896, "Philosophy in its National Developments."

lation. India, assured of the justice inherent in the British Empire, will await the time when she will have fitted herself to take a part in the destinies to which her patient loyalty and national thought shall entitle her. The loyalty of India has astounded those who knew nothing of her deep-ingrained nobility and chivalry, which pay a willing and grateful tribute of recognition to a nation infused with the love of justice and fair play. For those in India who care not for the Kshatriya, or warrior element of life, there is the certainty that in the future, as in the past, their religious beliefs, whatever form they may assume, will be recognized by the British Empire in India to be as much India's sacred heritages of the past as are to the West her own religious beliefs and faiths. Above all, India knows that the sanctity of her household life is as secure against intrusion as are the portals of the shrines of her deities.

In past days, "It was inevitable that, after the novelty of British rule, of the law and order and security for life and property which it had established, had gradually worn away, those who had never experienced the evils from which it had freed India should begin to chafe under the restraints which it imposed. What is disheartening and alarming are the lengths to which this reaction has been carried. For among the younger generation of Hindus there has unquestionably grown up a deep-seated and bitter hostility not only to British rule and to British methods of administration, but to all the influences of

Western civilization, and the rehabilitation of Hindu customs and beliefs has proceeded *pari passu* with the growth of political disaffection."[1] So far as philosophic thought is concerned, it is often, both in the East and in the West, merely in a state of transition from dogma to criticism leading to reconstruction. In India it has always been undergoing a process of change and growth. The history of philosophic thought in India, and of the religious beliefs based thereon, is a striking instance of the truism that "the introduction of a new type of civilization in the midst of an old one has at times touched the latter in its deepest parts. It has occasionally quickened the development of powers which have been latent for centuries."[2] Although philosophic speculation in India has advanced along her own national current of thought, under the impress of climatic and racial influences, she has never failed to absorb the best of those outside intellectual truths and spiritual ideals with which she was brought into contact, so long as they did not necessitate an abandonment of her own traditional modes of thought. Indians, who in increasing numbers are students of Indian and Western philosophies, might even hold that modern philosophic thought tends more towards the strengthening and vivifying that of India than towards its entire refutation and rejection.

India in her search for a solution of the mystery of

[1] "Unrest in India," Sir Valentine Chirol, pp. 26-7.

[2] Knight, *Mind*, 1896.

RAMES'VARA TEMPLE.

To face p. 11.

the Universe found a problem over which the early dreamers and ascetic hermits spent ceaseless broodings. It was one to which Kshatriya warriors brought the vigour of independent thought untrammelled by dogma or priestcraft. It was one which sent the yellow robes and begging dishes of Buddhist monks abroad through India, and to the further East, as symbols that the problem could only be solved in renunciation of life, which was endless sorrow of birth, life, and death. The quest brought forth the revival songs of mystic and lyric poets of the early Middle Ages, an echo of whose sweet-linked melodies reaches us to-day in the poems and prose of Sir Rabindranath Tagore: "Examples unique in our time, rare in any time, of this synthetic mysticism, a whole and balanced attitude to the infinite and intimate, transcendent and immanent reality of God, as they speak to us out of life itself, yet not out of the thin and restless plan of existence which we call by that august name."[1]

[1] "Autobiography of Devendranath Tagore," Int., p. xv.

CHAPTER II

THE VĒDAS

THE DAWN OF THOUGHT

THE earliest efforts of thought, in India, to solve the problem of the Universe are found in the Vedic hymns of an invading Aryan race. These Indo-Aryans, as they became, had left their ancestral homes—somewhere in Asia—where they had spoken a language the common source of the Vedic Sanskrit and of the modern Aryan languages of Europe. Driven, through some cataclysm of nature, or through pressure from invading forces, the Aryans journeyed with their flocks towards the further East. On their long marches amid new lands they had but little time for thought. They had to fight their way through opposing foes and gain new pasture lands for their flocks. Some 2000 or 1500 years B.C. they reached the upper reaches of the Indus and there took up their abode. Amid the plenty and rest in these fertile river valleys they sang songs of praise to their deities. These hymns were known as Brahmans, and their composers became, in later times, known as Brāhmans. In the sun-lit

INDRA.

To face p. 13.

plains of India, the torrid heat and sudden storms, the starry depths of heaven, aroused new wonder, and the hymns telling their glories grew in number. The first bands of Aryan settlers were not left long in their new homes. New and less civilized bands of invading Aryans swept down through the north-west passes and took possession of the lands along the Indus. The early Aryans were forced further East, and finally rested in the rich river valleys between the Ganges and Jumna. These new homes were known as the Midland. Here, about 1000 or 800 B.C., some 1,000 hymns were collected and compiled into the Rig Vēda, ever since known as the Hymn Wisdom of India. The Brāhmans became the hereditary custodians of these hymns, and in their memories alone retained the words of the hymns and the correct intonation of their chants. These hymns have been described as presenting "to us an earlier stage in the evolution of beliefs based on the personification and worship of natural phenomena than any other literary monument of the world. To this oldest phase can be traced by uninterrupted development the germs of the religious beliefs of the great majority of modern Indians."[1]

In the Vedic hymns the gods were simple personifications of the forces of nature. There were gods who moved in the heavens and ruled the course of the sun and myriad stars, gods who rode on the storms and lived in the friendly fire and moved

[1] Macdonell, "Vedic Mythology," p. 2.

in the waters, gods of disease and wrath. All nature was swayed by the deities who were fashioned in the minds of the people as men. Their attributes were glorified and magnified until each god in turn seems to rise, in the imagination of the poet who sings his praise, to equal rank with all the other deities. These gods, although they possessed human attributes, were deemed to be immortal. Sacrifices of burnt flesh and intoxicating Soma juice, pleasing to man, were offered to them to induce them to grant the wishes of their worshippers. Invocations to the gods to aid the Aryans in warfare and to vanquish their enemies fill the hymns of the Rig Vēda.

In the earliest thought of India it was from these deities, or personified agencies, that the Cosmos was created and held on its course. To the minds of the early Aryans the wonder-working forces of nature which they saw around them, the long dawn, the evening sunset over the far-off hills, the sudden storms and hail which devastated their cattle folds, the unknown terrors of the night, with its ghostly fears, were all manifestations of deities beyond which the mind sought for no unifying cause. The fire which was a friend to the Aryans and cleared the dense forests, driving away the lurking fever, was in itself a personal deity, Agni.

In the West, in later times, the more practical Greek Hylicists held that it was real elements, such as fire and water, from which creation arose. Thus Thales taught that all that existed sprung originally from water.

Anaximander held that all things arose from primitive matter, which underwent a process of differentiation by heat and cold. Anaximenes thought that air engendered everything, while Heraclitus was content to view fire as the symbol of the ceaseless flux of impermanence brooding over all things. In one Vedic verse the Indian conception of a cosmos seems to be almost the same as that of the Greek Hylicists, for this verse says that in the opinion of some people water was the primal source of all things, but that in the opinion of others fire was the primal element. The thought of the time, however, soon drifts back to the idea of a cosmos energized by personified agencies. It is said, in one verse, that in the beginning the waters pervaded the universe and generated fire from which the spirit of the gods arose.

The universe lay spread out before man, diversified in name and form. How did it assume name and form, and out of what was it created? Man fashions a house, and therein he abides to see a family grow up round him. Perhaps the world was fashioned as a man fashions a house, or perhaps it was created by a union of some male and female agencies. Such were the two fundamental ideas which presented themselves to early Vedic thought. How did diversity first arise, and out of what? Before diversity arose, there must have been a time, the Vedic poet[1] imagined, "When there was neither existent nor non-existent, no air, no sky above. What then held it all? Who ruled it all? Did deep waters brood every-

[1] x. 129.

where? Then there could have been neither death nor non-death. There was no division of night or day. Then all that was One breathed of itself; beyond this there was nothing. Darkness was wrapped in darkness. In that void of waters perhaps creation arose by warmth (tapas—fervent austerity or meditation). Perhaps Desire first arose. If wise men inquire of themselves they will know the birth of Being from non-Being."

The problem found no satisfactory solution, for the poet continues: "Who knows and who can tell how all arose or whence it came? The gods themselves know not, for they were born later. He in the highest heaven knows the source whence came all things. He knows if there was creation or non-creation, or perchance He knows not."

Two verses[1] ask:—

"That which is earlier than this earth and heaven, before the Asuras and gods had being,—
What was the germ primeval which the waters received where all the gods were seen together?
The waters, they received that germ, primeval, wherein the gods were gathered all together.
It rested upon the Unborn's navel, that One wherein abide all things existing."

Here is the tradition that on the waters rested the Unborn, the Nārāyaṇa, of a later period, to whose resting-place all men go, and that from the navel of Nārāyaṇa

[1] Griffith, tr. Benares, 1891, "Rig Vēda," x. 82, 5 and 6.

BRAHMĀ.

To face p. 17.

arose Brahmā, the primal Creator. The vague speculations of the Rig Vēda concern themselves with the nature and origins of these gods and their powers. In one verse, amid the praises of the gods, the question is asked: "Who are these gods and whence came they?" In another hymn the singer pauses to inquire: "Who created these gods and how were they created?" The question was evidently one which had been raised by many inquirers, for in the same hymn the challenge is sent forth: "Does *anyone* know who created the gods or how they were created?" As in Greece, in later times, questionings arose as to how changes first occurred in the primal condition of all things, and if there was any primal cause which produced this change. The question is asked, "Who has created the heavens and the earth?" and again, "Were the heavens created before the earth, how were they created, and what was the power of the god wherewith he created?"

The answer is that the gods fashioned forth the heavens and the earth just as a man builds his own primitive wooden house. Therefore the question arises: "Where was the tree and whence came the wood wherewith the world was fashioned and set firm for ever? Was it Indra, the mighty god of war, who fighting against chaos spread out the earth and propped up the heavens? Had he alone brought forth the sun and set a limit to the heavens and to the earth? On what was Indra supported, and where did he take his stand, when he created all things?"

This search after a primal cause and Creator was a search which one hymn says would never be solved, for "No one knows how amid the chaos of void and formlessness *motion* was caused from which ensued Creation." The gods, the hymn continues, "were created subsequent to this change, and even they know not how it was produced." Another verse asks what conception can the mind have of a primal condition when there was "no air, no sky, no division of day or night, no death, no immortality. What then enveloped the world? Where did it rest in the abyss of space?" The answer is that then there could only have been that which was neither Existent nor non-Existent.

This answer implies that a Beginning is undefinable and beyond the power of man to describe as Existent. It also holds that the Beginning was not a Void, for it was not non-Existent.

The regular rising of the sun and its setting first gave birth to the idea that there was some principle of causation, some law, course, or norm eternally unchanging, running through all nature and through the course of nature.

This unchanging Norm or Rule was conceived as presiding over the course of the sacrifice. It is said to regulate the return of day and night, to regulate the seasons, to be a divine truth underlying all things. A conception which was to dominate much of the afterthought of India is reached when it is said that the gods act through the occult power of Māyā, a principle which is good in the case of deities and evil in the case of demons.

Another conception which rises to importance in the after religious thought of India can be traced back to the Rig Vēda, where Faith, or Confidence, is personified and invoked by the mystery of prayer. Faith is asked to inspire faith. It is invoked at the rising of the sun, at noon, and at the setting of the sun. It is represented as a cause sufficient to kindle the sacred fire, and through faith the oblation to the deities is offered.

Not only did the ancient Vedic metaphysicians endeavour to grasp the meaning of a Beginning and of a primal cause, but towards the end of the early Vedic period, in the later hymns, they sought a principle of Unity underlying all the gods. The deities are grouped together as those belonging to the heavens and those belonging to the earth. Three deities are said to dwell in the solar regions, and seven in the heavenly spheres. Again, the gods are divided into classes, dwelling in the heavens, on earth, and in the intermediate regions, eleven gods in each, thirty-three in all. Finally, the conception of Unity is reached when one hymn says that "Wise men give many a name to that which is only One; although it is only One they call it the god of fire, or of the atmosphere, or of death." Many verses even gather all the gods together under one name of the Golden Germ, the Maker of all things, the Creator.

The gods of the Vedic period are only figuratively anthropomorphic; they have human attributes, but only as illustrative of their powers. The arms of Vishṇu are the rays of the sun, the tongue of Agni breathes out fire. "The fingers of Trita are referred to only in order to illustrate his character as a preparer of Soma, and the belly of Indra only to emphasize his powers of drinking Soma. . . . It is easy to understand that in the case of deities whose outward shape was so vaguely conceived, and whose connection with natural phenomena was, in many instances, still clear, no mention of either images or temples is found in the Rig Vēda."[1]

Each poet as he sang the praises of each god exalted the god he sacrificed to as highest above all others. This belief in individual gods alternately regarded as the highest, has been termed Henotheism. It has, however, been pointed out that this Henotheism, or the regarding of each god addressed as divinely supreme, is "An appearance rather than a reality produced by the indefiniteness due to undeveloped anthropomorphism, by the lack of any Vedic god occupying the position of a Zeus as the constant head of the pantheon, by the natural tendency of the priest or singer in extolling a particular god to exaggerate his greatness and to ignore other gods, and by the growing belief in the unity of the gods, each of whom might be regarded as a type of the divine. Henotheism might, however, be justified as a term to express the tendency of the Rig Vēda towards a kind

[1] "Vedic Mythology," Macdonell, p. 17.

VARUṆA.

To face p. 21.

of monotheism."[1] In one verse[2] the Sun is called "The life (Ātman) of all that moveth and moveth not," and in another verse[3] it is said of the Sun:

"They call him Indra, Mitra, Varuna, Agni, and he is the strong winged Garutmān.
To what is one (ēkam santam) wise men give many names; they call it Agni, Yama, Mātarisvan."

From a vague searching towards monotheism, out of the polytheism of the Vedic period, the mind again turns to a pantheistic conception of the universe, when[4] it is said of the goddess Aditi:—

"Aditi is the heaven, Aditi is mid air, Aditi is mother, father and son.
Aditi is all the gods, all classes of men, is all that has been born and shall be born."

The idea that the universe is generated by heat and light and moisture leads to the idea that the heavens and earth are capable of producing all things. The heavens and earth produced the gods, and then the gods created all things. This difficulty troubled not the imaginative mind of the early Vedic poet, who sees no difficulty in children begetting their own parents in the mystic dream of creation, for[5] "Indra begat his father and his mother from his own body." The

[1] Op. cit. p. 17.
[2] i. 115. 1.
[3] i. 164. 46.
[4] i. 89. 10.
[5] x. 54. 3. See "Cosmology of the Rig Vēda," Wallis, p. 32.

first-born of Heaven and Earth was the Sun, the Hiranyagarbha, or Golden Germ, the Prajāpati, the Lord of all things born.

In one verse[1] Prajāpati, the Lord of Creation, is addressed as Supreme Deity and as containing in himself all things:—

> "When the august waters went, receiving the germ of all and producing Fire; thence arose the living spirit of the gods. What God shall we honour with sacrifice?
>
> Who surveyed with power the mighty waters, when they received productive energy and begat sacrifice; who alone is god over the gods?
>
> Prajāpati, no other than thou art become lord over all these productions; grant us our desire when we call upon thee: may we be possessors of wealth."[2]

When early Vedic thought turned its attention from the purely cosmological view of the universe, the idea arose that just as the breath of man is that vital principle through which he lives and has his being, so likewise it was Breath which went forth in the Beginning to create all things. The Breath or Ātman was in later times to become the Self or Soul or Ātman of all things created and of man. The immanence of the universe in God is foreshadowed in

[1] x. 121. 7–10.

[2] "Cosmology of the Rig Vēda," Wallis, pp. 51–2.

the verse[1] which declares that "the Ātman, or Breath, of all that moves or moves not, is the Sun that created all things and filled the air, the earth, and the heavens."

The first and earliest place where the Ātman or Soul is held to be the psychic principle of all things is in the Atharva Vēda:[2] "Free from desire, wise, immortal, self-existent, satisfied with sap, not deficient in any respect—knowing that wise, young Soul, one is not afraid of death."

The Brahman, the power of prayer, becomes in the Atharva Vēda the cosmological principle of the universe, half personified as its soul: "Whoever know the Brahman in man, they know the most exalted One; whoever knows the most exalted One, and whoever knows Prājapati, they know also the universe."

It was these two ideas, of Brahman as a cosmological principle immanent in the universe, and of an Ātman or Soul as psychic principle underlying all things, on which were based the whole after pantheistic conceptions of a Supreme Soul as Soul of the universe and as the soul within man.

The Rig Vēda gives no trace of an early Aryan belief in Transmigrations of the soul after death. The soul (asu or manas), after death, retains its individuality, and passing by the ancient path marked out by the fathers, ascends in glorified form of the old body, to the Heaven of Yama to rejoice with the

[1] i. 115. [2] Whitney and Lanman, "Atharva Vēda," x. 8. 44.

forefathers. Of Death, Yama, it is said that "his two envoys, two dogs, four-eyed, dark-hued, insatiate, with distended nostrils, roam among the people. May they restore to us a fair existence here and to-day, that we may see the sunlight." [1]

The evidences for belief in a hell, in the Rig Vēda, are vague. There is mention of an endless abyss and of an underground darkness for the evil. The later period of the Brāhmanas gives the doctrine that good and bad after death undergo rebirths, in the next world, allotted according to their good or evil deeds in this world.

The Vedic period collected the ancient hymns of the Indo-Aryans into the verses of the Rig Vēda, and those of the Sāma Vēda, used as chants during the sacrifice, and those of the Yajur Vēda as the ritual for sacrifice. The fourth or Atharva Vēda contained many verses of the older Rig Vēda, mingled with ancient spells and charms and incantations of witchcraft.

In these Vēdas the Vedic sacrifice was the only mode of winning the favour of the gods, and the priests were the only mediators between the people and their deities. Those who give liberally to the priests are praised. Those who abstain from the sacrifice are cursed:—

"Make their wealth flee who yield us not wealth, for
through our hymns they enjoy their riches.

[1] "Rig Vēda," Griffith, Benares, 1891, vol. iv, p. 129.

Far from the sun keep those who hate devotion, for
they are godless and prosper in their work."[1]

The warrior who served the gods and rewarded the priests is said to take the food of those who worship not and his joint-family are blessed:—

"He with his folk, his house, his family, his sons,
gains booty for himself and, with the heroes, wealth,
Who with oblation and a true believing heart serves
Brāhmanaspati, the father of the gods."[2]

It is also to the Vedic hymns that the two chief gods of modern Hinduism, Vishṇu and S'iva, trace their origin.

The Vedic Vishṇu, the god of preservation of the world, is a Solar deity. As a Solar deity he was always associated with the three strides which he takes; two strides in passing over the earth, when he is seen by man, the third stride in his abode in heaven. His three strides denote the idea of the sun passing in his course through the three divisions of the universe, or else the rising, culmination, and setting of the sun.

One hymn sets forth the praises of Vishṇu, the Supreme God of Hindu Vaishnavism:—

"1 I will declare the mighty deeds of Vishṇu, of him
who measured out the earthly regions,
Who propped the highest place of heaven, thrice
setting down his footstep, widely striding.

[1] v. 42. 9. [2] ii. 26. 3.

2 For this, his mighty deed, is Vishṇu lauded, like some wild beast, dread, prowling, mountain roaming;
He within whose three wide-extended paces all living creatures have their habitation.

3 Let the hymn lift itself as strength to Vishṇu, the Bull far-striding, dwelling on the mountains,
Him who alone with triple step hath measured this common dwelling-place, long, far extended.

4 Him whose three places that are filled with sweetness, imperishable, joy as it may list them,
Who verily alone upholds the threefold, the earth, the heaven, and all living creatures.

5 May I attain to that his well loved mansion where men devoted to the gods are happy.
Fast joined to that, the seat supreme of Vishṇu the mighty-strider, is the well of nectar.

6 Fain would we go unto your dwelling-places where there are many-horned and nimble oxen,
For mightily, there, shineth down upon us the widely striding Bull's sublimest mansion."[1]

S'iva, the third god of the Hindu trinity—Brahmā, the Creator; Vishṇu, the Preserver; and S'iva, the

[1] "Rig Vēda," Griffith, Benares, 1889, vol. i.

Destroyer of the Universe—appears in the Vedic hymns as Rudra.

Rudra, in the early hymns, is similar to S'iva of modern India, as having had three mothers (tryambaka), or as born from the three-fold universe. In the Vēdas, Rudra, like S'iva, shines like gold; he has braided hair and wears a wondrous necklace; he is of red colour and has a blue neck. Rudra bears a thunderbolt, yet is auspicious (S'iva). He is said "to come from heaven, self-bright, auspicious, strong to guard."[1] He is fierce, and is associated with illness and fever. He is a slayer of cattle and a lord of robbers. Rudra as S'iva was therefore, evidently, a deity of non-Aryan folk, and was admitted into Brāhmanism only as a compromise with the beliefs and worship of powerful aboriginal foes.

The Brahman, or prayer, was in the Vedic period the hymn or invocation to the gods, the magic spell uttered by the priest at the sacrifice. Brahman was originally a neuter word derived from a verbal root meaning to grow, to spread. In course of time it came to signify the power of prayer, which spread everywhere, and eventually it became the substratum on which was based the entire universe. Every letter and syllable and word of the Brahman, or invocation, possessed a supernatural potency that placed the Brāhman, or presiding priest at the sacrifice, in communion with the deity to whom the sacrifice was offered.

This conception of the Brahman, or prayer, "as a kind

[1] Rig Vēda, x. 92. 9.

of magical invocation, possessing magical power, is one of the most ancient and highly elaborated in Vedic literature."[1]

In the later Upanishad period the Brahman, or prayer, is identified with Speech. It is said to be of the very nature of Speech: "Speech is the highest Brahman."[2] In the Rig Vēda, Speech, or the voice of the hymn, becomes personified as a female deity, Vāc, Voice, which is the voice in the wind and in the storm, the voice that rang from the heavens throughout the primeval universe. This Voice, or goddess of Speech, is held[3] not only to sound throughout the universe but to have created all things. Later, in the Brāhmanas, this goddess of Speech became the wife of the Creator, "in unison with whom and by whom the Creator accomplishes His creation, yea, Vāc, Voice, is even finally the most spiritual begetter, and now and then she is placed absolutely at the beginning of all things."[4]

In the Mahābhārata[5] it is said that the Eternal Word, without beginning or end, was created from before all time by the Self-Existent.

The conception of this sacred and revealed sound of the Vedic prayer became in time inextricably inter-

[1] Geden, "Studies in the Religions of the East," p. 237.
[2] Brih. Up. iv. 1. 2.
[3] Rig Vēda, x. 125.
[4] Garbe on Vāch and λόγος, "Philosophy of Ancient India," p. 53.
[5] viii. 533.

woven with the conception of the deity as a personification of the Brahman, or prayer, and of all knowledge. Not only in the Brahman, or prayer, do all the gods rest, but the prayer is personified as the Lord of Prayer, the Lord of Beings, the All-Maker, the Golden Germ, even as Brahmā, the personal Creator of the universe. As the Brahman, or prayer, became the personification of all creative power and of all knowledge, so likewise the Brāhmans, as composers or invokers of the Brahman, came to be considered as very personifications of all revealed lore and of all divine powers. Thence the belief arose that the "visible manifestation of the world to come, in the midst of the present world, is the caste of the Brāhmans, who have knowledge and power, who can open and shut to man the approach to the gods, and make friends or enemies for him above."[1]

The Brāhmans claimed not only a divine power, but held that divinity could only manifest itself here on earth in their own class or caste. In the Atharva Vēda the Brāhmans are hailed as "kinsmen of the gods." In the same Vēda (Book XII) curses are fulminated against anyone who reviles the Brāhmans or even touches their wealth and property. The gods are invoked: "To cut up and cast out and burn those who revile the Brāhmans; to smite them so that they may go down from Death's abode to evil places. Smite off their shoulder-blades, strip off their skin,

[1] Oldenberg, "Buddha," p. 13.

cut their flesh in pieces, wrench their sinews, burn them up. With a hundred-pointed, razor-edged thunderbolt slay them." In the Rig Vēda, the divine origin of the Brāhmanic caste is traced back to an ancient period when the common custom of early human sacrifice was in vogue. Here the gods are represented as sacrificing a giant, a being called Purusha, the source of all creation. The account[1] itself is not old, but traces back to an early period the dependence of all creation on the sacrifice. The account declares that:—

> "The man (purusha) had a thousand heads, a thousand eyes, and a thousand feet; he covered the earth in all directions, and extended ten finger-breadths beyond. . . .
>
> As a victim on the sacrificial grass they anointed the man who was born in the beginning, him the gods sacrificed. . . .
>
> When they disposed the man, into how many parts did they form him? What are his mouth, his arms, his thighs, and his feet called?
>
> His mouth was the Brāhman, his arms were made the Rājanya (or warriors), his thighs were the Vaisyas (traders and cultivators), and the Sūdra (the servile class) was born from his feet."

The Brāhmans, with divine power and magic spells, could alone gain for those who rewarded them with

[1] Rig Vēda, x. 90.

grain, cattle, or gold, prosperity here on earth and in a life hereafter ample rewards. For those who performed not the costly Brāhmanic sacrifices, there was soon to be established a belief that they were doomed to endless transmigrations of their souls into future lower and polluted forms of existences here on earth.

The time came, almost two thousand years ago, when the Law-Book of Manu held that: "Whatever exists in the universe, is all in effect, though not in form, the wealth of the Brāhmans, since the Brāhman is entitled to it by his primogeniture and eminence of birth."

The result to-day is that "the Brāhman, humble as his worldly status may be, retains an undisputed pre-eminence, which he never forgets or allows to be forgotten"; and further that "neither the triumph of Buddhism, which lasted for nearly five hundred years, nor successive waves of Mahommedan conquest availed to destroy the power of Brāhmanism, nor has it been broken by British supremacy."[1]

No priestly assumption of hereditary divinity could have won for Brāhmanic culture the victory which it won in India over primitive animism and uncultured thought. It may be a matter for doubt if any Aryan in India to-day can claim pure Aryan descent. A cultured Aryan language and literature has, however, Aryanized all North India. In South India early Jain, Buddhist, and Brāhmanic influences grafted on to the

[1] "Indian Unrest," Sir V. Chirol, p. 34.

early indigenous literature all that makes it worthy of taking a place in the record of the best that man has thought. It has been said of the Aryans in India that "perhaps no race has shown a greater aptitude for civilization. . . . After its settlement in India it advanced normally along the path of civilization. Its customs grew into laws and were consolidated in codes. It imagined the division of labour. It created poetry and philosophy and the beginnings of science. Out of its bosom sprang a mighty religious reform called Buddhism, which remains to this day one of the leading religious systems of the world. So far, then, it resembled those gifted races which created our own civilization." [1]

The social and religious life of Hindu India traces itself back to Aryan culture and Vedic times. S'iva is still the Rudra of the Vēdas, and Vishṇu is the Sun-god who strode across the heavens and firmament and earth in three strides. In social life the joint-family still survives, knit together as the type of a union wherein all of kith and kin will be united in an indissoluble union hereafter. Many in India to-day dread the idea that the social and religious life of the people is drifting away from the ancient traditions and beliefs of the past. The spiritual view of life remained India's sheet-anchor, in former days, when she lay open to the storm of alien encroaching faiths and beliefs. Her idealism makes her view the real, relatively, as of minor

[1] "Expansion of England," Seeley, p. 279.

importance. India still holds sacred her Vedic revelation, and idealizes her epic traditions and the stories telling the deeds of her bygone heroes and self-sacrificing women. The people of India still worship in their temples the memory of the early saints and sages who travailed long in piety and asceticism to attune their lives and thoughts to the spiritual that abides in the heavens and lives in the moral nature of man. To the spiritual idealism of India Western civilization brings its own heritage, and with it "a larger stock of demonstrated truth, and therefore infinitely more of practical power."

India still holds that knowledge of the spiritual has been revealed to her as much as it has been to the West, and as to demonstrated truth, the West too often loses sight of the fact that "the poetic or mystic philosopher is by no means disposed to regard demonstrated truth with reverence; he is rather apt to call it shallow, and to sneer at its practical triumphs, while he revels for his part in reverie and the luxury of unbounded speculation." [1]

[1] Seeley, op. cit. p. 283.

CHAPTER III

THE BRĀHMANAS

THE PRIEST AND SACRIFICE

THE abiding stronghold of Aryan civilization was in the Midland, in the rich plains between the Ganges and Jumna, extending as far east as Prayāga or Allahabad. It was here that Brāhmanism first asserted spiritual dominion all over India. When the hymns of the Rig Vēda were compiled in the Midland the Brāhmans, as descendants of the earlier composers of these hymns, claimed for themselves a right to be their hereditary custodians. These hymns, with their sacred chants and long-sounding words of the Vedic-Sanskrit, became, in popular imagination, capable of swaying the gods for good or evil. The Brāhman families, who alone retained the tradition of the correct chant and inner meaning of the Vedic hymn, rose to supreme influence and importance. The sacrifice to the god was valueless were a single syllable or word of the accompanying Vedic hymn falsely intoned. For centuries the Vedic sacrifices to the gods, the Vedic hymn, and the intonation of the presiding Brāhman dominated India. The welfare of kings and people depended on the efficacy of the Vedic sacrifice and on the power of the Brāhman over the ways of the gods. The whole sacrificial cult and its ritual were elaborately set forth in prose Books of Ritual, or Brāhmanas, from about 800 to 500 B.C. These Brāhmanas have been described as "the intellectual activity of a sacerdotal caste which, by turning to account the religious instincts of a gifted and naturally devout race, had succeeded in transforming a primitive worship of the powers of nature into a highly artificial system of sacrificial ceremonies, and was ever intent on deepening and extending its hold on the minds of the people by surrounding its own vocation with a halo of sanctity and divine inspiration."[1] The Brāhman, as priest presiding over the long drawn-out ritual of the sacrifice to the deities, became, in the minds of the people, the very personification of divinity and of the efficacy of the Vedic hymn. The early Book of Ritual known as the "Brāhmana of 100 Paths" says: "Verily there are two kinds of gods; for, indeed, the gods are the gods; and the Brāhmans who have studied and teach sacred lore are the human gods. The sacrifice of these is divided into two kinds: oblations constitute the sacrifice to the gods; and gifts to the priests that to the human gods, the Brāhmans who have studied and teach sacred lore."[2] Not only the Brāhman priest, but also the Vedic hymn, or Brahman, became divine, as the creative source and

[1] S.B.E., vol. xii. p. ix.

[2] S'at. Br. ii. 2. 2. 6.

primal cause of all things. The "Brāhmana of 100 Paths" declares that: "Verily, in the Beginning, this Universe was the Brahman."[1] Again it says: "In the Beginning, indeed, the gods were mortal, and only when they became possessed of the Brahman were they immortal."[2] More definite is the statement of the same Brāhmana that in the Beginning: "The Creator through austerity created first the prayer, the Brahman or Vēda, therefore the Brahman is the foundation of everything here."[3] The fifth and last books of this Brāhmana declare that the Brahman, or Vedic prayer, first created all the gods and then descended to earth and delivered all mankind into the hands of Death.

The early cosmological query of Rig-Vēda period, asking where was the tree and where was the wood out of which the world was created in the Beginning, is answered, in the Taittirīya Brāhmana, by saying that the Brahman, or Vedic prayer, was the tree and that Brahman was the wood out of which was created heaven and earth.

This early philosophic doctrine of the Brahman, or potency of the prayer, pervading the Universe as a cosmic principle is accompanied, in later time, by a doctrine of an Ātman, Self, or Soul, pervading all things as a psychic principle. This Ātman meant nothing more in early Vedic times than wind, breath, or life-breath. Ātman, by itself, has a reflexive signification meaning Self. In the "Brāhmana of 100 Paths" the Ātman

[1] xi. 2. 3. 1. [2] xi. 2. 3. 6. [3] vi. 1. 1. 8.

is said to be the Self of the Universe. It is said to reside in the heart of man and goes out as the spirit of man on death. Therefore, on death, it is said that the "part of the vital air which is immortal streams out by upward breathings."[1] The same Brāhmana teaches that: "The divine inspirers are the vital airs, for they inspire all thoughts."[2] The vital airs are also said to be "the highest thing of all this Universe";[3] they are "the gods of the gods,"[4] and "they are neither in the sky, nor on earth, whatever breathes therein they are,"[5] for "In the Beginning Prajāpati was both mortal and immortal, his vital airs were alone immortal, his body mortal."[6] Therefore it is said: "Hail to the vital airs; the over-lord of the vital airs is the Soul (mind)."[7]

With the gradual development of these two ideas of a Brahman, or creative power, pervading the Universe, and that of an Ātman, or Soul, pervading all things as Self, there is associated the idea of the Transmigration of the Ātman or Soul of man after death. Life after death, in early Vedic times, meant that the good went to the happy abode of the gods and that the bad passed into outer darkness. In the Brāhmana period there is the added doctrine that man is liable to retribution for his good or evil deeds. It is, however, only in the other world that he is doomed to repeated births and rebirths as expiations for actions done in this world. The full doctrine of Transmigration, which influenced the whole

[1] S'at. Br. vi. 7. 1. 11. [2] vii. 1. 1. 24. [3] viii. 7. 4. 21.
[4] ix. 2. 1. 14. [5] ix. 2. 1. 15. [6] x. 1. 4. 1. [7] xiv. 3. 2. 3.

life and thought of India down to the present day, is that retribution, for actions, for good or evil deeds, is not restricted to repeated rebirths of the Soul in the other world, but that the Soul must come again on earth to work out the reward or penalty which good or evil deeds necessitate.

This Indian doctrine of Transmigrations of the Soul as the result of action or Karma differs much from the animistic beliefs of primitive folk. Animism implies the transfer of man's life or spirit into other objects and involves no doctrine of retribution. Primitive folk propitiate animals (such as snakes) which are inimical to them and worship animals (such as cows) or things (such as trees) which they find serviceable. The idea thus arises that animals, or objects, are endowed with spirit life. This spirit being viewed as an entity, and having independent existence, is supposed to be capable of passing from object to object. This spirit, being attenuated, is supposed, by primitive folk, to pass from man's body during sleep, or in trance, or on death. Efforts are therefore always made to woo the spirit back to the body it is supposed to have only temporarily left. In times of excitement the spirit—generally symbolized as a dove or a butterfly or pigeon—is liable to escape from the body. Even to-day the custom survives of throwing rice during a wedding festival so as to keep the spirit, as a dove, from wandering, under unwonted excitement, out of the body of the bride. On death the church bells are tolled to call the spirit back to its former abode in the body, which rests awaiting the return of the soul at the lych-gate.

The full Indian doctrine of Transmigrations of the Soul into new existences, as retributive justice, is evidently distinct from, and was not borrowed from, the surrounding animistic beliefs of the aborigines. It is a doctrine which is not fully developed until the period of the Upanishads, somewhere about 500 B.C. So individualistic and distinctive is the doctrine that it has been held that Pythagoras borrowed it from India, which he is said to have visited before 529 B.C. There is, however, no reliable evidence that Pythagoras ever visited India. There is further no evidence that similar ideas may not arise in different parts of the world, in the minds of different people cogitating more or less on parallel lines on the same fundamental problems. There are striking resemblances between many Indian and Greek ideas which it is easier to accept as independently developed than to assume that they are borrowed one from the other. Not only is there the Indian and Pythagorean idea of Transmigration, there is also the theory of five primitive elements, the fifth being the Indian ākās'a—ether or empty space. Further, there is the common prohibition against eating beans, which is also found in many other parts of the world. There is also the common problem of the irrational number $\sqrt{2}$ which is dealt with in Indian geometry in the Sulva Sūtras. The whole question of the probability of any borrowings between India and Greece has been ably and exhaustively examined, with the result that: "It is perhaps disappointing to find that we cannot trace to India the beginnings of a philosophy which undoubtedly influenced Greece and has found a place in both the systems of Plato and Aristotle, but it is impossible to maintain that opinion in the face of the evidence for the present available." [1]

The story of a primeval Flood, as narrated in the "Brāhmana of 100 Paths," is evidently an account of a universally accepted tradition. In this account it is told how "Manu, the first of mortals, was one day washing his hands and by chance grasped a fish. In compassion, he reared the fish, and when the fish grew big it said to Manu: 'In such and such a year a flood will come. Therefore make ready a ship, and when the waters rise enter into the ship and I shall save you.' So he prepared a ship, and when the waters rose he entered into it. The fish then tied the ship to its horn and swam with the ship to yonder northern mountain." [2] The story is told in the Brāhmana to glorify the efficacy of the sacrifice, for it was only after Manu had performed Vedic sacrifices that a daughter was produced and so he re-peopled the world.

Another world-wide tradition, of the creation of the world from a Golden Egg, is also preserved in an account in the same "Brāhmana of 100 Paths." This is a tradition known not only in early times in India but

[1] Keith, J.R.A.S., 1909, p. 601. [2] S'at. Br. i. 8. 1. 4.

THE FLOOD AND THE FISH.

To face p. 40.

also in Babylon, Egypt, Phœnicia, Persia, and among the Greeks. Gomperz[1] traces the origin of the idea to a primitive thought that as the heavens are rounded like an egg there must have been an egg, in the beginning, which burst asunder, the upper part to form the heavens, the lower the earth. When this idea first arose is unknown. In Greece, in the sixth century B.C., it appears in Orphic theogony under the idea of a Mundane Egg. In the beginning of all things, it is told, Chronos, the Time principle, existed. From this Time principle matter arose, having as its basis light or fire, known as Ether. From Ether a Silver Egg was formed by Chronos. The contents of this Silver Egg was a dark mist, from which all things arose. At about the same period of time when this story of a creation was told in Greece, it was also told in the Indian Brāhmana. In the beginning there was, according to the Indian story, nothing but a sea of waters, and the waters desired ardently to reproduce. So after one year a Golden Egg was produced. This Golden Egg was broken open by the Lord of Creation, Prajāpati, after he had evolved the power of reproduction. It is strange that the Indian account says that the Creator, after having created, lamented that his creation turned against him and went from him, for having created the Asuras, or evil spirits, he knew: "Verily I have created evil for myself, since, after creating, there has come to me, as it were, darkness. Even then he smote them with evil,

[1] Gomperz, "Greek Thinkers," p. 92.

and owing to this they were overcome; whence people say: Not true is that regarding the fight between the gods and Asuras which is related partly in the tale and partly in the legend."[1]

A story is told in the S'atapatha Brāhmana of Vishṇu which shows how this god of Hinduism was associated with the sun as a personified solar deity. It is told[2] that the gods were performing a sacrifice at Kurukshetra, which was the gods' place of divine worship on earth, and: "They agreed whoever of us, through austerity, fervour, faith, sacrifice, and oblations, shall first compass the end of the sacrifice, he shall be the most excellent of us. Vishṇu first attained it, and he became the most excellent of the gods. . . . But Vishṇu was unable to control that love of glory of his; and so even now not every one can control that glory of his." The account then states that Vishṇu stood before the gods with strung bow with three arrows, and the gods dared not attack him. So the gods bribed the ants with promises of perpetual food and water, and the ants gnawed the bow-string of Vishṇu so that "the ends of the bow, springing asunder, cut off Vishṇu's head." It fell with the sound of "grn," and "on falling it became yonder sun." Then the body of Vishṇu lay stretched out to the east and Indra came and gobbled it up, so that he became possessed of the glory of Vishṇu, "and he who knows this becomes possessed of that glory which Indra is possessed of." There may be some explanation of this contest between

[1] S'at. Br. xi. 1. 6. 9.   [2] xiv. 1. 1. 4.

the gods and Vishṇu, but none is given. The account in the Brāhmana only says that Vishṇu is the same as the sacrifice, and therefore when Indra became possessed of Vishṇu he is mystically called the Great Lord, which is the same as possessed of the sacrifice.

The story is told in order to glorify the sacrifice, which rose in the Brāhmana period to be the one bond which united heaven and earth, and the sole means whereby kings and people could win the willing aid of the gods. It has been pointed out that in the Brāhmana period the Brāhmans "devoted the whole of their energies to the examination of the nature of the sacrifice, and their speculative activity took a wide range and resulted in many theories. They thus developed the doctrine of the substitution of the animal or cereal offering for the human, which, they argued, was the more primitive, and, again, they enunciated the doctrine of the efficacy of the sacrifice in the maintenance of the world." [1]

[1] Keith, J.R.A.S., 1915, p. 129.

CHAPTER IV

THE UPANISHADS

I. Theism, Pantheism, and Idealism

The sacred home of the Brāhmanic sacrifice had been in the Midland, the land stretching between the Ganges and Jumna as far east as the modern Allahabad. From their early homes in the Midland and North-west the Aryans spread far and wide over India. Warrior chieftains, of Kshatriya rank, won for themselves principalities far removed from the Midland. Powerful aboriginal rulers of contending tribes formed alliances with the Aryans and, as they increased in wealth and importance, claimed Kshatriya origin. These outlying princes and rulers of aboriginal or mixed-Aryan descent were glad to welcome to their courts Brāhmans skilled in the mysteries of the sacrifice and clever in composing verse. The Brāhmans could by their sacrifices and prayers summon the gods to the aid of their patrons. When victory was won, the Brāhman could proclaim in song the prowess of the victor and extol his deeds. The Brāhman could alone civilize the ruder aborigines, win them from their savage rites of human sacrifice and worship of crude woodland deities.

The wide gulf that lay between the aboriginal dark-skinned races and the Aryans was always in danger of being bridged by matrimonial and other alliances. The Brāhmans, intent on preserving their own claims as a divinely instituted caste, strove to strengthen the caste system so that it might form a barrier against the breaking down of social and racial differences. In South India, where, from the late arrival of the Aryans, the origin and growth of the caste system can be more clearly traced than in the north, it has been pointed out that: "The social standing of those men who had been following occupations indispensable to the well-being of the Brāhmans rose high in the long run, and they now pass for high-caste Hindus. Of course, learned Brāhmans discovered decent Hindu pedigrees for the low but highly serviceable tribes and stamped them with the seal of sanctity."[1] This division of the people, in the south, into hereditary castes not only led to incessant faction fights and feuds between caste and caste, but also to enmity against the Brāhmans. The same account gives an instance of a tribe in Malabar which still considers the entrance of a Brāhman into their houses so polluting that the houses have to be purified after such entry. On the other hand, the Pariyas, who now form 50 per cent. of the labouring class, were independent and stubborn enough to resist Brāhmanic claims, and are now considered so degraded

[1] M. Srinivāsa Aiyangar, "Tamil Studies," p. 81.

that they are not allowed to approach nearer to a high-caste Hindu than thirty yards. In cases of caste pollution it may be held that "the degree of the pollution varies inversely with the degree of adoption of the Brāhmanical customs and manners."[1] In the south, as in the north, the more powerful and influential indigenous rulers and chieftains were classed as Aryan Kshatriyas and "the Brāhmans got up for them genealogies which traced their ancestry to the sun, the moon, or the fire."[2]

Aryanism in the home of the Brāhmanic sacrifice, the Midland, had endeavoured to keep itself free from contact with the aboriginal races and to preserve its isolation by a class or caste system. So that the sacred traditions and Vedic literature should remain the birthright of the Aryans, every Aryan youth had to be received within the pale of Aryanism by a symbolic rebirth, wherein he was invested with an emblem of birth, a sacred covering or thread. He then became entitled to instruction in the Vedic scriptures, which were taught to him by the Brāhman who had invested him with a new birthright. Every twice-born Aryan was enjoined to divide his life into four ās'ramas, or periods. The first period, that of youth, had to be passed in study with his spiritual father, a Brāhman learned in the scriptures and ritual of the sacrifice. The second period of manhood had to be spent in married life, performing, under Brāhmanic guidance, the daily and occasional offerings to the gods. His life's work cul-

[1] Ibid., op. cit. p. 90. [2] Ibid., op. cit p. 61.

minated in the S'rāddha ceremonies, wherein, on the death of his father, he offered for ten days water and piṇḍas, or cakes of rice, to speed the soul of the deceased to the abode of the ancestors of the family. On the eleventh day of the S'rāddha ceremonies all entitled to rank within the family bond assembled together to present offerings to the souls of the ancestors. The round of S'rāddha ceremonies had to be repeated monthly and then yearly. In the declining period of life the ideal for all Aryans, and the duty of all Brāhmans, was to sever themselves from the concerns of life, leave their homes and family, and live a hermit life in a forest retreat, engaged in meditation, and instructing pupils in the oral traditions of the Vedic school to which they belonged. The last stage of life was to be spent as a homeless ascetic wandering throughout the land. For those who lived as hermits in the forest the Āranyakas or Forest Books were compiled, containing the treasured lore of centuries regarding the full significance and recondite meaning of the sacrifices. To these Forest Books were appended Upanishads, or books of secret knowledge. The earliest Upanishads date back to some six hundred years before our era. On these early Upanishads rests almost all of the philosophic, and much of the religious, thought of India of to-day. The chief aim of life, according to Brāhmanic tradition, was to free the soul during its endless transmigrations from rebirth in abodes of punishment, or from rebirths on earth in the body of a man of lower caste or in a degrading animal existence. This could only be attained through the *Doctrine of Works*. If a man obeyed the will of the gods, revered the Brāhmans, performed fitly all religious duties, and observed the laws and ordinances of his caste, his soul would gain rewards in heaven and be reborn on earth in an ennobled bodily frame, perhaps even in the body of a Brāhman.

Respecting the transcendental ideas of God and the Soul the Upanishads teach doctrines which at times appear opposed one to the other. In the poetic and cryptic imaginings of the Upanishads the intuitive thought of man strives to express its conception of the spiritual which throbbed through all creation and in the heart of man. Speculations as to the why and wherefore of the universe are at first vaguely formulated, discussed, and brooded over until they are finally taught as definite and assured beliefs and faiths of varied schools of thought.

Sometimes God is declared to be a personal God presiding over the world and the soul of man. Sometimes God is held to transcend the world, abiding above and apart from the world of phenomena. Finally God becomes purely spiritual and the world unreal in a spiritual unity of all.

The question which Upanishad thought set itself to solve was how, if in the Beginning there was One only, he had resolved himself in a known world of phenomena. What was the material out of which a spiritual Being had created a world of reality? If there existed matter, how had that matter been created by a God who was One only?

The answers of the Upanishads are held by orthodox thought in India not to rest solely on abstract metaphysical reasoning, but to be divine revelations. The Upanishads, however, contain many solutions of the universe, idealistic, pantheistic, and theistic. The question, therefore, which Indian thought had to answer was how, if the Upanishads hold a divine revelation, their speculations respecting God and the soul can be reconciled one with the other and be shown to contain only one consistent divine revelation.

Whatever the answer may be, orthodox thought in India holds that the nature of God is known and can be explained only through the correct interpretation of texts of Vēdas and Upanishads, or of other works as are of such undisputed authority as to be considered revelation.

In Western thought, as expressed by Kant, there are three subjects which transcend experience: namely, God, the Soul, and the freedom of the will. Kant therefore held that "after we have satisfied ourselves of the vanity of all the ambitious attempts of reason to fly beyond the bonds of experience . . . the belief in a God and in another world is so interwoven with my moral nature that the former can no more vanish than the latter can ever be torn from me."

Kant found a basis for a moral law in the somewhat insecure evidence of his own moral nature, and, as he said, "Two things fill my mind with ever renewed wonder and awe the more often and deeper I dwell on them—the starry heavens above me and the moral law within me."

It must be remembered that "Kant inherited from Plato through Berkeley, and transmitted to Hegel and Schopenhauer, the doctrine that man is the maker of his own universe, and so destroyed the sense of reality."[1] Schopenhauer, while pondering over these Kantian transcendental ideals of thought, gained some slight knowledge of the teachings of the Upanishads, and held that: "In the whole world there is no study so beneficial and so elevating as that of the Upanishads. It has been the solace of my life, it will be the solace of my death."

Max Müller, who knew more of the Upanishads than did Schopenhauer, stated in a lecture before the Royal Institution, that "If Philosophy is meant to be a preparation for a happy death, or Euthanasia, I know of no better preparation for it than the Vēdānta philosophy."

In India of to-day, to orthodox thought, the Upanishads are held to be as full of spiritual life and philosophic thought as they were through the past ages. Bengal's recent laureate poet, Sir Rabindranath Tagore, has said that to him the Upanishads "have ever been things of the spirit, and therefore endowed with vital growth, and I have ever used them both in my

[1] "Evolution and the War," Chalmers Mitchell, p. 105.

own life and in my preaching as being instinct with individual meaning for me as for others."[1]

The vague cosmological guesses of early Vedic times give place in the Upanishads to the assured belief that the universe throbs with the very spirit of God, in whom all things live and persist. The world is held to be immanent in, and pervaded by, God, as the cosmic principle Brahman. Side by side with this cosmic potency of Brahman there arises the conception of the universe pervaded by a Soul or Spirit as a psychic principle underlying all things. The universe, therefore, is not only transfused with God as the cosmic principle Brahman, but it also is spiritual with the spirit of God as the Ātman, spirit, or soul of the universe. This spiritual view of the universe is clearly a later conception than the cosmological view of the world as immanent in the cosmic Brahman. In the Upanishads it is said that the knowledge of the universe being permeated by a Soul or Spirit was never in the possession of the Brāhmans until it was taught to an assembly of Brāhmans by a Kshatriya. In the Rig Vēda the Ātman was merely the vital breath of man. In the Brāhmana period the Ātman is held to pervade everything as the Self of the universe. In one of the earliest Upanishads, if not the earliest, it is taught that: "In the Beginning all this universe was Ātman, or Self. There was nothing else blinking. He thought, Shall I create worlds? He created these worlds."[2] In another

[1] "Sādhana," p. viii.

[2] Ait. Up. ii. 4. 1.

Upanishad, held by some scholars to be the oldest Upanishad, it is taught that in the Beginning there was only Ātman, or Self, which, looking round, could see no second. Then this Ātman, or Self, entered into all things as male and female, as they were spread out in name and form.[1] It is then said that this Ātman, or Self, which existed from before all time, entered into all things as the Brahman or first principle of the universe. Here the Ātman and the Brahman come to express one and the same idea. This Ātman or Brahman is said to pervade the universe just as the vital life (vāyu or prāṇa) pervades man. Sometimes the Ātman or Brahman is termed "It,"[2] sometimes "He."[3] The Brahman is further said to have "created whatever is. Having created, he entered into it and became what is manifest and unmanifest, what is defined and undefined, what is knowledge and not knowledge, what is real and unreal."[4] The same Upanishad also asks: "Who could breathe, who could breathe forth if that bliss, or Brahman, was not in the ether in the heart?"[5] From the primeval Ātman, or Self, is said to have sprung "ether, then from ether air, fire, water, earth. From earth herbs, from herbs food, from food seed, from seed man."[6] In an earlier Upanishad[7] the Ātman is said to have created first these worlds, then primal man or Being (purusha or

[1] Brih. Up. i. 4.
[2] Chānd. Up. vi. 21.
[3] Taitt. Up. ii. 6.
[4] Ibid. ii. 6.
[5] Ibid. ii. 7.
[6] Ibid. ii. 1.
[7] Ait. Up. ii. 4. 3.

virāj), and then the deities. It is through these deities that the creative force enters into the universe. The Ātman then entered man: "having split open the top of the skull, he entered that way." Having thus entered man, the Ātman or Soul of the universe abides in the heart of man in the three stages of waking, dreaming, or deep, dreamless sleep. Therefore, in deep, dreamless sleep the soul of man is said to become united with the Brahman or Ātman in the ether in the heart. When a man dreams he is then freed from the senses, but his soul is associated with his mind, and so he is capable of remembering the impressions received when awake.

In the Chāndogya Upanishad[1] a father instructs his son S'vetaketu in the knowledge that the Ātman, or Self, abides in man as his own soul, or self, just as salt mingled in water, although unseen as salt, remains as the real essence of the salt water. This Upanishad, therefore, says: "Here also, in this body, forsooth, you do not perceive the True, my son; but there it is. That which is the subtle essence, in it all that exists has its Self. That is the True. That is the Self, and Thou art That." The earlier Aitareya Upanishad[2] teaches of the Sun that: "What I am, he is; what he is, I am." The Rig Vēda had already taught that the Sun was the Self of all that moves and moves not, therefore the above Upanishad[3] says that this Self should be meditated on, for it is "all that breathes,

[1] iv. 13. [2] ii. 2. 4. [3] ii. 6.

whether it walks or flies, and all that is movable and immovable."

The same Upanishad asks: "Who is he whom we meditate on as the self? Which is that self? . . . That self is Brahman, Indra, Prajāpati, all the gods, the five great elements. . . . All that is guided by knowledge, it rests on knowledge. The world is guided by knowledge. Knowledge is its foundation. Knowledge is Brahman. He by his knowing self having left this world and having obtained all delights in the world of heaven, became immortal." It is no doubt difficult to know whether a monism of knowledge is here taught or a dualism. Professor Keith, the translator of the Aitareya Āranyaka,[1] where this teaching occurs, says that: "The question is whether this justifies an attribution to the author of the doctrine that knowledge alone exists. . . . The self or god is conceived as creating the material world as a reality, but the exact nature of the creation is left vague. The relation of Brahman and Ātman is likewise left vague, a mere identification such as may have been made being of little value."

The Upanishad of the Aitareya Āranyaka [2] also states: "Let him know that the person within all beings who is not heard, not reached, not thought, not subdued, not seen, not understood, not classified, but who hears, thinks, sees, classifies, sounds, understands, and knows is his own self." Here, as pointed

[1] "Anecdota Oxoniensis," pt. ix. note, p. 236. [2] iii. 2. 4.

out by the translator,[1] the Ātman is not object but subject only, and: "This occurs frequently later, and with it the doctrine that the Self cannot be known." Professor Keith states, however, that "the Aitareya is consistently pantheistic or cosmogonic. The Ātman is the world or produces it, but its reality is not impugned." Further he says: "We have in the Āranyaka a pantheistic view older than the idealistic, and if we accept this result we will be inclined to interpret the Upanishads generally either pantheistically or idealistically, as may best suit each passage. Indeed, probably the idealistic view is the rarer, as it is the more subtle."[2]

The Upanishads become theistic when they teach not only the immanence of the world in God but the distinction of Brahman from the world, in the words: "He who dwelling in the earth is distinct from it, whom the earth does not know, whose body the earth is, and who within controls the earth, he is thyself, the ruling immortal soul."[3] The S'vetās'vatara Upanishad[4] teaches the most marked theistic doctrine of the Upanishads in the words: "Two birds, bosom friends, move round the one tree; one eats the fruit, the other looks on. On the tree man sits in illusion, weak, having no Lord, but when he worships the other Lord, and knows His glory, his grief departs." This Upanishad further teaches devotion—bhakti—to

[1] "Aitareya Āranyaka," Keith, note, p. 254.

[2] J.R.A.S., 1906, p. 494. [3] Brih. Up. iii. 7. 3. [4] iv. 6–7.

Rudra-S'iva, the after God of Hindu India, along with Vishṇu, and it declares that if the truths it reveals "have been told to a high-minded man, who feels the highest devotion to God, and for his Guru as for God, then these truths will indeed shine forth."[1]

II. The World Unreal

When thought in the Upanishads turned from the objective to the subjective side of consciousness, the inevitable result was that the objective appearances of reality faded from sight. In dreamless sleep all appearances of reality are absent, and the soul of man is said to have passed into union with the Supreme Ātman or Soul of the universe. Man therefore, when awake, may likewise reject the entire objective reality of the universe, and seek for his soul rest in a mystic trance of union with the Supreme Soul. The spiritual then reigns supreme, freed from all the contaminations and entanglements of matter. When the mind has emptied itself of contemplation of phenomena, or appearances of things, then arises the cry, so often repeated in India, that: "The world is false, Brahman is true. There is One only and no Second." The words "there is One only and no Second" have been held to mean that nothing exists outside Brahman and that the world is a pure illusion. In such a conception Brahman remains unrealized

[1] vi. 23.

and unrealizable in any external phenomena of experience, which are merely a delusion of ignorance. Existence or Being is thus left void of even the attributes of thought and extension, assigned by Spinoza to Being, so as to form a basis for consciousness and body in mankind. The doctrine of the non-reality of the world, when carried to the logical conclusion that all things are illusions, was one widely accepted in India. It has been held that: "This metaphysical theory has had a considerable influence in Hindu life and thought, and it has undoubtedly retarded natural development and to some extent moral progress, though the facts of life have been too strong for it. But, whatever the exact significance of the doctrine, it is clear that Yājñavalkya, and those who followed him, did, in some sense or other, hold that the world was unreal, a view which is not in any true sense Kantian." [1]

To Kant, things as manifested in the world were manifestations or forms in which these things appear, subject to the limitations of human knowledge and the mind's conceptions of time and space. Beyond knowledge of the appearances of things, manifesting themselves under mental limitations of time and space, there is no possibility of an absolute knowledge of things as they exist in absolute time and space. Therefore there is, to Kant, no possibility of knowledge of a Lord or Īs'vara, a knowledge which is claimed to be

[1] "Ait. Ār.," Keith, p. 42.

attainable by concentration of thought on the spiritual as inculcated by Indian sages in the Yoga and Vēdānta Paths of Knowledge.

In the Brihadāranyaka Upanishad, the sage Yājña-valkya is described as leaving his wife Maitrēyī to take up his abode in the forest to meditate on the Supreme Soul, or Self, of all things. He teaches his wife in many ways the doctrine that the Ātman, or Self, is the sole reality. This knowing Self within man being subject, and not object, of thought is unknowable. He says to Maitrēyī that[1]: "As a mass of salt has neither inside nor outside, but is altogether a mass of taste, thus indeed has that Self neither inside nor outside, but is altogether a mass of knowledge; and having risen from out these elements vanishes again in them. . . . For when there is, *as it were*, duality, then one sees the other, one hears the other, one perceives the other, one touches the other, one knows the other; but when the Self only is all this, how should he see another, how should he hear another, how should he touch another, how should he know another? How should he know Him by whom he knows all this? That Self is to be described as 'No, no.' He is incomprehensible, for he cannot be comprehended; he is imperishable, for he cannot perish; he is unattached, for he does not attach himself; unfettered, he does not suffer, he does not fail. How, O beloved, should he know the knower? Thus far goes immor-

[1] iv. 5. 13.

tality." Again he teaches[1]: "If a man understands the Self, saying 'I am He,' desiring what or for the love of whom should he weary his body? . . . By the mind alone the Self is to be perceived, there is in it no diversity. He who perceives therein any diversity goes from death to death."

Therefore, if a man knows that the world is unreal in the idealistic conception that the Spirit, or Ātman, is the sole reality, the result follows, as Yājñavalkya[2] declares: "Knowing this, the people of old did not wish for offspring. What shall we do with offspring, they said, we who have this Self and this world of Brahman? And they, having risen above the desire for sons, wealth, and new worlds, wander about as mendicants. . . . This great, unborn Self, undecaying, undying, immortal, fearless, is indeed Brahman. Fearless is Brahman, and he who knows this becomes Brahman."

A later Upanishad declares that: "There is no effect and no cause known of Him. . . . He is the one God, hidden in all things, the Self within all Beings, the witness, the only One."[3]

This doctrine of non-duality, the doctrine that all appearances are unreal, is in another late Upanishad illustrated by the analogy of a fiery circle (alāta cakram) produced by sparks of a whirling fire-brand, for "having cut through ignorance he saw Brahman flashing

[1] iv. 4. 12 and 19.

[2] Op. cit. iv. 22.

[3] S'vet. Up. vi. 8–11

like a wheel on fire, and having seen Him he obtained immortality."[1]

Here it is clear that the fiery circle produced by the fire-brand is the effect of an illusion, and not, as the Buddhists (vijñānavādins) contended, an illustration of their doctrine that reality, or continuity of life, is a mere succession of momentary flash-points of consciousnesses.

Brahman, as taught in many Upanishads, is the Supreme Soul, "without parts, without actions, tranquil, without fault, without taint."[2] Brahman is defined as neither coarse nor fine, neither short nor long,[3] as: He who is without and within unproduced,[4] and as, "this great unborn Self, undecaying, undying, immortal, fearless, this indeed is Brahman."[5]

Brahman is the Self within all things, and, like the ether, is omnipresent and eternal,[6] and the Self of all the universe is Brahman,[7] so that "Brahman is present everywhere, within everything, the Self of everything." Therefore, once there arises knowledge that Brahman is the Soul or Self of everyone, "there is no going out of the Soul, either before or after death; the Soul is in itself Brahman and abides as Brahman."

The earlier Aitareya Upanishad teaches the same doctrine that "on the death of him who desires the Ātman only, his vital spirits do not go elsewhere. . . . Being Brahman he goes to Brahman." This Upanishad

[1] Mait. Up. vi. 24. [2] S'vet. Up. vi. 19. [3] Brih. Up. iii. 8. 8.
[4] Mund. Up. ii. 1. 2. [5] Brih. Up. iv. 4. 25.
[6] Ibid. iii. 4. [7] Chānd. Up. vii. 25. 2.

also states that "when all desires which entered the heart are undone, then does the mortal become immortal, then he obtains Brahman," for "he who sees all as Self, and his own Self as the infinite Self or Ātman, has gained all knowledge and is for ever free from evil."

The unison between the Self of man and the Self of all things is taught where it is said: "When he finds freedom from fear and rests in that which is invisible, incorporeal, undefined, unsupported, then he has obtained the fearless. For if he makes but the smallest distinction in it, there is fear for him. But that fear exists not for the wise man."

In the Chāndogya Upanishad Death appears on the scene as giving instruction regarding the immortality of the Soul.

Death teaches that the Soul "is not born, it dies not; it sprung from nothing, nothing springs from it; this Ancient is unborn, eternal, and everlasting. It is smaller than small, it is greater than great, it is hidden in the heart . . . he who knows this is freed from death." Here the Soul of the universe and the Soul of man blend in unity beyond which there is no duality. They both rest for ever in unconscious Oneness, pure subjectivity, never more to awake to the illusion of objectivity. No longer can diversity crowd in to keep the Soul from its eternal rest, for "just as a razor is placed in a razor-case or fire in a receptacle of fire, so the intelligent Self enters into the corporeal Self."[1] In this inseparable

[1] Sānkh. Up. v. 5-8.

unity there is, it is said, no becoming greater of the Self by good works or less through evil deed. Therefore, it is also said that when the Self is known as "I am that," the Self is "harmed by no deed whatsoever, neither by theft, nor slaying the babe unborn, nor by slaying his mother, nor by slaying his father. Nor when he has done evil deeds does the bloom leave his face."

This means that in the higher knowledge of God as all in One no action is possible, for no duality and no objectivity exists. Actions have no longer reality. The Soul and all things have passed away into a monism of unconscious abstract subject of thought. When the reality of the world, even as phenomenal, drifts away from before the recluse whose mind is concentrated in meditation on the Supreme Soul as the One Existent, then: "The wise who knows the Self as bodiless within the bodies, as unchanging among changing things, as great and omnipresent, does never grieve. That Self cannot be gained by the Vēda, nor by understanding, nor by much learning. He whom the Self chooses, by him the Self can be gained. The Self chooses him as his own. But he who has not first turned away from his wickedness, who is not tranquil and subdued, or whose mind is not at rest, he can never attain the Self—even by knowledge."

The same Upanishad[1] teaches that: "The knowing Self is not born, it dies not; it springs from nothing, nothing sprang from it. The Ancient is unborn, eternal,

[1] Katha Up. 1. 2. 18 and 19, S.B.E., vol. xv.

everlasting; he is not killed, though the body is killed. If the killer thinks that he kills, if the killed thinks that he is killed, they do not understand; for this one does not kill, nor is that one killed."

Another Upanishad[1] says: "As the flowing rivers disappear in the sea, losing their name and form, thus a wise man freed from name and form goes to the Divine Person, who is greater than the great. He who knows that highest Brahman becomes even Brahman. In his race no one is born ignorant of Brahman. He overcomes grief, he overcomes evil; free from the fetters of the heart, he becomes immortal."

Disentangled from the diffuse and obscure wording of the Upanishads, the teaching of this culminating doctrine is that there is no duality in the universe, that when the Self is known all is known; the soul of man is indeed that Ātman, that immortal, that Brahman, it is indeed All. This Self, in the words of one Upanishad, "Is the Brahman without cause and without effect, without anything inside or outside, omnipresent and omniscient."

The idealistic teachings of the Upanishads in driving back thought to an unconscious subjectivity void of outside objective reality, reach a point where knowledge ceases to have intelligent meaning. Knowledge, for Kant, was based on sense perceptions united with the mind's potential impressions of relations of co-existence and succession. Undoubtedly the Upanishad teaching

[1] Mund. Up. iii. 2.

of all reality being an illusion would approach the teaching of Kant were not the flux of sensations, according to Kant, provided with a unifying principle so that they may persist in time. Therefore: "It is easy to say that substance is a fiction of thought; Kant's reply to that charge is, that to treat successive sensations as having one source common to them (which we must constantly do in our experience) implies as a ground of its possibility *an identity or persistency in the consciousness* which serves as the common vehicle of the successive feelings. Unless thought supplied this persistent, permanent background, it would be impossible for us to realize the relations in time known as succession and simultaneity."[1] Kant therefore begins with time and cause as innate functions of the brain, which, coupled with the senses and objects of experience, give the intellect knowledge. He ends by holding God and the soul as transcendental ideals unknowable by intellectual speculation. The immortality of the soul, however, he asserts, must be assumed, as all *a priori* arguments for or against its immortality end in fallacies, and further because the very moral nature of man demands immortality for the soul.

The idealistic and illusory doctrines of the Vēdānta, taught by S'ankara, as being the ultimate transcendental teachings of the Upanishads, deny the evidences of the senses of a real or phenomenal world. They, however, accept God and the soul as knowable from the

[1] "Kant," Wallace, p. 175.

revelation contained in the Upanishads respecting their nature. The difficulty thus arises of how to reconcile the contradictory views of the Upanishads respecting the true nature of the universe and of the relationship of God to man.

An idealism, which holds all things to be illusions, deprives the mind of all sources of knowledge. The Upanishads, however, also teach in many places that the world is phenomenally real. With the reality of the world are taught dualistic conceptions of God and the soul of man. At other times, although the universe remains immanent in God, still God by His nature is held to transcend the world. The Upanishads further teach the worship of a personal God who does not transcend the world nor the thoughts of those who worship Him by devout meditation and purity of heart. In the S'vetās'vatara Upanishad this personal God is to be believed in through faith.

When they teach: "The absorption of the individual soul into the Supreme as of a river into the ocean, and the unconsciousness of the soul when everything but himself fades away from his knowledge," then, "In this respect the doctrine may be regarded as Pantheistic, or as setting forth the illusory character of all phenomena. Speculation in the Upanishad times was very free, and it veered round even to the denial of the soul as a substance." [1]

The mingling of varied doctrines such as these in

[1] Bhandarkar, "Vais'navism, etc.," p. 2.

the Upanishads which form, with all Vedic literature, the foundations for the philosophic thought on which modern Hinduism is based, has resulted in infusing the religious beliefs of to-day with an irresistible tendency towards Advaita, or non-duality, where realism is lost in a sea of spiritual idealism. At times it seems almost a hopeless task to trace the philosophic conceptions underlying the worship of Vishṇu and S'iva to anything but a Vēdāntic idealism. Vaishnavism and S'aivism bring the individual soul in salvation "very near" to the Supreme Soul; they only stop short of the idealism of Yājñavalkya in not equating the absolute union and identity of the soul of man with the Supreme Soul.

As with the Upanishad teachings, so likewise Hinduism of to-day passes from theism to pantheism, thence to spiritual idealism. Sometimes God is a personal God, creating a real world. Sometimes God transfuses himself into the whole universe in an all-absorbing pantheism, which then fades away in the idea of the unreality of everything. This is seen in one Upanishad,[1] which teaches that "He who dwelling in the earth is within the earth, whom the earth does not know, whose body is the earth, who within rules the earth, is thy soul, the Inner Ruler, the immortal.

He who dwelling in the heavens is within the heavens, whom the heavens do not know, whose body

[1] Brih. Up. iii. 7.

are the heavens, who from within rules the heavens is thy soul, the Inner Ruler, immortal."

The Upanishad then continues to declare that he, the controlling Soul, dwells in and controls the sun, the quarters, the moon and stars, the ether, the darkness, the light, the elements, the vital air, speech in the Vēdas and sacrifices, and this Soul "is thy soul, the Inner Ruler, immortal. Unseen he sees, unheard he hears, unminded he minds, unknown he knows. There is none that sees, but he; there is none that hears, but he; there is none that minds, but he; there is none that knows, but he. He is thy soul, the Inner Ruler, immortal. What is different from him is perishable."

Here the knowing Soul in man and the Soul which pervades and sustains the world alone exist as One, and in this knowledge everything is known. The whole universe fades away before such a conception of ideal oneness of Soul. Should, however, the universe be viewed as existing outside the Supreme Soul, but pervaded and identical in true essence and nature with that Supreme Soul, then abstract idealism drifts back into pantheism. If, however, it be held that the Supreme Soul created the universe, as self-existent, and then that the universe became immanent in the Supreme Soul or Being, who produced the cosmos, then there is a pure dualism so long as the universe exists as created from the beginning.

The Upanishads are the record of the free speculations of the period untrammelled by Brāhmanic dogmas respecting the spiritual efficacy of the prayer and of the sacrificial cult. Kshatriyas of outlying courts indulged freely in these speculations, some of which are said to have never been known to Brāhmans until they were proclaimed by Kshatriyas.

It has been contended that the whole purport of the Upanishads is to teach that the world is real and that the Lord and Creator holds within Himself omnipotent powers of realizing Himself in the universe and in the Soul of man. This view holds that the Upanishads reveal the Lord to the loving faith of those who seek Him and that He realizes Himself in the activities of man and in the ceaseless desires of the Soul.

On the other hand, it has been held that the sole purport and aim of the Upanishads is to teach an idealistic monism wherein the soul of man is one with the soul of all things, and that "the older the texts of the Upanishads are, the more uncompromisingly and expressly do they maintain this illusory character of the world of experience."[1] This doctrine of the illusion of all appearances of reality follows naturally and logically from the repeated teachings in the Upanishads regarding the non-duality of the Self or Ātman, or Brahman, as the sole reality in the universe.

The Soul or Self emerges, in such a doctrine, as a pure, knowing subject outside of which there is no object of

[1] Deussen, "Philosophy of the Upanishads," p. 228.

knowledge. The knowing Self is reduced to abstract consciousness without anything to be conscious of, an abstraction beyond all power of definition or conception. Such a condition of the Soul can only be defined—according to the doctrine of unreality—by assigning to it attributes and then denying that these attributes exist in the words "No, no."

This regress towards a notional abstract Self or Ego has been described as a process wherein "you first eliminate corporeal feeling; you then eliminate all the contents of memory and your position as a particular 'this' in the general world, and the result is that your Ego comes to disclose itself as a mere asymptotic regress towards a notional pure subject of knowledge—a thinker without thoughts, an abstraction, nothing at all."[1] Although the S'vetās'vatara Upanishad, in common with other Upanishads, teaches the monism or unity of souls in Brahman as the Supreme one and only Soul, still it is equally strong in inculcating the personality of a Lord or Īs'vara whom he addresses as Hara, Bhagavat, Rudra, or S'iva. This seeming contradiction raises the whole question which has divided Indian thought into conflicting schools, one holding to realism, the other to idealism. According to the former the universe is an evolution, or Parināma, of Brahman, and is a real universe. According to the idealistic school, Brahman, as Spiritual monism, remains abstract consciousness, pure subject matter of thought, and any

[1] Haldane, "Pathway to Reality," p. 154.

appearance of a universe can only be a "turning aside," or Vivarta, of Brahman or the Spiritual, so that the universe becomes nothing but an illusion.

The Upanishads are the Vēdānta, the End, or consummation of Vedic thought, and so sacred were they that their teachings were condensed into short sentences, or strings, or sūtras, so that future generations might have a record of them handed down in the memory of those Brāhmans whose duty it was to learn them by heart. These sūtras are known as the Vēdānta Sūtras or Brahma Sūtras. A long line of commentators has endeavoured to explain the full meaning of these mnemonic sentences, and to show that they express the full and consistent exposition of all Upanishad teaching. The first great commentator was S'ankarācārya, and he undertook the task of proving that the problem of the universe could only be solved in an idealistic monism of Brahman. All reality was an uneasy dream conjured forth by a delusion which permeated all things and the soul of man, so as to make them imagine they were separate from unconscious rest in Brahman.

Many Indians and many scholars in the West maintain that S'ankara's interpretation of the Vēdānta in his commentary on the Vēdānta Sūtras, unduly strained the real meaning of the Upanishads and Sūtras thereon. It has been held that "the true Vēdāntists always held that behind the relatively real there was the absolutely real, that behind the phenomenal world there was the full reality of Brahman."[1] S'ankara, however, held that the Brahman of the Vēdānta was "in itself impersonal, a homogeneous mass of objectless thought, transcending all attributes; a personal God it becomes only through its association with the unreal principle of Māyā, so that, strictly speaking, S'ankara's personal God, his Īs'vara, is himself something unreal."[2] Therefore those who gain the highest knowledge of Brahman, "whose soul has become enlightened by the texts embodying the higher knowledge of Brahman, whom passages, such as the great saying, 'Thou art that,' have taught that there is no difference between his true Self and the highest, obtain at the moment of death immediate final release, a withdrawal altogether from the influence of Māyā, and the Soul asserts itself in its true nature, which is nothing else but the absolute highest Brahman." Those who continue to believe in a real or phenomenal world remain under the influence of ignorance, and by devout meditation of the lower Brahman, or Lord, remain subject to the limitations (upādhis) of the soul, and to transmigrations until they gain perfect knowledge.

The question for the future thought of India to consider is if the conclusions of S'ankara rest on a foundation of philosophic reasoning sound enough to support the vast structure of Hinduism which has been erected thereon. The contest between those who hold

[1] "Vēdānta Philosophy," Max Müller, p. 130.

[2] "Vēdānta Sūtras," Thibaut, p. xxx.

to the teachings of S'ankara and those who oppose them is being waged fiercely in India of to-day. So fierce is this contest that it has been recently recorded that a leader, prominent in the S'aiva Siddhānta school of thought of South India, wrote: "I would rather see all India become Christian than that it should fall a prey to the Vēdānta of S'ankara." [1]

[1] "Der S'aiva Siddhānta," Schomerus, 1912, p. 20.

CHAPTER V

VĒDĀNTA

I. Limitations of Knowledge

Hume held that there were some "remote and abstruse subjects" for which the human understanding was by no means fitted. He considered that it would be well for the world if once for all a serious inquiry were made into the limitations and nature of the human understanding. If this were done there might perhaps no longer be occasion for the "plausible objection against a considerable part of metaphysics that they are not properly a science, but arise from the fruitless efforts of a human vanity, which would penetrate into subjects utterly inaccessible to the understanding, or from the craft of popular superstitions." Kant, who made an inquiry into the human understanding, found that "on the great questions of metaphysics—Immortality, Freedom, God—scientific knowledge is hopeless." [1]

S'ankara, in the same way, in the beginning of his commentary on the Vēdānta, or end of the Vēdas,

[1] Wallace, "Kant," p. 188.

says that learned men have in the past argued and reasoned over these metaphysical speculations concerning God and the Soul, but all these arguments have over and over again been refuted and new ones set up, all ingenious but all fallacious.

Kant held that a knowledge of God could be got only in the moral life. S'ankara held that it could only be got by "a presentation before the mind which is effected by meditation and devotion," that is, in his moral nature. He therefore, in inquiring into the nature of Brahman and its relation to the universe, rejects all the methods of ordinary Indian proof, such as perception and inferences therefrom. His body of proof lies in the Vedic teachings down to the Upanishads, and all succeeding books which give evidence of their being scriptural.

S'ankara held that, "as Brahman is not an object of sense, it has no connection with other means of knowledge. For the senses have, according to their nature, only external things for their objects, not Brahman." Therefore the true nature of God and the Soul can never be known "either by inference or by the other means of right knowledge." [1]

So important were the Upanishads considered that their main teachings were summarized in 555 short sentences to be learned by heart, and so carried in the memory. These short sentences were clues wherefrom the full meaning of the original Upanishad teachings

[1] S'ankarācārya, Commentary: Brahma Sūtras i. 1. 2.

might be expanded by teachers, or gurus (ācāryas), who held traditional expositions from previous teachers.

In India definite philosophical systems were not worked out by any single individual. They are the outcome of discussions and arguments carried on from generation to generation by ascetic sages learned in one or other school of Vedic tradition. From teacher to disciple definite traditional lines of thought were handed on and preserved. These teachings in course of time had to encounter opposition, and it is not until every possible argument of opponents had been controverted that the teachings assume the form of a system of philosophic thought. Some gifted teachers or the leading disciples of a system assembled together, then systematized the teachings into short sentences, strings, or sūtras, to form a text-book to which the name of some more or less mythical founder of the system of philosophy is given. The Vēdānta Sūtras have attached to them the name of Vyāsa (compiler) and Bādarāyaṇa, and are known as the Vēdānta System of Indian philosophy. When they were first formulated is unknown.

Professor A. Berriedale Keith[1] holds that "the date of Bādarāyaṇa is admittedly doubtful, but it is becoming more and more probable that he cannot be dated after the Christian era. Bühler pointed out that Āpastamba seems to have known some exposition of a Vēdānta doctrine in sūtras which may even have been

[1] J.R.A.S., 1907, p. 492.

the Brahma Sūtras, and Āpastamba can hardly be dated later than the third century B.C."

It has, however, been held that the Vēdānta, as well as the Nyāya system, could not have been composed earlier than 200 to 450 A.D.[1] The Vēdānta system naturally carries on the continuity of Vedic and Upanishad thought. Therefore, as Max Müller said,[2] for those "who care only for the growth of philosophic thought on the ancient soil of India the Vēdānta is clearly the first growth, and the question whether Kapila lived before Bādarāyaṇa, or whether the systematic teaching of the Sānkhya took place before that of the Vēdānta, can hardly arise."

Professor Garbe holds that the Sānkhya system takes precedence in priority of time over the Vēdānta. He holds[3] that the well-known references to the Vēdānta in the Bhagavad Gītā (especially Brahma sūtra padāni, xiii. 4) are all late additions grafted on to an early monotheistic deification of Krishṇa, as the Bhagavat or Adorable Lord, who became worshipped as early as the third or fourth century B.C.

On the rise of the Gupta dynasty to power, during the fifth century of our era, Brāhmanism once again asserted its spiritual supremacy over the people who had drifted from the early ideals of Buddhism to the worship of idols of Buddha and his incarnations. The

[1] Jacobi, J.A.O.S., vol. 31, p. 29.

[2] "Six Systems of Indian Philosophy," p. 151.

[3] "Bhagavad Gītā," 1905.

indigenous faiths and beliefs of the people and their worship of local deities received Brāhmanic sanction. Temples arose for the worship of these gods. Purānas were written, under Brāhmanic guidance, telling of the Vedic lineage of the gods, and magnifying the traditions of every indigenous shrine and deity worshipped therein. A new Hinduism arose, for which Brāhmanism had to establish a philosophic basis. In order to do this, the whole philosophic reasoning on which Buddhism was established had to be refuted. A reformed Hindu theism had to find its source in Vedic and Upanishad teachings, so that it might receive the stamp of Brāhmanic orthodoxy. The Vēdānta Sūtras were traditionally held to contain the very essence of all Vedic and Upanishad teachings in their 555 mnemonic sentences. Commentator after commentator on these sūtras arose, each essaying to explain their full meaning and endeavouring to prove that his own interpretation was the only valid one which was consistent with the true meaning of Vedic tradition. Some commentators held that the Vēdānta was a revelation, from before all time, of One Supreme Spiritual Being which alone existed, and could not be evolved into anything but the Spiritual. Such a universe could have no taint in it of matter or reality. The world was spiritual, and all appearances of reality were illusions. Other commentators held that the whole past thought of India had been to teach a theism wherein the world was real and created by a beneficent Creator knowable to the faith and devotion of His worshippers.

Hinduism of to-day accepts and rests on these interpretations of the Vēdānta. Irreconcilable as the two views may seem to be, the first a Spiritual monism, the second a more or less modified theism or pantheism, they both supply the philosophic basis on which Hinduism justifies itself. The transcendental Spiritual monism of the universe was taught by S'ankarācārya, a Brāhman of South India, born about 800 A.D. With Brāhmanic keenness of genius he saw that Buddhism could only be defeated on traditional lines of Indian thought. Once Hinduism and Brāhmanism could prove that Buddhism was based on metaphysical reasoning opposed to the whole current of Indian thought from Vedic times, it inevitably followed that the fate of Buddhism was sealed among all reasoning minds in India. S'ankara therefore undertook the task of proving that the doctrines of Buddhism were opposed to the entire revelation of Vedic scriptures, and afforded no basis for a metaphysical conception of the universe. Buddhism had taught as its highest ideal a Nirvāna or freedom from the potentiality of Karma, or action, which necessitated the continuation of existence which was full of suffering and sorrow, of birth, old age, and death. S'ankarācārya taught that all these sufferings and sorrows of Buddhism were delusions. The Vedic scriptures had revealed God as Supreme Soul of the universe. The soul of man could free itself from all

BUDDHA TEACHING.

To face p. 78.

sorrow and suffering, not in the Buddhist ideal of cessation from action, but in the knowledge that all life was an illusion, in the higher knowledge that God as Spiritual could never evolve out of the Spiritual anything pertaining to the non-spiritual. Buddhism, as its highest ideal, aspired to a Nirvāna wherein neither Spiritual nor real persists to arouse mankind to hopes, aspirations, or actions. S'ankarācārya refuted Buddhism by teaching that only the Spiritual exists, wherein all reality and actions become sublimated in a Nirvāna of Spiritual oneness of all things. So close do the two ideals of Buddhism and Spiritual monism assimilate themselves one to the other, that S'ankarācārya was often denounced as a crypto or disguised Buddhist. S'ankarācārya in his search towards a Why and Wherefore of the universe, started from the same standpoint as Hegel in later days, which held that "if we saw the universe whole, as we may suppose God sees it, space and time and matter and evil and all striving and struggling would disappear, and we should see instead an eternal, perfect, unchanging spiritual entity."[1]

Similarly, S'ankara in his Commentary,[2] says that true knowledge would destroy this apparent world, which is founded only in ignorance, from which all actions and agents and result of actions arise. In support of this he quotes the Upanishad declaring[3]

[1] "Problems of Philosophy," Russell, p. 223.

[2] iii. 4. 16.

[3] Brih. Up. iv. 5. 15.

that all this ignorance passes away when there remains only one Self or Soul of all things. Again,[1] he repeats that the whole apparent diversity of the world of reality exists only in our ignorance. There can only be one sole unity, and when this is recognized as the only true knowledge, the ordinary world of experience vanishes. This fundamental Spiritual monism is insisted on over and over again by S'ankara. In one passage[2] he says, "You are to dissolve by true knowledge the universe of effects, which is the mere product of ignorance"; and again[3] he says, "It is impossible when one has gained true knowledge to pass again into the world of phenomena." Here there is a monism in which the One becomes only knowledge (jñāna) without any knower (jñātā), or anything knowable (jñēya).

S'ankara carried the teachings of Yājñavalkya—that Brahman was the sole reality absolutely identical with the universe—to their logical conclusion, and taught that the universe was an illusion. Like Giordano Bruno in his efforts to explain the nature of God and His relation to the world, S'ankara reduced "the idea of God to a meaningless and barren abstraction and the finite world to evanescence and unreality."[4] To S'ankara the absolute principle of unity was an abstract consciousness void of all objectivity. To S'ankara there was no relative knowledge, in which things appear as phenomena.

[1] Commentary, 1. 2. 20.
[2] Ibid. 1. 3. 1.
[3] Ibid. 3. 2. 9.
[4] Caird, "Spinoza," p. 82.

The universe was swept away as illusory, as were all actions, good or evil, all transmigrations of the soul, all ideas of an abiding personality here or hereafter. Dr. Thibaut, in his exhaustive notes attached to his translation of the Vēdānta and S'ankara's Commentary thereon, says[1] that "although this form of doctrine has ever since S'ankara's time been the one most generally accepted by Brāhmanic students of philosophy, it has never had any wide-reaching influence on the masses of India."

S'ankara knew that his metaphysical speculations could have no influence on the mass of the people. He excluded the mass of the people from any participation in such a transcendental knowledge. It was a knowledge that presupposed a long course of mental and moral discipline. S'ankara taught that a necessary preliminary to any such knowledge must be a clear recognition of the difference between the spiritual and the temporal. There must be a previous discipline of renunciation, resignation, concentration of thought and belief. These in themselves excluded the mass of the people from any hope of ever arriving at the higher knowledge of Brahman. S'ankara even went farther: he closed the gates to higher knowledge against the mass of the people seeking to throw down the heavy burden of their evil deeds and to find salvation in a path of knowledge. In this world both women and Sūdras, and the mass of the people, have been born

[1] S.B.E., vol. 34, p. cxxvii.

thus in consequence of evil deeds of the past; therefore their ears must remain for ever closed to hearing the sacred words of the Scriptures which alone teach the higher knowledge of Brahman. S'ankara, like every other idealistic philosopher, however, recognized that there was a real world of ordinary opinion. Thus in arguing[1] against the Buddhists (vijñānavādins) who maintained the sole existence of thought, he says: "The non-existence of external things cannot be maintained, because we are conscious of external things. In every act of perception we are conscious of some external thing corresponding to the idea." Therefore he says,[2] "as long as true knowledge does not present itself, there is no reason why the ordinary course of secular and religious activity should not hold on undisturbed."

His object was to defeat Buddhism on its own line of metaphysical reasoning and at the same time to establish Hinduism and the worship of a personal God as the ordinary faith of the mass of the people.

To S'ankara the world of ordinary opinion and belief was very real; it was a world worth winning back, by all the force of his subtle reasoning, from Buddhism to Brāhmanism. So real was this world to S'ankara, that for those who could not rise to the metaphysical reasonings of a transcendental knowledge of a higher Brahman, S'ankara founded monasteries to win them from Buddhism, and he incessantly laboured for the restoration and pre-

[1] ii. 2. 28. [2] ii. 1. 14.

TEMPLE AT MADURA.

To face p. 83.

servation of Hindu temples. Even to-day the heads of four of his great monasteries bear the revered name of S'ankara. The Smārta sect of Brāhmans, who follow the teachings of S'ankara, accept Vishṇu and S'iva as being identical with Brahman.

The Vēdānta is based on the evidence of scriptural authority, which might at first seem as if it merely was a system of religion and not of free philosophic thought. Still, as Max Müller said, the claim to infallibility need only be waived to find in the Vēdānta "a real philosophy, a complete view of the Kosmos in which we live, like those that have been put forward by the great thinkers of the philosophical countries of the world, Greece, Italy, Germany, France, and England."[1]

II. The World as Illusion

The object of S'ankarācārya in formulating philosophic principles—in opposition to those held by Buddhism—on which the religious beliefs of the people might be based was to give to all inquiring minds an answer to the problem: "Can thought compass a conception which will read a meaning at once into—

"1. The featureless, moveless Infinite whose eternal repose no breath of living thought or feeling can disturb, and

"2. Into the Infinite who knows and loves Himself in His creatures with an infinite intellectual love?"[2]

[1] "Six Systems of Indian Philosophy," p. 280.

[2] Caird, "Spinoza," pp. 308–9.

Or, as it has been further asked, is it possible to harmonize the conceptions of God?—"who must be conceived as the negation of finite thought and being, yet who expresses, or reveals, Himself in nature and in the human mind." S'ankara taught that God is abstract subjective Self, beyond which there is no objectivity nor reality. His Commentary also accepts the leading statement of the Vēdānta that God is an intelligent Creator from whom proceeds "the origin, subsistence, and dissolution of this universe." [1]

The whole of the religious beliefs of Hindu India of to-day are divided into sectarian differences owing to contending opinions as to the true and full meaning of this scriptural passage. Rāmānuja, who wrote an able and voluminous Commentary on the Vēdānta Sūtras, maintained that the clear meaning and entire purport of the passage was to declare that God as highest Spirit had intelligence as His highest attribute. Therefore Rāmānuja held that all scripture culminates in teaching a God who has in His own nature all possibilities of self-realization in the objective reality of the world. This fundamental doctrine is accepted, in more or less modified forms, by all teachers of orthodox theism or of pantheism. S'ankara, on the other hand, maintained that the passage refers only to a lower knowledge of a qualified Lord as an object of worship. He held that this "scriptural doctrine of Creation does not refer to the highest reality; it refers to the apparent world only, which is characterized

[1] 1. 1. 2.

by name and form, the figments of ignorance."[1] Therefore, for S'ankara, there were two different knowledges taught in the Vēdānta. There was, first, a higher, metaphysical knowledge of an unconditioned Brahman, and secondly, a lower, or exoteric, knowledge of a Lord as a source of Creation. The higher Brahman is pure subject of thought, or abstract consciousness. According to this higher conception of Brahman, the Supreme is pure knowledge without any outside object of knowledge. Therefore there can be no duality existent in the world. For S'ankara, and for the many Brāhman thinkers in India to-day who follow his teachings, all in this world is non-duality (a-dvaitam). Brahman alone exists as "One only and no Second" (ēkam ēva a-dvitīyam). All phenomena, all appearances of reality, are therefore unreal, they are mere illusions, conceived, in ignorance, to be existing as objects of experience. These illusive appearances not only veil the true Unity of the universe, making it appear as diversity, they also veil the spiritual Unity of Brahman, which the ignorant view as a personal Creator or Lord.

This doctrine of a higher and lower knowledge is held to be further supported by the scriptural statement that "two Brahmans are to be known, the word Brahman and the highest Brahman; he who is perfect in the word Brahman attains the highest Brahman."[2]

Another late Upanishad also states that the Vēdas are the lower knowledge and the higher knowledge

[1] 2. 1. 33. [2] Mait. Up. vi. 22.

is that by which the absolute Brahman is apprehended.[1]

This higher knowledge of Brahman, as taught by S'ankara, sends back the inquirer after a first Cause to an infinite regression where the mind reaches a denial of everything except a mental abstraction of subjectivity void of any possibility of objectivity. Here Brahman transcends all thought: it is Being without cause or effect. Any conception the mind can frame regarding this higher Brahman can only be refuted by the ever-repeated "No; it is not such." Brahman, in the higher knowledge, is as unthinkable as was the Being of Parmenides, from which it is impossible to pass over into the world of Becoming. The Being of Parmenides, it is true, was "universal matter and universal spirit at once, but the matter is sterile because capable of no expansion and the spirit powerless because capable of no action."[2]

In the higher knowledge, as set forth by S'ankara, there can be no possible knowledge of any individual personality, such as Ego or Self, no more than there can be of any reality in the world of appearances. This metaphysical refusal to accept the evidence of the senses regarding external objects, and of the mind regarding personal existence, has been held to arise from the fact that if "the metaphysicians of ancient and modern times, dissatisfied with empirical knowledge, went on to metaphysics, this step is only to be explained by a more or less clear consciousness that all empirical investigation

[1] Mundaka Up. 1. 1. v. [2] Gomperz, "Greek Thinkers," p. 179.

and knowledge amounts in the end only to a great *deception* grounded in the nature of our knowing faculties, to open our eyes to which is the task of metaphysics." [1]

Knowledge of things seen in the universe is founded, according to Kant, on sensations regulated by mental faculties.

S'ankara held the very contrary. He held that no empirical investigation, or sensations, combined with any principles of the human intellect, could give any knowledge. To S'ankara, in true knowledge, all sensations are illusions. The human intellect has no principles, or functions, of any sort, simply because it is pure subject of thought without objectivity. He says in the introduction to his Commentary that subject and object are as much opposed to each other as light is opposed to darkness. The only knowable for S'ankara was Brahman as the Self of everyone. The existence of Brahman is knowable because it is revealed in the scriptures, and because "the existence of Brahman is known on the ground of its being the Self of everyone." [2] This Self, of higher knowledge, of man, is not the migratory Soul of ordinary opinion, according to S'ankara. It is not a Self arising from any duality, or from any reality of individual existence, for, as S'ankara says, "individual existence is apparent only, the product of Nescience." [3] For S'ankara the Self of man, in unison with the Self of the universe, remained One only, and

[1] Deussen, "Vēdānta," p. 47. [2] 1. 1. 1.

[3] Ibid.

all idea of duality was the result of ignorance of this knowledge.

This unreality of all empirical knowledge is not based, according to S'ankara, on the human faculties or understanding. It arises from the potency of an all-pervading principle of cosmic ignorance. This idea of cosmic ignorance, acting on the mind and everywhere in the universe, stands aloof from any phases of ancient or modern Western thought. It springs naturally from the past thought of India, and only carries that thought to a logical conclusion. The early Vedic period had closed, about 800 B.C., in the virtual spiritualizing of the cosmos. In the Brāhmana period the conception developed that the universe and the gods were swayed and ruled by the spiritual power of the priest and sacrifice. The prayer, or Brahman, transfused itself as an active agency throughout all things. A Lord of Prayer, as Brahmanas-pati, became the Supreme Spirit, as manifest throughout the universe. This spiritualizing of the universe included the spiritualizing of man, whose Self or Soul was merged in oneness with the Self or Soul of the universe. Thought had followed the spiritual until it had lost sight of the real. The natural result was that all that was real, all appearances of things and the universe, were viewed as spiritual. There was only one Soul or Spirit, into which all things were sublimated as into a dream of mystic rapture. Reality had faded away into the mists of a spiritual monism, wherein no current of

S'IVA AND PĀRVATĪ.

To face p. 89.

unrest could arise to disturb the mind of the dreamer. All appearances of reality, in such a dream, were caused by ignorance. If this ignorance, as a cause, produced this effect, it must, according to Indian thought of the period, be conceived as an agency, or potency, persisting in the effect. Ignorance, in itself, was an abstract idea. Abstract ideas such as Faith, Anger, Desire, or Love had been personified, in early Vedic times, as agencies or deities. Speech had been personified as Vāc, which was a female deity, or S'akti, or potency associated in the Beginning with a creative Lord. This idea of a female principle being associated with a creative god or deity is one of the early conceptions of Indo-Germanic thought. In one of the earliest Upanishads it is stated that "in the Beginning there was Self only. . . . He then made this Self fall in two, and thence arose man and wife."[1] The same account then says that it was this female principle which went forth throughout the universe as the abiding force of the Creator in the world, so that "verily in the Beginning this was Brahman, from it all this sprang."[2]

The ignorance which, in the teaching of S'ankara, pervades the universe and makes things appear as if they were real, is a creative principle. This cosmic ignorance is personified as a feminine abstract principle called Māyā, or Illusion, just as Vāc was personified as a female principle of speech in early Vedic times.

[1] Brih. Up. 1. 4. 3. [2] Ibid. 1. 4. 10.

It is this Māyā, this all-pervading principle of ignorance, in the world, which deludes the mind and makes it imagine the appearances it sees to be realities. Māyā weaves a veil before man, through which few see the eternal unison of One in All, in which knowledge all realities fade away as unrealities and the Soul rests in a sea of unconscious bliss. This doctrine of Māyā eliminates even the certainty held by Descartes: "I think, therefore I am, or, *Cogito, ergo sum.*" It would eliminate even the converse: "I am, therefore I think." Still the doctrine, in other respects, approaches close to a doctrine of illusion as held possible by Descartes, who "gradually became convinced that the only existence of which he could be quite certain was his own. He imagined a deceitful demon, who presented unreal things to his senses in perpetual phantasmagoria; it might be very improbable that such a demon existed, but still it was possible, and, therefore, doubt concerning things perceived by the senses was possible."[1] This "deceitful demon" was known from the earliest times in Indian thought. In the Rig Vēda it appears as Māyā, and "the divine dominion of Varuna and Mitra is often referred to with the word Māyā. This term signifies occult power, applicable in a good sense to gods or in a bad sense to demons."[2] At a later period it is taught that all appearances of reality arise from the Lord being

[1] Russell, "Problems of Philosophy," p. 28.

[2] Macdonell, "Vedic Mythology," p. 24.

associated with Māyā, "from which the Maker (Māyin) sends forth all the prayers, the sacrifices, the past and the future and all the Vēdas."[1] S'ankarācārya taught that Māyā as a cosmic principle of ignorance, in some indescribable (anirvachanīya) manner, veils the true non-duality of Brahman, making Brahman appear, to ordinary opinion, as a creative Lord or Ruler, Īs'vara. Māyā further draws the veil of ignorance over the Soul of man and makes it appear as a limited individual Soul, separate from Brahman, in a universe of seeming reality of objects denoted by names and forms. Brahman remains unchanged and unchangeable by the potency of Māyā throughout the universe. Brahman is the sole entity in the universe, which universe is a mere turning aside (vivarta) of Brahman. The world is woven out in name and form, to the ignorant, by a magic vesture of diversity which emanates from Brahman as though he were a magician, through his association with the s'akti, or deluding influence, of Māyā. S'ankara in his Commentary says that "the magician is not affected by the illusion produced by himself, because the illusion is unreal, so the Brahman as highest Self is not affected by the illusion of a world."

This action of Māyā can only be explained by assuming that Māyā, or illusion, is as unreal as is the whole apparent world of reality. S'ankara teaches that the whole world of name and form, of ordinary

[1] S'vet. Up. iv. 9.

opinion, arises from Brahman being fictitiously connected with Māyā (a vidyā prati upasthāpita nāmā rūpa māyā). From this connection of Māyā with Brahman, a real world of ordinary opinion remains for mankind to accept as a manifestation, or turning aside, of Brahman. S'ankara therefore held that, accepting things as real, according to ordinary opinion, though higher knowledge knows all things to be One, the creation of the universe occurs because there are "belonging to the Self, *as it were*, of the omniscient Lord, name and form (figments of non-knowledge). These names and forms are, however, not to be defined as Brahman, or as different from Brahman." They are "the germs of the entire expanse of the phenomenal world."

In support of this teaching the scriptures and Manu are quoted by S'ankara as declaring that: "In the Beginning the Lord shaped from the words of the Vēdas the names and forms of all beings and the procedure of all actions."[1] He further says that from the eternal words of the Vēdas the definite species, as opposed to the genus, of all things were produced. Also that, before the Creation, the words of the Vēdas became manifest to the Creator, and that all things were created to correspond to these words. Here a definite ideal, or norm, is set forth, according to which a real world of ordinary opinion was created. The words are not the material cause of the world,[2] but things were created to corre-

[1] 1. 3. 28. [2] Ibid.

spond with the ideas conveyed by the words. Here the teaching of the Vēdānta comes close to the theory of Ideas of Plato. The Idea of Plato was, however, not a mere form or norm, as is usually held, but a power or force.[1] To Plato the world was appearance, not reality, but by the force of the Idea "the excellence or beauty of every structure, animate or inanimate, and of every action of man, is relative to the use to which nature or the artist has intended it."[2] In the Vēdānta the world was fashioned forth by the eternal words of the Vēdas, which foreshadowed, in the mind of the Creator, the ideas on which things were created.

When true knowledge arises and the Spiritual Oneness of all things is apparent, then these names and forms are said not to be "not absolute non-existence, but to be only a different quality or state, the state of name and form being unevolved." In this undeveloped condition name and form are said to be "identical with the cause." Therefore it is declared, by S'ankara, that when the higher knowledge arises "the creative quality of Brahman vanishes at once."[3]

S'ankara in the passage[4] already quoted says "that before the Creation the Vedic words became manifest in the mind of the Creator, and after that He created the things corresponding to those words." Not only does this passage make the word of the Vēda real and eternal, but S'ankara bases the whole of the doctrine

[1] See Kallem on Bergson, *Mind*, 1914, vol. xxiii. p. 208.
[2] "Republic," ch. 10. [3] ii. 1. 22. [4] i. 3. 28.

of the unreality of the world on the eternal verity of the Vedic scriptures. The monistic doctrine of the unity of all in One here rests on Vedic revelation. S'ankara in his Commentary[1] declares that "the fact of everything having its Self in Brahman cannot be grasped without the aid of the scriptural passage: Thou art That."

It would seem here as if S'ankara established the whole of his doctrine of illusion on evidence which is in itself illusion. S'ankara meets this objection by replying[2]: "Nor do we mind your objection that if perception, etc., ceases to be valid, scripture itself ceases to be so, for this conclusion is just what we assume." In support of this he quotes scripture,[3] which declares that, when true knowledge arises, "Then a father is not a father, a mother not a mother, the worlds not worlds, the gods not gods, the Vēdas not Vēdas."

Nevertheless, so long as man does not attain to the highest spiritual knowledge of Brahman the world is real. If the world be real, then there must be some explanation forthcoming as to how the evil and sorrows and sufferings of the world arose. S'ankara held that no Creation could be considered "essential goodness" if it was designedly created full of pain and regrets. He says of the Lord, that "as the infliction of pain and the final destruction of all creatures would then form part of His dispensation, He would have to be taxed with great cruelty, a quality abhorred by low people

[1] 1. 1. 4. [2] iv. 1. 3. [3] Brih. Up. iv. 3. 22.

even."[1] S'ankara, in his doctrine of a higher knowledge in which the whole world was illusion, had opposed the Buddhist doctrine that the world was a ceaseless flux of momentary consciousnesses. In his doctrine of a lower knowledge of a creative Lord he had sought to re-establish Hinduism in its worship of gods as gods, and the Vēdas as Vēdas, as beliefs on which all orthodox religious duties and beliefs should be based. In opposing the Buddhist doctrine of suffering and sorrow in the world being due to ignorance of the Four Noble Truths and as arising from the chain of causation, he fell back on the almost universally believed doctrine of the Transmigration of Souls as a reward or punishment for good or evil deeds. He therefore holds that the Creator in His Creation is bound to allot good and evil according to the merit or demerit of individuals in previous rebirths in the great periods (kalpas) of creation. The opponent of this doctrine naturally asks how the Creator was justified in the beginning of all Creation, when there was neither merit nor demerit of individual souls to condition the Lord, "who knows and loves Himself in His creatures with an infinite intellectual love." Could not the Creator, then, in the infinite Beginning, have created a world free from all sorrow and suffering? S'ankara replies that such an argument brings those who urge it into an antinomy of thought, for "without merit and demerit nobody can come into existence, and, again, without a body merit and demerit cannot be formed;

[1] ii. 1. 34.

so that on the doctrine of the world having a beginning, we are led into a logical see-saw."[1]

S'ankara therefore holds that the world, as viewed in ordinary opinion as a real world, must have existed from before all time without a beginning. The Vēdānta Sūtra[2] is relied on by S'ankara as conclusive assurance on this doctrine of Hinduism, as it states that "the Beginninglessness of the world recommends itself to reason, and is as such revealed in the scriptures." S'ankara, in his commentary on this passage of the Vēdānta, says that reason supports the conclusion that the world had no Beginning, because it cannot be conceived as having a Beginning, for in such a case "there would exist no determining cause of the unequal dispensation of pleasure and pain, and we should have to acquiesce in the doctrine of rewards and punishments being allotted without reference to good or bad deeds." From the dawn of thought in India the abiding faith of the people has been this one firm and assured belief that it is only through good deeds that a man can be born, or can become, good, and that by bad deeds he becomes bad. Buddhism had held that the influence of good and evil deeds could only be annihilated by the renunciation of all action. The Vēdānta and S'ankara, and, even before S'ankara, Kumārila Bhaṭṭa, called on the people to believe that in a blameless life, worshipping the gods of their forefathers and performing all duly ordained religious rites and ceremonies, they could lay up

[1] ii. 1. 36. [2] Ibid.

for themselves a treasure of good deeds, the full fruit of which would be reaped throughout countless generations. When the doctrine of the undying potency of Karma or actions first arose in India, it was whispered in secret as overriding the pretensions of priests and priestcraft to spiritual dominion over the people. In one of the earliest Upanishads, if not the earliest, the sage Yājñavalkya was asked what became of a man when he died. He replied: "'Let not this question be discussed in public.' Then the two went out and argued, and what they said was Karma (deed) and what they praised was Karma, which is to say, that a man becomes good by good deeds and bad by bad deeds."[1] S'ankarācārya taught as the highest ideal for India, that man, beyond all the appearances of reality, should seek the Spiritual. In this spiritual all reality would fade away into an eternal rest of idealistic monism. This spiritual idealism was essentially Indian. It was far removed in thought from the idealism of Leibnitz, or even of Berkeley, which would not deny that our sense data are signs of something which exists independently of our private sensations.[2] Kant held that if it were not for our perceptions of things, they would remain as unreal abstractions, and time and space and all would end in illusion. Absolute time and space, therefore, for Western thought, would seem to remain as mere indefinitely extended forms of our perceptions of finite time and space. According to S'ankara, time and

[1] Brih. Up. iii. 2. 13.

[2] Russell, op. cit. p. 56.

space, in the higher knowledge, are not transcendental ideals; they do not exist, they are illusions fashioned forth by cosmic ignorance. In the lower knowledge, of ordinary opinion, S'ankara held that time and space exist in themselves. He held in opposition to the Buddhists that "with regard to space it cannot be maintained that it is not definable, since substantiality can be established in the case of space no less than in the case of the two so-called nonentities, time and cause."[1] Here S'ankara approaches closer to the views of modern thought than did Kant, for: "Upon the view put forward by Riemann and adopted by Clifford, the essential properties of space have to be regarded as things still unknown, which we may one day hope to find out by closer observation and more patient reflection, and not as anxious to be accepted on the authority of universal experience or of the inner consciousness."[2] It has further been recently pointed out that "the reasons for regarding space and time as unreal have become inoperative."[3]

III. The World as Magic—Māyā

To many it might appear that the teachings of S'ankara were inconsistent, because they taught a higher knowledge of a higher Brahman, wherein the world was illusion,

[1] ii. 2. 24.

[2] Tucker, "Mathematical Papers by Clifford," p. xl.

[3] Russell, "Problems of Philosophy," p. 229.

and also taught a lower knowledge of a conditioned Lord, wherein the world is real. Parmenides, however, held, much as S'ankara did, that sense perceptions are illusory; nevertheless he also held that the world, so far as there were sense perceptions, in ordinary opinion, required an explanation. Parmenides took for granted the ordinary beliefs and opinions of men.

He accepted them "with the specific warning not to yield to them unquestioning credence; he spoke of the misleading structure of his theory, and called his expositions plausible or acceptable in contrast with the convincing force of truth which belongs to ideal reason." Similarly Kant's doctrine that "only the thing in itself" possessed objective reality, need not have prevented his derivation of the solar system from a primeval nebula.[1] S'ankara in a similar manner says that "the entire complex of phenomenal existence is considered as true as long as the knowledge of Brahman being the self of all has not arisen, just as the phantoms of a dream are considered to be true until the sleeper wakes."[2] Further, in the same connection he says: "Hence as long as true knowledge does not present itself, there is no reason why the ordinary course of secular and religious activity should not hold on undisturbed." Again, in arguing[3] against the class of Buddhists who assert that thought only is real (Vijñānavādins), and against those who assert that everything is a void and that nothing is real

[1] Gomperz, op. cit. p. 180. [2] ii. 1. 14. [3] ii. 2. 18.

(Mādhyamikas), he says: "The non-existence of external things cannot be maintained, because we are conscious of external things."

Therefore, so long as a man does not realize the ultimate truth of non-duality the world remains real. This reality is not an erroneous truth (Samvṛiti satya of Nāgārjuna), like that of the Mahāyāna Buddhist; it is truth until and up to the arising of a truer knowledge of universal Unity. So long as the world is held to be as it appears, so long man must remain under the influence of actions which lead to transmigrations of the Soul. S'ankara says that "the highest Lord may, when he pleases, assume a bodily shape formed of Māyā in order to gratify thereby his devout worshippers." [1]

This Ruler, although he creates, in association with Māyā, a world of names and forms, for those plunged in ignorance of the Lord's higher unqualified nature, remains himself omniscient and omnipotent, unaffected by the evolution of a world. These worlds are evolved again and again in great periods of time (kalpas), so that there is an endless series of evolutions, preservations of the world, and retractions. The Lord should therefore be worshipped as a deity possessing attributes, who has woven over the unity of Brahman the appearance of a phenomenal world wherein individual souls gain experiences through the senses. From the Lord, who is Brahman, conjoined with the potency of Māyā, issue the subtle elements or essences, the "things in themselves,"

[1] i. 1. 20.

ether, fire, air, water, earth. As each essence emanates from the preceding essence, the Universal Self, Brahman, enters each in turn and becomes the Self of that essence or element. So Brahman is immanent in the Universe from the beginning of all things. It is this entering of Brahman into the elements which enables them to enter on their activity.[1] From Brahman there come eleven vital airs, which are minute in size, being the subtle essences, faculties, or functions. These subtle faculties are five of the senses, five of action, and the Mind, which has many functions and is designated in various ways (manas, mind; buddhi, intellect; ahaṃkāra, egoism; citta, thought). This mind is said to be "the abode of the energy which acts through the means of right knowledge."[2] Above all presides the chief vital air or breath, with its functions of aspiration, inspiration, restraining, ascending, and all pervading. This chief vital air, together with the other vital airs, and Mind, form a subtle body or ghost in which the Soul is enclosed.

The Self, or the Soul of man, is a sentient principle which "rules the body and is connected with the fruit of actions."[3] It is eternal, self-existent, and is not like the other elements making up the body, which are mere products. It is in itself Brahman, the Ātman. So long as the world of illusion is viewed as real the Soul remains enclosed in a subtle ghost body, surrounded by a world of phenomena, and therefore partakes in actions and is liable to transmigrations. The Soul, surrounded by its

[1] ii. 3. 13. [2] ii. 3. 7. [3] ii. 3. 17.

subtle body, or ghost, resides in the heart, and from there it presides over the entire body. The Soul is, in its freed and essential nature, eternal. It does not emanate from the Universal Self or Lord. The associated subtle or ghost body is the product of Illusion, and the Soul, because of its being surrounded by the subtle body, takes part in the activities of the world as created through Māyā. True knowledge can alone enable the Soul to free itself from its surrounding bondage of the subtle body and to recognize the whole world as an illusion. Not only men, but the gods, not only animals, but plants, possess souls, for into their bodies the transmigrating Soul of man may pass so long as its subtle body clings to it. Thus it is said that the Soul can be reborn "in a dog, or a hog, or in an outcast."

The lower knowledge of Brahman as a Lord associated with Māyā, from which the world of ordinary opinion emanates, may enable the Soul to do good deeds and thus effect the cessation of its transmigrations. The Soul which has done good deeds and has gained the lower knowledge of the Lord passes on death out of the body. Then the Soul, surrounded by its subtle body, its still abiding ignorance of the higher knowledge, its good and evil deeds, joined with the impress of the deeds done in former births, is led by the chief up-breathing vital air to the abode of the gods. The passing of the Soul from the body, with its surrounding subtle body, is said to be by way of the 101st artery, which is in the head. The Soul thence passes beyond the days, beyond the moon and the sun, till it is received by "the guardians of the path of the gods," or by "a man who is not a man." It is then led to the Lord in the heaven of Indra, Varuna, or Prajāpati. Here the Soul abides in power and majesty for all time. It does not return to this world, but by the favour of Brahman it gains, in time, the higher knowledge of non-duality and rests in the annihilation of individuality. The souls of those who fail to gain this lower knowledge, but who still perform religious sacrifices, do good deeds and practise charity, pass on death, through the hundred arteries of the body, to the moon. Here they gain companionship with the gods, the impress of part of their deeds fades away, but enough remains stamped on the soul to necessitate a rebirth. So the subtle body has again to bear the soul through the ether, wind, smoke, mist, and rain, whence it finds its way through plant life into the embryo, to become again associated with a body as a man and if its deeds were meritorious even as a Brāhman. Those who gain no knowledge, who perform no religious rites, who are evil, descend into one of the seven hells of death there to suffer torment. From these hells they descend again to the earth through the rain, their subtle body bearing the soul into plant life, which when devoured by man passes, in some unexplained way, into a new human body.

All Vēdāntic thought culminates in mystic raptures over the tranquillity of rest which lies before those who gain the higher knowledge of the Higher Brahman and pierce the veil of Māyā. To gain this haven of rest no religious rites, no vain strivings to tread the thorny path of morality, are necessary. These avail nothing to guide the pilgrim one iota, even the size of a mustard seed, nearer his longed-for trance. No mental activity, no endeavouring after, or avoiding, the knowledge that man is caught in the snares of delusion, can bring nearer the eternal peace of Nirvāna. Strenuous meditation endows the soul with supernatural powers and insight. Supreme knowledge of the identity of Self with the Self of the universe, and the awakening from the dream of an empirical world, can only flow from the favour of the Lord " with a view to former actions." The knowledge is held by S'ankara to be completely revealed in the Vedic scriptures; it can, however, be borne in on the soul by the favour of the deity. When the knowledge is thus gained, the knowledge itself illuminates the whole mystery of delusion, and ignorance passes away like the empty imagery of a dream. Unless the knowledge be thus revealed to the soul, it may strive eternally to know Brahman, to know the emptiness of the figment of a world; it can never do either one or the other. When the Soul becomes conscious that there can be no abiding principle of duality in the world, then no evidence of the scriptures or any methods of knowledge are valid. They can no longer remain valid when the power of Māyā is dissolved, and nothing remains but an objectless Self of the universe. The dreamer may dream dreams and imagine the visions seen therein are true, but to the soul, when it reaches the full knowledge of Brahman, the whole of phenomenal existence is untrue. The Commentary of S'ankara on the Bādarāyaṇa Sūtras states that just as rivers lose their identity and individuality on passing into the sea, so the soul loses its individuality on its becoming merged into Brahman.

The crown and chief glory of the Vēdānta is said to be that as soon as full knowledge is reached all duties come to an end and actions have no further meaning or result. One verse of the early Upanishads [1] taught that if the Soul of man recognizes that it is Brahman, desiring what or for the love of whom should it weary itself? In Buddhism the doctrine of Nirvāna was the death-knell of all action. Still the individual who gained Nirvāna remained associated with a body for a time. In the Vēdānta, in conformity with the teaching of the Bhagavad Gītā, true knowledge is indifferent to acts. The sublime ecstasy of the soul when it gains the divine vision of the pure light of Unity with Brahman sublates into nothing the body and its acts. Then the soul lays aside its endless questionings and all duty is over and all work is ended. The body may indeed persist, for a time, to bear its burden of results of past and present deeds, just as the potter's wheel continues to revolve under the impetus that first set it in motion. Soon this potentiality runs down and the body decays. The result of all past good and evil deeds is dissipated.

[1] See *ante*, p. 59.

Those relations who were loved receive the result of the good deeds the Soul may have participated in, those who were not loved obtain the result of the bad deeds.

The Soul has gained the Highest Knowledge of Spiritual Oneness of all things. It is a knowledge wherein there is nothing to know and no knower. It is a knowledge which brings ecstasy where there is nothing to be ecstatic over. The mind has reached a condition where it finds only an abstract notional subject of thought.

The higher knowledge, or esoteric teaching, of S'ankara is based on the doctrine of non-causation, which ends in the effect being the same as the cause.

Brahman can undergo no change. The universe can only be a turning aside (vivarta) of Brahman. If ordinary opinion holds that there is diversity and reality in the seeming world of appearance, this opinion can only arise through some universal principle of ignorance which pervades all things and the mind of man. This ignorance can only be Māyā or Illusion. Māyā is not Being, for Brahman connotes all that is Being, beyond which there is no possibility of an Existent. On the other hand, it is not non-Being, for to the ignorant it produces a world of phenomena which remains a real world of ordinary experience and belief until it becomes sublimated in the higher spiritual knowledge of the Oneness of all things, a belief which rings through India of to-day in the incessant cry, "Brahman is true, the World is false. There is One only and no Second."

S'ankarācārya's doctrine of Māyā and his interpretation of the Vēdānta Sūtras of Bādarāyaṇa have been ably summed up as follows: "There are two doctrines indicative of the relation of God to the world, the so-called Parināmavāda and the Vivartavāda. The former implies real development and the latter an illusive development. This last is the doctrine of S'ankarācārya, wherefore his system should be called Singularism rather than Spiritual monism; while the first is that clearly held by the author of the Sūtras. This is evident from his very definition of Brahman as that from which everything originates, in which everything lives, and into which everything resolves itself in the end. . . . S'ankarācārya himself acknowledges . . . that the author of the Sūtras follows the Parināma doctrine, though to save his theory he imagines, without any grounds, that Bādarāyaṇa has in view the ordinary or illusory condition of things in doing so. S'ankarācārya's Vivartavāda it was which the later schools of Vaishnavism and S'aivism contended against; for even according to him it leaves no scope for the relation of the ruler and the ruled, i.e. God and the devotee, in the condition of reality when all illusion is dispelled and one spirit alone exists."[1]

[1] Bhandarkar, op. cit. p. 160.

IV. Quenching the Fire-brand

S'ankarācārya had sent his message throughout India, for after ages to ponder over, when he taught that this world was unreal, the mere figment of a passing dream, delusive as the tricks conjured up by a magician, and that the only truth our limited experience could give us was that:—

> "The cloud-capp'd towers, the gorgeous palaces,
> The solemn temples, the great globe itself,
> Yea, all which it inherit, shall dissolve,
> And, like this insubstantial pageant faded,
> Leave not a rack behind. We are such stuff
> As dreams are made of, and our little life
> Is rounded with a sleep."

The task which S'ankarācārya had set before himself was to defeat Buddhism on its own chosen ground and to re-establish Brāhmanism on an incontrovertible basis. Buddhism had declared that existence was only momentary flashpoints of consciousness. The Buddhists (vijñānavādins) had held that life was like the glowing end of a torch, which, when whirled round, gave the appearance of continuity, but that in reality there was only a circle of continuing momentary sparks. S'ankarācārya's answer was that if the torch is held at rest, the Buddhist theory of life vanishes. The Buddhist illustration of life as a circle of never-abiding consciousnesses merely means that the Buddhist con-

MAITREYA. THE FUTURE BUDDHA.

To face p. 109.

ception of life amounts to its being a pure illusion, just as much as the fiery circle of the burning torch is produced by the trick of moving the torch quickly in a circle or along a straight line.

The age in which S'ankarācārya lived was an age of bitter and vehement opposition to Buddhism. Orthodox sacerdotal Brāhmanism had found a champion in Kumārila Bhaṭṭa, who about 700 A.D. resuscitated the doctrine of works by his Commentary on the philosophy of the sacrifice, and was followed in about 800 A.D. by S'ankarācārya, who led the attack on Buddhism by striving to undermine the philosophic principles on which Buddhism then rested. The whole of India was alive, during these centuries, with opposition to Buddhism. The whole trend of the times was back to Brāhmanism and to a revived worship of the ancient deities of India, Vishṇu and S'iva. S'ankarācārya came to his task ably equipped in philosophic subtleties. His spiritual preceptor had been one Govinda, whose spiritual preceptor was Gauḍapāda. The latter had written a treatise of two hundred stanzas or Kārikās, which have been well described as "one of the most remarkable products of Indian philosophy."[1]

S'ankarācārya wrote a short commentary on these stanzas, which are considered so authoritative as to be termed a Upanishad. The stanzas are divided into four chapters. The stanzas of Gauḍapāda are full of quaint

[1] Macdonell, "Sanskrit Literature," p. 241.

conceits. Philosophic arguments are supported by analogies drawn from the most unexpected sources. These analogies, at times, would almost seem to indicate that the doctrine of Māyā, and of the world being merely illusively conjured forth by a magician, may have originated from observing the tricks of illusion of conjurors, which seem to have been believed in, during the eighth century, when Gauḍapāda lived, and to have excited as much wonder as they do to-day. The trick of suspending a rope in the sky and descending thereby is only to be explained as an illusion. Gauḍapāda says in one of his many analogies[1] that for anyone to hold the world to be a real appearance would be the same as calling a magic elephant (māyā hasti) a real elephant. This trick of making to appear a magic elephant does not seem to be performed in India of to-day. S'ankarācārya in his Commentary shows that the trick was well known at the beginning of the ninth century. He says that for anyone to believe this unreal world to be real would be similar to believing the elephant of illusion (Māyā) to be a real elephant. People knew the magic world and magic elephant as real, and, he continues, so real does the magic elephant appear that people tie it up and mount on it.

In another stanza Gauḍapāda says that all things in the world are produced by illusion (māyā), just as from magic (māyā) seeds are produced magic (māyā)

[1] Dvivedi, Bombay, 1894, 4. 44.

sprouts. This illustration clearly refers to the well-known mango trick. John Fryer, who travelled in the East from 1672 to 1681, tells that in India he saw a conjuror produce "a mock creation of a mango-tree arising from the stone in a short space, with fruit green and ripe; so that a man must stretch his fancy to imagine it witchcraft; though the common sort think no less."[1] The significance of the trick, as being an illustration of magic, or māyā, is seldom noted by Europeans and would be lost if performed in this country. The conjuror's object is not to perform the trick as one of sleight-of-hand, but to arouse the idea that the whole appearance of the mango-tree is an illusion. For this purpose the trick is usually, and best, performed in a part of the country where the mango-tree is not in blossom or bearing fruit; the conjuror, however, manages somehow to produce from distant places the flower and fruit of the mango-tree.

This doctrine of illusion is again illustrated by the reflection seen in a mirror. An individual, seeing this reflection, imagines that it is himself; but when the mirror is broken it is seen that the reflection gave only an illusion of duality. In the same manner the self of man disappears in the absolute abstract Self of all things when ignorance is destroyed. There abides no more reality in the world than there is in a dream, or in a town in the air or mirage[2] (gandharva nagaram). There is no birth, no production (ajāti). The individual

[1] Hakluyt Society, vol. xx., p. 105. [2] 2. 31.

soul is neither a part nor a production of the Soul of the universe, no more than space confined in a jar is a production of space.[1] To seek for causation would be "expecting to find a footprint in the sky" (pas'yanti yē jātim svē vai pas'yanti tē padam).[2]

The doctrine that to those who gained true knowledge the world was seen to be an illusion did not mean for Gauḍapāda, no more than it did for S'ankara, that there did not remain a very real world of ordinary opinion until true knowledge arose. Gauḍapāda teaches[3] that so long as man rests in ignorance, the world is real. In this real world devotion to God and good deeds are enjoined by the scriptures, out of the pure grace of God, so that the Soul may become contemplative and pierce through unreality to absolute truth. When the Soul gains true knowledge of the absolute Brahman, then "one should abide in it and rest in it, and not, like those of less intelligence, in the objects of the senses."[4] Gauḍapāda teaches that if it were not for the mind of man there would be no appearance of duality in the world. S'ankara, in his commentary on this teaching, states that it is self-evident that all duality is mental (dvaitam sarvam manas).

S'ankara argues that if any one imagines an absence of mind, then there could be no duality and everything would be an illusion. Again, when the mind is asleep there is no object for thought and consequently no

[1] 2. 7. [2] 4. 28. [3] 3. 16. [4] 2. 38.

duality. S'ankarācārya therefore holds that those Buddhists (vijñānavādins) who say that the mind is a production and full of sorrow and momentariness (kshaṇikatvam) are talking in vain. If they (Mādhyamika Buddhists) teach that all is a void, they might as well teach that they can hold the heavens in the palm of their hand. Gauḍapāda holds, as against the Buddhists, that the idea of momentary consciousness is a pure illusion. It is the effect of Māyā, universal ignorance, which produces the illusions of change, of birth or production. The whole of the delusion is mental, arising in some unaccountable way.

S'ankarācārya asserts, in his Commentary on Gauḍapāda,[1] that the Buddhists have no more valid grounds for believing in passing phases of the mind's momentary consciousness than they would have for asserting the mind's non-existence. When the fire-brand is at rest after it has been whirled round, the fiery circle is quenched and known to have been unreal, an illusion. Therefore the Upanishad[2] is quoted to prove that when the Self pierces through Māyā and is freed from ignorance, it sees not an unreal fiery circle, of continuing sparks of fire or consciousnesses, "it sees Brahman, where there is unity and no duality, flashing like a wheel on fire, and having seen Brahman, obtains immortality."

[1] 4. 28. [2] Mait Up. vi. 26.

CHAPTER VI

SĀNKHYA

THE WORLD AS MATTER

THE Sānkhya metaphysical speculations started with possibly the fewest assumptions that any pre-Buddhist inquirer into the how and why of the universe could make. It takes for granted the existence of matter and of a soul within man.

Souls, or purushas, of men are eternal, different from matter, being self-existent and in eternal rest in their original condition. When at rest in its primal condition the Soul is immaterial, subtle, inactive, pure light, passive. The existence of innumerable individual souls is taken as self-evident. It is held as ample proof of their existence that their existence is never denied. Further, it is held that their existence is proved from the design of the world which was made for the experience of souls, so that they might rise supreme above it and find eternal rest. The 21st verse of the Sānkhya Kārikā, which is the standard authority and dates from the fifth century A.D., says that, "for the soul's contemplation of nature and for its separation therefrom, a union of both takes place, as of a lame man and a blind man, and by that union creation is formed."

The commentary of Gauḍapāda to this verse says that, "as the birth of a child proceeds from the union of male and female, so the production of creation results from the connection of nature and soul." Here, for the first time in Indian metaphysics, there is no assumption or mention of a God or of a Creator of matter, or of the universe.

The question the Sānkhya had to answer was how the world of effects was produced. The mind of man naturally concludes, when it sees an effect, that the effect must have a cause. Kant held that causality was an innate function of the brain. Hume had held that there was no necessity, so far as absolute or metaphysical necessity is concerned, why existence should begin with a cause. To early thought the cause always remains immanent in the effect. The Sānkhya system assumed matter at rest as the least possible assumption from which to start in order to explain therefrom the evolution of the universe. Why the mind of man should consider the idea of matter at rest more simple to conceive than matter in motion is in itself a mystery. Leucippus and Democritus saw no difficulty in conceiving primal matter as an infinite number of atoms always in motion. In India, the Sānkhya system took primal matter at rest as its ultimate assumption. From this abstraction from the totality of the experiences of reality it proceeded to reconstruct the universe. This primal matter is held to be so subtle as to be beyond the apprehension of the senses. As effects are seen in the world, the Sānkhya held that these effects must imply a cause, and that this cause must be contained in the primal matter.

So far as there was no God or Creator, the Sānkhya abstraction reached a materialistic regressus of thought. Still, as it held to the current belief of souls, it also held to the equally old idea of three essences, or guṇas, of goodness, passion, and darkness, pervading everything and causing, by their want of stable equilibrium, disturbances and activities in the universe. It was therefore assumed that primal matter must also have three essences, constituents, or factors, namely: first, that of goodness, or brightness, or truth, or being; second, that of passion or energy; and third, an element of gloom or darkness. These three factors are assumed because, it is said, they transfuse everything. In ultimate primal matter, before any evolution of a universe takes place, these three constituents are held to be in equilibrium. Primal matter therefore, in this condition, is inert and powerless. The essences, or three constituents, of this dead matter when at rest are united like three strands of a rope.

The Sānkhya holds that in primal matter, when a disturbance in the equilibrium of the three guṇas takes place, the factor of energy causes primal matter to assume activity. Three arguments are stated, in the Sānkhya, as possible to be raised against this assumption. First, how could an unintelligent principle, such as primal matter, create an intelligent world, of the complexity of which not even the most ingenious workman could form a conception? Second, how could any want of equilibrium among the three constituents of primal matter lead to action in matter; and, third, how can the three constituents of matter return to rest once they have been moved to activity? These arguments are answered by saying that a non-intelligent principle can produce an intelligent design, just as rain acts for the benefit of the world and non-intelligent milk acts for the benefit of a calf. This only means that whatever exists in the effect must have existed in the cause. Therefore the three constituents of primal matter persist in the effect, and are immanent throughout the universe in different proportions.

The whole of the disturbance in the equilibrium and primeval quiescent condition of matter is said to be caused by the near approach to it of Souls, which arouses it to activity. The soul, then, exercises a magnetic influence on matter, and the three qualities of goodness, passion, and darkness come into operative force.

When primal matter is aroused into activity by the near proximity of Soul, there emanates from matter the subtlest form of matter, which is known as the Great principle,

Buddhi, Consciousness, or Intelligence, which passes into the universe. From Consciousness emanates Egoism, which produces the internal organ Mind, the faculty of receiving sensations and discriminating thereon. From Egoism are also produced the five organs of knowledge and the five organs of action, and five subtle elements (tanmātras) of ether, air, fire, water, and earth. From these five subtle elements arise the gross elements forming the body. The subtle elements (tanmātras) are the essences, or imperceptible subjects, of the visible elements, and are explained by Vijñāna Bhikshu, in his Commentary, to be "the subjects of the species of sound, touch, colour, taste, and smell; they are the rudiments of the elements." They are, in fact, the "things in themselves" of these elements. Of these Sānkhya principles eight are producers: Primal Matter, Consciousness, Egoism, and the five subtle elements. The other sixteen are productions. These twenty-four with Soul are the Twenty-five Principles. As expressed by Gauḍapāda in his Commentary: "He who knows the Twenty-five Principles, whatever order of life he may be in, be he an Ascetic, a Brāhman, or even a Buddhist, he is free: of this there is no doubt." The Soul, by the creation of a world, is involved in a threefold suffering. First, there is suffering of the body and mind; second, there is suffering from the outside world; and third, there is suffering from supernatural causes. The Sānkhya therefore seeks, like Buddhism, to find a refuge from these sorrows of a world. The Sānkhya teaches that the world exists so that the Soul may know its true nature and free itself from the sorrows of the existent. By freedom from the entanglements of matter the Soul gains a knowledge of its own essentially eternal isolation. This knowledge could only be gained by perception, by authoritative teaching, or by reasoning. No religious rites, no help from Brāhman priests or from sacrifices, could aid the Soul to regain eternal rest. Religious observances gave no abiding freedom to the Soul from the sorrows of the world. The residuum of actions would cling to it even after repeated transmigrations. Sacrifices were held to be impure as they necessitated the shedding of blood. The Soul, surrounded by the body and organs, internal and external, receives from Consciousness, or Buddhi, reflections of the impress made on it by outside objects. These outside objects are experienced by the activity (vṛitti) of the sense organs, which project themselves outward on to the object of experience. The internal sense organ, Manas, or Mind, receives these impressions, which thence pass into Consciousness. The reflections of an outside world, when received in Consciousness, are taken by the Soul as real objects of its own individuality through Egoism. Thus the Soul is drawn into a false connection with an outside world simply through the fictitious reflections shed upon it by Buddhi or Consciousness. The Soul remains passive, receiving from the Mind, which is called the doorkeeper of the senses, messages from the world of experience which pass to Consciousness and Egoism. The Soul is conscious of nothing except what it receives through the senses. The Egoism takes these sensations as referring to its own individuality, and Consciousness sends back messages of likes or dislikes, from which ensue actions. Sensations are received by the organs of sense projecting themselves on to the object. Thus, if the eye of a cat be seen in the dark, the rays of light may be seen going to the object. Similarly, in the case of fire the eye projects itself onto the object of fire. Although these sensations are presented to the Soul, by its unconsciousness being lit up by the influence of the Soul's own pure light, still the Soul remains in its absolute condition as pure light or thought. The Soul is thus surrounded by a fine body of matter, or ghost, which consists of the eighteen products of matter: Consciousness, Egoism, the Mind, the ten senses and the five subtle elements. This ghost body clings to the Soul and bears it through transmigrations as the result of its material nature. This subtle, or ghost, body of the Soul is the familiar ghost believed in all over India, which lurks everywhere and haunts the imagination of all simple folk. If a pack of dogs be taken, when hunting, near a burning-ground of the dead, it will generally be found that the dogs raise their heads and mournfully howl. If any simple villager be asked why they stand still and howl, the reply will be that the dogs can see what is invisible to man, and that they howl because they see the ghost bodies of the dead hovering over the burning-ground. The Soul, when it roused primal matter from its primeval rest, became encased in this fine or subtle body, its ghost. This subtle body presents the universe to the Soul, as a spectacle to view. Hence arise likes and dislikes and consequent actions. These, in turn, affect the intellectual constituent, the ghost body, which is thereby indelibly impressed, so that each ghost gains its own individual characteristics and is urged forth to new actions. The soul is thus caught in the trammels of matter.

After death it is surrounded by its ghost or subtle covering, which determines, by the impress of action it bears, whether the soul is to be carried to the heavens or hell or is to be reborn in a body to correspond with its past deeds. If the soul had not influenced matter there would have been no emanation from matter; so far as the soul was concerned it would have remained eternally pure and in unconscious rest: matter would have remained inert. By its fateful magnetic influence on matter, and by shedding the radiance of its consciousness on the emanations of matter, it has become subject to action through its surrounding ghost, subject to transmigrations in higher or lower forms of gods, men, or animals. By the good deeds of the ghost it may be carried to one of the eight heavens, or the bad deeds may have so left their impress as to characterize the ghost as an individual fit only for a lower hell or for an impure rebirth. The Sānkhya system has here reached its culminating point. The whole secret of nature is declared to be laid bare and knowledge has been gained. Matter has danced the dance of life for the benefit of the soul. The soul, wearied of the dance of life, sinks backs to dream of unconscious rest. Nature, like a loved one who has revealed her charms and finds her lover satiated, retires in modesty. So long, however, as life lasts the soul finds no eternal rest. For this it must wait until death. Then alone, for all, comes a Nirvāna of rest. The Sānkhya had cut off all refuge for a wearied soul. Religious rites were useless. Sacrifices and blood-offerings were declared unclean. Their efficacy was denied, for they affected rich and poor unequally. Those who were rich could offer most and gain most. It had damped the ardour of the ascetic, for his vain efforts to rise above the allurements of the senses could only gain for him a transient salvation. There was left no hope for anyone that his soul could gain knowledge, and come nearer to, or merge into, the infinite Soul of the universe. In the Sānkhya there was only soul and matter eternally separate from before all time. The soul could only hope for a return to solitary unconscious isolation. Freed from matter, it could only become freed from suffering, bodily or mental.

It was left to later times to fill up the gap left by the early Sānkhya by endowing it with a personal God. When this was done the Bhagavad Gītā or Song of the Lord[1] says that it is only the ignorant who can see a difference between the teachings of the Sānkya and those of its sister system, the Yoga, where the

[1] v. 4.

ascetic gains for his soul isolation from the dance of life by mortification (tapas) of the body.

To some the term Sānkhya, which means number, has suggested the idea that the system was derived from the Pythagorean school, which taught that number was the essence of all things. It seems much more possible that the term Sānkhya was used on account of the number of topics it discussed. A knowledge of the Sānkhya requires a knowledge of the total number of principles discussed, and these are: twenty-four primary principles, of which eight are producers and sixteen productions, which with Soul bring up the number to twenty-five.

CHAPTER VII

VAIS'ĒSHIKA AND NYĀYA

THE WORLD AS ATOMS

THERE was one last possible explanation of the riddle of the universe to be essayed by Indian thought. The Sānkhya had found its ultimate source, from which all things were evolved, in primal matter. Not content with this, the Vais'ēshika and its sister system, the Nyāya, sought to trace the beginning of all things to some ultimate particle of matter. The mind of man could hardly drive its conception of matter further back than the invisible and indivisible atom of matter. It was, however, no new theory in the history of man's efforts to solve the universe. Leucippus had framed a theory of the universe on the conception of primal atoms in a state of motion. There can be no doubt that "the Indian atomistic systems, Vais'ēshika and Nyāya, were conceived a long time after Leucippus and Democritus."[1] There can, however, be no question as to any borrowing of the idea of the atomic

[1] Garbe, *Monist*, 1893, p. 178.

theory of the universe by India from Greece. It is only one more example of the innumerable instances where the mind of man has solved problems in a similar manner in different parts of the world. The Greek atomic theory accepted atoms in a state of motion as the ultimate condition of matter. If this theory had been borrowed by India from Greece it can hardly be imagined that the very essence of the early Greek conception of atoms as in *motion*, not at *rest*, as in the Indian conception, should have been lost in the journey from Greece to India. In India the atomic theory was based—like the Sānkhya theory of primal matter, on the assumption that "a state of rest was more natural to matter than a state of motion, or even that it was absurd to consider motion as a part of the primordial endowment of matter."[1] In India the thought of the time was that the cause remained always immanent in the effect. The universe lives and moves in the cause from which it has its being. When Indian thought, in the atomic theory, had to solve the universe as an evolution from matter, it had to empty matter of all cause and therefore of all motion.

The atomic theory in India is ascribed to Kanāḍa, called, no doubt in derision, the Feeder on Atoms. The system dates from some time, probably, between 200 and 450 A.D.[2] The invisible, intangible, and indivisible atoms of Kanāḍa have the power of

[1] Gomperz, op. cit. p. 344. [2] Jacobi, J.A.O.S., vol. 31.

combining in aggregates of two. The smallest visible combination of atoms is a mote, or combination of three double atoms. This mote, as seen in a sun-beam, is just barely visible. In the Greek theory of atoms of Democritus, the atoms had no function of grouping themselves together, nor did they ever join so as to become visible. In the Indian doctrine the atoms, by some unseen virtue, or, as it is said, by some other competent cause, unite to form earth, water, light, air, and mind. The concurrence of two atoms forms a double atom of earth, and so on, till by combination gross, grosser, and grossest masses are produced. The unseen force, or virtue, or influence producing these combinations is the force of actions or deeds done during previous existences. The whole object of the system is to set before the soul of man the true nature of existence. Existence is suffering; there are the sorrows of the world, the pains of birth and death. Individual souls are eternal and infinite; they are diffused through all time and space. It is only by the evolution from atoms of the universe and the body of man that the soul gains the means of perceiving things and of having activities. Soul is merely the basis for qualities and actions. The compassion of Kanāḍa, it is said, has given mankind a knowledge of the true nature of the world. The soul can therefore attain to a presentation of its own true and essential nature, and by such knowledge it becomes freed from suffering and gains release. To attain to this knowledge, man must be perfected in all revealed knowledge, he must have acquired merit by good deeds done in this or in a previous existence. Then, and then alone, man can realize the truth of the analysis of existence as set forth under six heads or categories by Kanāḍa, on the attainment of which knowledge all false knowledge vanishes, and there is an eternal end to birth, activities, and suffering, and supreme bliss to the soul ensues. The whole of existence, knowledge of which gives release to the soul, is summed up under the six heads of substance, quality, action or motion, identity or generality, difference or particularity, and finally inherence or inseparability. A later category was added under the head of non-existence. Under these heads Kanāḍa develops his own peculiar metaphysics and psychology. Under the category of substances is taught the knowledge of the origin and nature of earth, water, light, air, ether, time and space, the soul and the mind. Air, although it transcends sense perception, and is invisible, still from its motion must be of the nature of substance. Time and space are held to be eternal substances and infinite. Mind is a substance of atomic dimensions and capable of receiving but one sensation at one time. Conjoined with the body, it is nevertheless eternally distinct. The one interesting point in the system is the development of the theory of sensation and perception. In the case of vision the sight organ consists of fire or light, which may be seen in the eye of a cat in the dark. The organ of vision is therefore said to be fire, clear as the light of a lamp. This fire of the eye, by going forth from the eye and by conjunction with the object viewed produces an impression on the mind. This impression is transmitted by the mind to the eye. This theory of vision, where the organ of sight consists of fire which combines with the object viewed and takes its shape, has been pointed out[1] to be remarkably similar to the theory of vision of Alcmæon of Croton, a younger contemporary of Pythagoras. In Greece, "Alcmæon was the first to turn his attention to the subjective impressions of sense, thus opening the path which was ultimately to lead to a deeper insight into the nature of the act of perception and of the process of cognition in general. . . . His curiosity was aroused by the photopsy in an eye which has received a heavy blow, and this phenomenon stimulated his powers of scientific imagination. It forms, we conceive, no mean evidence of Alcmæon's genius for science that he realized the significance of this rare and abnormal phenomenon and regarded it as the key to the normal act of vision. It was inevitable that his explanation should be crude and childish in character. He seized on a purely material factor, where we speak of the specific energy of the nerve of sense."[2]

The system of Kanāḍa endeavoured to make a scientific analysis—so far as ascertained fact would

[1] Gomperz, op. cit. p. 549. [2] Ibid. p. 149.

permit at that time—of the underlying nature of the universe and of man's relationship thereto. It was an endeavour to reconcile the seeming conflict between man's ideals of justice and the stern reality of a world, wherein retribution often falls on the undeserving. Metaphysical attempts to solve the problem of the universe are attempts where the philosopher "is expected to tell us something about the nature of the universe as a whole, and to give grounds for either optimism or pessimism. Both these expectations seem to me to be mistaken . . . and I believe the question of optimism and pessimism to be one which the philosopher will regard as outside his scope, except, possibly, to the extent of maintaining that it is insoluble."[1]

In the system of Kanāḍa the whole reality of matter drifts back to the mental abstraction of atoms. The soul when it realizes this knowledge remains passive in isolated unconscious bliss. It remains unaffected by the flux and change in atomic matter, evolving, through the influence of some mysterious cause, scenes, sensations and activities, all ending in sadness, and endless transmigrations of the soul through births and rebirths. To fill up the gap left in this system, the religious and ethical ideas of after ages (twelfth century) joined to it the conception of a Deity or Supreme Soul

[1] Bertrand Russell, "Scientific Method in Philosophy," 1914, p. 4.

possessing power and knowledge for the creation and preservation of the world.

Nyāya

The Nyāya, which develops the system of Kanāḍa, is held in respect in India more for its system of formal logic than for any distinctive philosophic teachings. Ascribed to a Brāhman teacher called Gotama, its formal thought follows close on that of the Sānkhya. The text-book of the Nyāya school has but five chapters, each divided into two lessons.

The system postulates the existence of a Supreme Creator, a soul of eternal knowledge. Individual souls, which are eternal and infinite, are the substratum of the attributes of knowledge, desire, aversion, volition, pain, and pleasure. They are subject to transmigrations through different bodies. The emancipation of the soul from the body and its attainment of eternal bliss follow on a knowledge of the twelve objects of knowledge taught by the system, which depend on four methods of proof—revelation and authority, perception, inference, and similarity. The twelve objects of which knowledge has to be gained are the soul, the body, the senses, and the objects of the senses, intellect, mind, production, fault, transmigration, retribution, pain, and emancipation. Ignorance of the full knowledge of these twelve objects of knowledge arouses feelings of likes and dislikes in the individual, whence action ensues, leading to birth and death, pain and sorrow. The Nyāya differs from the Sānkhya in deriving the five sense organs not from intelligence or consciousness, but directly from the five gross elements of matter. The mind, further, in the Nyāya is eternally distinct from the soul, being of atomic size, its functions being to receive sensations for presentation to the soul.

The Nyāya Sūtras of Gotama were commented upon by Vātsyāyana, whose commentary was in turn commented on by Dignāga, who probably lived in the sixth century. Vātsyāyana must therefore have lived before the beginning of the sixth century and possibly before the second half of the fifth century.[1]

[1] L. Suali, "Filosofia Indiana," p. 14.

CHAPTER VIII

YOGA

ASCETICISM

THE formulated system of the Yoga philosophy cannot be traced back further than the fourth or fifth centuries of our era.

The first rule of the earliest known formulated doctrines of the Yoga, as set forth in the Sūtras of Patañjali, states that "when there is restriction of all the fluctuations of the mind-stuff there is the concentration in which there is no consciousness of an object." [1]

The Yoga teaches the attainment of a super-personal condition of the mind wherein it reaches what has been called the subconscious or subliminal self.

That such a state exists has been held to be proved; [2] "If we are to believe the Hindu philosophers, at least those of them who have, in addition to theoretical knowledge, practical experience as well, i.e. the Yogins

[1] "Yoga System of Patañjali," Professor J. H. Woods, Harvard, 1914, p. 4.

[2] "Kashmir Shaivism," Chatterji, Kashmir, 1914, p. 101.

of the right kind (not those distorters and torturers of the body and performers of juggling, hypnotizing, and such-like feats for the delectation of the public, who also have come to be known as Yogins, especially to the Western tourist), and who repeatedly assert the possibility and truth of such experience. While the Yogins claim—they having trained their whole life, spiritual, mental, moral, and physical, in a particular way—to be able to have this experience at will, others, even in the West, would seem to have had it as occasional glimpses over which they have little control."

The Yoga accepts the teachings of the Sānkhya, but points the way to the release of the soul from matter by asceticism. It further adds a belief in a Lord or Īs'vara, who in grace and mercy aids the soul in concentration of thought through asceticism.

Asceticism, or tapas, originally meant to burn, or to ardently mortify the body and suppress all desires. An ascetic in India has always been viewed as endowed with supernatural powers, as one whose wrath was to be feared and whose goodwill was to be sought by worship and gifts.

The word Yoga means yoking or uniting, and in the system of Patañjali implies yoking the mind to the subject of matter and the soul's release. The system defines Yoga as the suspension of the principle of consciousness, or "repression of the activities of Buddhi." The Yoga practices can only be fully taught by a guru, or teacher, to a disciple, and if no teacher can be found, then the grace of the Lord, or of Vishṇu or S'iva, must be sought. There are said to be mysteries connected with Yoga over and above the principles laid down in the text-books, and these must be kept secret by the teacher and only communicated to a suitable and loved disciple (chela). The Yoga system has a lower teaching, that of Kriyā or Hatha Yoga, and a final teaching, that of Rāja, or Kingly, Yoga. A modern text-book of the Hatha Yoga, by a perfected Yogin, Swātmā rām Swāmi, states "that suspension of the mental activity will cause the three worlds to disappear with their misery. By the knowledge of controlling the mind all occult powers are acquired."[1] India to-day is thronged with followers of the Yoga—some sincere, some charlatan, some even demented from their self-inflicted tortures. Some are to be found with their arms uplifted, for years, until the arms have become immovable. Some are seated amid surrounding fires gazing with unmoving eyes into the glare of a midday sun. Some wander about with the fire of madness in their mind, the fire of hunger in their bodies, the fire of intoxicating drugs in their brains, crying on the gods in their frenzied imaginations. The Hatha Yoga Pradīpikā says that the disciple seeking knowledge of how to free his soul should always reside in a small cell, and the Commentary adds: "He should depict on the walls a burning-ground and the hells or places of purification after death, so

[1] p. iii.

that his mind will conceive a horror and dislike of this worldly life." There are eight fundamental rules, or practices, enjoined for all who follow the First or Lower Yoga. These are: (1) Restraint from destroying life, from falsehood, from unchastity and non-liberality. (2) Subduing oneself by ascetic practices, by ever repeating the mystic syllable "Om," and by devotion to God. (3) Definite postures are to be assumed during meditation. (4) Regulating the retention of the breath. (5) Regulating its inspiration and expiration. (6) Abstraction. (7) Firmness, and (8) Meditation.

The rules regarding the control of the breath depend on the general Indian belief that the Soul enters and escapes from the body by an artery running from the forehead to the heart, where the Soul abides. Should this artery be closed by regulating the breath, by inspiration and expiration, the breathing ceases and the Soul can escape, for ever or for a time, from the body through the artery. Some of the practices inculcated in the Hatha Yoga seem impossible, some are indescribable. The following are a few of the simpler and milder practices. One should sit with the heels placed on the stomach, the chin fixed on the breast, and the eyes fixed on the spot between the eyebrows, for a period of twelve years. The Yogi then, ever contemplating the Soul, will gain magic powers of mind and body.

To become free from old age and death the membrane of the tongue should be daily gradually cut until it is severed and can be turned upwards. To purify the mind a piece of cloth four fingers broad and fifteen spans long should be swallowed and then drawn out again.

These are but preliminary stages towards the final aim of the Yoga, the isolation of the soul from matter. This last stage is that of the Rāja or Kingly Yoga. The Yoga here fixes its attention on the freedom of the Soul from the first emanation of primal matter, the Buddhi, Intelligence or Consciousness, which is the subtlest form of matter. The practices of the Kriyā Yoga end in the withdrawal of all the senses into pure Consciousness. Physical disciplines prepare the disciple for Kingly Yoga, but any seeking after magic or occult powers has the effect of retarding the disciple in his progress towards the final isolation of his soul from Consciousness.

The first stage in the final Yoga is Dhāraṇa, or intense concentration, so as to limit Consciousness to consciousness of one object only. The next stage is Dhyāna, or deep meditation, after which is reached the final stage of Samādhi. The Samādhi at first is not completed, for still in the Consciousness abide the conformations, or impress, of former deeds which may act as the seeds of further actions. Supreme Samādhi is reached when even this impress fades and the Soul stands freed from the last taint of matter. In the state of conscious Samādhi the consciousness has lost all objectivity and self-identity. It becomes what it meditates upon. All past transmigrations, and their full meaning, illuminate consciousness. In Madras, local interest was greatly aroused a few years ago (in 1910) by the case of a Yogi who was stated to have reached Samādhi. The *Siddhānta Dīpikā* (August, September, October 1910) states that when red-hot cinders were applied to the eyes of the Yogi he never spoke. He had passed the danger point of conscious Samādhi by not yielding to the fascination of exercising supernatural powers, for, as the *Dīpikā* wrote, if these powers are not used, "they yield their full strength to you, and merge themselves in you and become part of you as the conqueror." The Yogi, it was further said, could therefore "think and act in a higher plane without being encumbered with the natural organs of thought."

Huxley[1] has in a few words expressed what some may deem not inapplicable to the more extreme phases of the Yoga: "No more thorough mortification of the flesh has ever been attempted than that achieved by the Indian ascetic anchorite; no later monachism has so nearly succeeded in reducing the human mind to that condition of impassive quasi-somnambulism which, but for its acknowledged holiness, might run the risk of being confounded with idiocy."

The Greek historians who accompanied Alexander the Great on his invasion of India in 327 B.C. wrote accounts of the Yogis they had seen in India. Onesikritos left the record that a Hindu sage named Kalanos followed Alexander the Great on the march back from India as far as Persepolis, and there finding,

[1] "Evolution and Ethics," p. 17.

as Arrian wrote, that he became ill and could no longer follow a life of meditation, he gave his rug and begging bowl to the onlookers and mounted a funeral pyre, and was burnt to death in the presence of the wondering army. Eusebius Renaudot, in a translation of the travels of two Muhammadans who visited India in the ninth century, records of the Yogis in India that "some of them are quite naked, or have only a leopard's skin thrown over them, and in this plight keep standing with their faces turned to the sun. I formerly saw one in the posture I have described, and on returning to India about sixteen years afterwards I found him in the very same attitude, and was astonished he had not lost his eyesight by the heat of the sun." Marco Polo recorded that he saw many Yogis in India who were said to have lived one hundred and fifty and two hundred years drinking an elixir of life composed of sulphur and quicksilver: "And they would rather die than do what they deem their law pronounces a sin . . . and they sleep on the ground stark naked, without a scrap of clothing on them or under them, so that it is a marvel they don't all die. . . . They fast every day in the year and drink nought but water." Marco Polo said they wear a pewter or gold image of an ox which they worship, tied over their forehead.

A very full account of two Yogis is given by Jonathan Duncan from his observations of them at Benares in 1792. He presented the Asiatic Society of Bengal with drawings of these Yogis which he had made himself. In one picture the Yogi has his arms fixed immovable over his head. The arm is atrophied, mere skin and bone, the finger nails long and twisted. This Yogi commenced his austerities at the age of nine. He travelled, with his arms immovably fixed above his head, through all the holy places of India; from Benares to the temple of Jagannath in Orissa, down to the South to view the bridge said to have been built from India to Ceylon by the army of monkeys which brought cyclopean rocks to enable Rāma to rescue Sītā from the demon Rāvana. Thence he travelled back to gaze on the spot where the sacred Ganges springs from the snowclad Himālaya, on to Kabul and Bamian, viewing on his way the remains of the Buddhist monasteries so as to keep in mind the instability of all things. He then travelled on to Moscow, back to Tibet and Nepal, to take up his abode at the holy city of Benares.

The second Yogi described was a Yajur Vēda Brāhman who at the age of ten had commenced his life of mortification of the flesh so as to free himself for meditation. In Nepal, at the holy lake Manuswara, he studied under Mahātmas who had advanced so far in the science of the Yoga as to be able to perform miracles. He returned to Benares, where he continued his austerities. In the hot weather he sat, without clothing, with the sun pouring down on him, with four fires kept constantly burning round him. His bed, on which he always lay without covering, was studded with sharp iron spikes. In the cold weather a stream of water flowed continuously on his head from a perforated pot. Mill in his "History of India"[1] records of Yogis in India that: "Of all the phenomena of nature none appears, at first view, more extraordinary than the self-inflicted torment of the holy saints of Hindustan. Some of them keep their hands closed till they are pierced through by the growth of the nails; others hold them above their heads till the power of the arms is extinguished. . . . Other penitents bury themselves up to the neck in the ground, or even wholly below it, leaving only a little hole through which they may breathe. They tear themselves with whips; they repose on beds of iron spikes, they chain themselves for life to the foot of a tree. . . . They fix their eyes on the blazing sun till the power of vision is extinguished."

[1] Vol. i. 153

CHAPTER IX

BUDDHISM

I. The Warrior becomes a Monk

In early India, some 2,500 years ago, there was a general belief that there was an abiding principle, a Self or Soul, within man which persisted after death. The Soul received rewards in heaven and rebirth on earth in ameliorated conditions of life, if the Karma, or action of previous existences, had been good. It was awarded penalties in hell and rebirth in degraded conditions of life if its actions had been evil. Therefore extreme asceticism came to be an ideal whereby man could free his Soul from both good and evil actions. In the midst of such beliefs the Buddha, or Enlightened One, was born about 560 B.C. He was son of a ruling chieftain of a Kshatriya clan living where now there are forest-covered ruins, about one hundred miles north of Benares, as the lowlands sink into the Tarai of Nepal at the foot of the mountain ranges of North India. When he reached the age of twenty-nine he abandoned his home, his wife, and child son, and, until he reached the age of eighty, when he died, he never ceased teaching that life was fleeting and full of sorrow. As the weeping philosopher Heraclitus said, according to Lucian, so might the Buddha have said: "To me it is a sorrow that there is nothing fixed or secure, and that all things are thrown confusedly together, so that pleasure and pain, knowledge and ignorance, the great and the small, are the same, ever circling round and passing one into the other in the sport of time."[1] So, likewise, the Buddha saw nothing abiding in this world. He held that the universe was a ceaseless ever-becoming, in which impermanence even the gods participated. In such a doctrine there could be no abiding principles such as God and the Soul, or Self. If this were so, it might be well asked why man should weary himself with good deeds or with asceticism. Actions can only lead to new existences, with their sufferings of birth, disease, sorrow, old age, and death. Were it not better to seclude oneself from the world and live a life of concentrated thought, wherein all attachment to fleeting pleasures of the senses might fade away and man gain a haven of rest in quietism? The problem and its solution is old and yet ever new. As has been said, "The mystery of existence, the unreality of what seems most real, the intangibility and evanescence of all things earthly—these thoughts obscurely echoing to us across the ages from Heraclitus, have remained, and always will remain, among the deepest and most insistent of the

[1] Marshall, "Greek Philosophy," p. 20.

world's thoughts, in its sincerest moments and in its greatest thinkers."[1]

In Benares many seekers after truth abandoned their asceticism and flocked to hear the new solution of the here and hereafter as taught by Buddha. It is recorded that, at Buddha Gayā, one thousand Brāhmans joined the middle path of monastic quietude. Throughout Bihar and Oudh the Buddha gathered in the people to listen to his teaching and to wonder at the yellow robes of his followers and at the wealth which was poured at their feet. The people had been accustomed to the proud reserve and vaunted divine knowledge of Brāhman priests. They had given alms to Jain ascetics and half-crazed Yogis. Men had worshipped the Brāhmans and their gods, they had lived in fear and trembling at the thought that their slightest neglect of reverence towards the Brāhmans and their sacrifices might doom their souls to perpetual torments in hells or to rebirth in foul and unclean new forms of life. All these terrors of life were now to be swept away and nothing abiding left of mind or matter, or of God or soul. All humanity was to receive, irrespective of caste distinctions, knowledge of a saddened world wherein there was no hope. Love towards each other and mutual forbearance could alone give some momentary relief from sorrow in a life which had no more permanency than had a quickly passing shadow.

[1] Marshall, op. cit. p. 21.

Buddha, before he left his home, his wife and child, had found that a continuing of life was but a continuing of sorrow. He is said to have turned from all visions of life with despair in his heart, and above all he saw with loathing the vision of old age and death. If life, so hopelessly full of sorrow, was to end inevitably in decaying powers of body and mind, why add to its sorrows by conjuring forth problems—which were insoluble—of God, the Soul, and the Hereafter? Amid conflicting authorities it is difficult to ascertain the exact ideas of Buddha on these questions of the How and Wherefore of the universe; "for although Buddha gives no place to a First Cause in his system, yet, as is well known, he nowhere expressly denies an Infinite First Cause or an unconditioned Being beyond the finite, and he is even represented as refusing to answer such questions on the ground that their discussion was unprofitable. In view of this apparent hesitancy and indecision he may be called an agnostic."[1] Buddha merely taught those who entered the Buddhist order that a monastic life of quietude and thought was preferable to a life in the world, while he told the lay members of the order, who lived a worldly life, to do good deeds of charity and kindness to all men, and not weary themselves with philosophic doubts and questionings. The Vēdānta taught its doctrines of God and the Soul, their spiritual

[1] Waddell, J.R.A.S., 1894, p. 384.

relations and their transcendental unity. Buddha fixed his gaze on life and taught that the problem of the universe was the problem of the present condition of that life which was ever flowing on with its heavy burden of suffering and sorrow. Such teaching could not admit of even a momentary abiding of consciousness within the mind of man from which he could postulate the existence of an I or Ego as a principle of thought. To Buddha the world was evasive and ever transient. He therefore taught that "in the whole universe there is nothing permanent, no eternal substance either of mind or matter." [1]

To S'ankara the whole universe was spiritual, outside of which everything was unreal and an illusion.

Buddha, in directing his view solely on the real, lost sight of the spiritual and so found the world very sad.

S'ankara, in fixing his gaze solely on the spiritual, lost sight of the real, which faded away as an illusion.

The two metaphysical abstractions of Buddha and S'ankara meet in a doctrine of a thirteenth-century sage of South India, Meykandar, the Seer of the Truth, which declares that the mind, becomes that with which it identifies itself most; spiritual if it identifies itself with the spiritual, realistic if it identifies itself with the real. He expresses this in the words "It becomes It" (Adu adu ādal).

[1] "Evolution and Ethics," Huxley, p. 20.

The Buddha in his doctrine of the evanescence of all things might blot out from abiding existence God, the soul, and the self of man, but there was one factor in Indian belief he could not view as momentary and transitory, and that was the effect of man's good and evil actions. To-day in India a man may be an agnostic as regards the existence of God and the Soul, yet he may remain an altruist, driven by an inexorable law of Evolution, his moral nature or intuition. The Buddha taught that the aim of life was a destruction of the ignorance which results in desires and cravings which lead to actions and continuous existence. To attain Nirvāna, the sublimest ideal of Buddhism, the cessation of the onward stream of life, all actions, deeds, or Karma, arising from ignorance, should be abandoned, as they only result in the continuing of existence. To gain Nirvāna, home, wife, and family should be forsaken, and the result of deeds, or Karma, be quenched in the secluded life of the monastic cell.

No metaphysical teachings respecting life and its ever becoming could have won the people of Kās'i and Kosala, where Buddha taught, to a reverence for his law and for the Buddhist monks. Indian thought from the very earliest times had seen the supernatural and spiritual underlying everything. Strenuous subduing of the desires, and of the senses, great gift of speech, piety, heroism,

JAIN TEMPLE, CALCUTTA.

To face p. 147.

and even eccentricity, were viewed as endowments of some inherent divinity in the person of those who rose above the ordinary lives of the people. Even to-day it has been said that "the ordinary householder looks upon the Sanyāsi, or mendicant, as an ideal of perfection. The conviction is so engrained in the Hindu mind, that let a man but wear the mendicant's garb and profess contempt for the world, he is at once installed as a spiritual guide and worshipped as such." [1]

Sooner or later, famed ascetic saints or renowned heroes became deities and found a place in the Hindu pantheon. Two other, later deified, saints or sages appeared in India much about the same time as Buddha. All three were Kshatriyas of clans living outside the Midland, where Brāhmanism had spread the cult of the sacrifice and claimed for itself divine birth.

In the lower Tarai of Nepal, between the Rohinī river and the higher reaches of the Rapti, the founder of Buddhism was born about 560 B.C. He was a Kshatriya son of the ruling chief of the Sākya clan. In Videha (Tirhut) the founder of Jainism was born about 599 B.C. He was a Kshatriya of the Jñātrika clan and was known as Jñātiputra. To the west the third, a Kshatriya of the Yādava or Sātvata clan, [2] was born in the third or fourth century B.C.

[1] S. N. Sastri, "Mission of the Brāhmo-Somaj," p. 58.

[2] Bhandarkar, "Vais'ṇavism," pp. 9, 11. See *post* pp. 200, 210; also Keith, J.R.A.S., 1915, p. 547.

He was known as Vāsudeva, the centre of a belief and faith in a personal God to be worshipped in devotion and love, a faith which afterwards became the basis of the religious beliefs of a great part of India.

Round the personality of Buddha the imagination and piety of after generations wove ever growing traditions of a miraculous birth and supernatural divinity.

As regards the Buddha it is almost certain that he never encouraged among his followers any philosophical discussions as to the how or why of the universe, and that he considered it useless to discuss any metaphysical speculations regarding the nature of God and of the soul.

Shortly after his death, in 483 B.C., a council of 500 monks assembled together at Rājagriha and there recited their master's Vinaya, or rules for the monastic order, and the Law, or Dhamma, for monks and lay members, so that there might remain a record thereof to be handed down for the guidance of future generations. One hundred years later a second council is said to have been held at Vais'ali to protest against the growing laxity of the Buddhist community in observing the laws of their order. The earliest written records of the teachings of the Buddha are contained in the Pāli Tripiṭakas, or Triple-baskets, the sacred records of the Buddhists of Ceylon. Two of these collections deal with the Vinaya, or rules for the Buddhist monks, and with the Sutta, or doctrines or discourses of the Buddha. These were not introduced into Ceylon until 241 B.C., and probably were not reduced to writing until 80 B.C.

The Pāli canon can therefore hardly be expected to give any reliable evidences of the exact teachings and words of Buddha. It has been held that "the words and theories put into the mouth of Buddha therein are largely the composition of monks who lived several centuries after Buddha's death." [1]

If too much reliance cannot be placed on the Pāli Piṭakas as a record of the teachings of the Buddha, nevertheless they show that his earnest endeavours were to establish an order of monastic mendicant monks bound to the strictest injunctions of a moral law and discipline. The Buddhist monk who entered the monastic order had to regard his property as distributed to others, and, if married, his marriage as dissolved. One eternal problem had to be solved: how to cut oneself adrift from all attachments leading to a craving for existence, thence to birth, suffering, death, and new existences. No life but a life of monastic seclusion with deep concentration of thought over the transitoriness of life could lead to that ineffable bliss wherein all suffering ceases, and a craving for pleasure or being becomes dormant. Karma, or action, fraught with desires and thirst for existence, leads through ignorance to re-birth. Huxley summed up the stoic apathy of the period when he

[1] Waddell, J.R.A.S., 1914, p. 661.

said that "The Vēdas and the Homeric epos set before us a world of rich and vigorous life, full of joyous fighting men—who were ready to brave the very gods themselves when their blood was up. A few centuries pass away and, under the influence of civilization, the descendants of these men are . . . frank pessimists, or at best make-believe optimists. The courage of the warlike stock may be as hardly tried as before, perhaps more hardly, but the enemy is self. The hero has become a monk. The man of action is replaced by the quietist."[1]

No northern race which has ever taken up its abode in southern or eastern climes has escaped the penalty of being "sicklied o'er with the pale cast of thought." Rome, when it fell to barbarian hosts, had long suffered beneath the deadly miasma of its malarious surroundings.

Buddhism, which taught an abandonment of home, wife, and child for a self-centred concentration of thought and an annihilation of all action, spread among a people whose environment was of the very nature of their saddened thoughts. The Buddha had been born in the then malarious, stricken surroundings of the lower Tarai of Nepal. Near to his home, beyond the Sadānīra river, was the land of the Videhas or modern Tirhut. The "Brāhmana of 100 Paths"[2] tells how Agni, or fire, had formerly not cleared the land of forest and jungle to the east of the

[1] "Evolution and Ethics," p. 29.

[2] 1. 4. 1.

Sadānīra, but that "nowadays, however, there are many Brāhmans to the east of it. At that time the land to the east of the Sadānīra was very uncultivated, very marshy, because it had not been tasted by Agni."

It requires but little imagination to picture the physical and mental condition of the people, immigrant Aryans and aborigines alike, who lived in a land such as this. Generation after generation had been born amid these marshy swamps before they had been gradually cleared, by fire, of forest and drained. The Atharva Vēda[1] calls forth all its subtlest spells to drive far away from the Aryans the devastating fever: "The fever of the third day, of two days out of three, the constant and the autumnal, the cold, the hot, that of the hot season, that of the rainy season, do thou cause to disappear." And again a spell is sought to drive downward "the fever that is spotted, speckled, ruddy, like a sprinkling."[2]

The most deadly form of malaria in sub-mountainous districts—at least in South India—is that which appears when a mountain river rushes down in spate from its source in far-off feverish jungle uplands. Then the bodies of those who drink its clear waters become speckled with small crimson spots, just as described in the above Vēda. Whole villages then lie silent, every individual who has drunk of the clear waters struggling with death. Those who survive bear for years the poison in their bodies and brains.

[1] v. 22. 13, Whitney and Lanman. Harvard. [2] v. 22. 3.

Again the fever in these eastern tracts is described[1] as making "all men yellow, heating up like fire, consuming." Spells are conjured forth to drive the fever to neighbouring tribes, for "In that thou being cold, then hot, didst cause trembling, together with cough —fearful are thy missiles, O fever."

It is always towards the outlands or to the despised east[2] that the fever is sought to be driven as its natural home, for[3] it is to "the Añgas, the Magadhas, like one sending a person a treasure do we commit the fever."

It was in this land of the Magadhas that the Buddha made his earliest converts and where he chiefly taught for the forty-five years of his wanderings. To some devout souls a severance from the world and a longing for the cessation of all existence may denote no brooding pessimism. For them such losses are counted as gains, and the victor's award, for conquest over the self, is the blissful assurance of an eternity of joy. The Buddhist pessimist could look to no award, no compensation for all his severance from the world and longings for cessation of existence. For the Buddhist recluse, "When the thunderclouds in the heaven beat the drum, when the floods of water choke the paths of the air, and the monk, in a mountain cave, surrenders himself to abstraction, he can have no greater joy."[4] The Buddha himself may have taught

[1] A. V., v. 22. 2. [2] v. 22. 10. [3] v. 22. 14.

[4] Oldenberg, op. cit. p. 315, quoting from Theragāthā.

nothing respecting the question of a hereafter. The Buddha knew that "there were enough, and more than enough, of hopes and wishes from which he who desired to follow the Sākya's son had to sever his heart. Why present to the weak the keen edge of truth: the victor's prize of the delivered is the Nothing? True, it is not permissible to put falsehood in the place of truth, but it is allowable to draw a well-meant veil over the picture of the truth, the sight of which threatens the destruction of the unprepared."[1] The subdued Buddhist quietists of Magadha may have been no more pessimistic and no more enervated by long residence in the further east than their brethren had become in the Midland and to the west. At the time of the rise of Buddhism in the east the pristine intellectual vigour of Brāhmanism had waned, even in its ancient homes to the northwest, and "the old Vedic religion had degenerated into the coldest formalism; the idea that the mechanical repetition of certain formulæ and verses and manual operations had a religious efficacy took firm hold of the Brāhmanic mind, and mysticism usurped the place of spiritual worship."[2] Buddhism arose at a period when the outlying clans, with their ruling Kshatriya chieftains, felt little inclined to submit to the growing priestcraft of the Brāhmans. The personality of Buddha, the socialistic simplicity of his teachings, and inculcation

[1] Oldenberg, op. cit. p. 274.

[2] Bhandarkar, "Search for Sanskrit MSS.," 1887, p. 38.

of high ethical standard of morals, added to the fact that he was of Kshatriya origin, all appealed with irresistible force not only to Kshatriyas and to those outside the pale of Brāhmanism, but also to many Brāhmans of Magadha, Kosala, and Videha.

It seems almost an insoluble mystery why Buddhism should have disappeared from India. The established order of mendicants were freed from the necessity of undergoing any manual labour. The monks were not subjected to any severe rules of discipline. They were "secured from want; some of them enjoyed the fascinating power of wealth, so completely contrary to all the principles of their religion and to the precepts laid down by their teacher for the attainment of spiritual progress; they are often lazy, and not seldom avaricious. But in Ceylon and Burma, at least, they are not, as a body, disgraced by gluttony or drunkenness."[1] When one wanders in India along the mountain sides and views the now deserted cells, hewn out of the solid rock, the abode in ages past of these mendicant monks, and then gazes on the rich river valleys teeming with ripening crops, one wonders why the cells are not still occupied. The mendicant monk had but to wander through the rich villages and hold out the begging bowl for it to be amply filled. The Brāhmans had taught, as the ultimate ideal, a hermit's life in the forest and a wandering, as an ascetic, throughout the world. The Jains, before the time of Buddha, had

[1] Rhys Davids, "Buddhism," p. 168.

AJANTA CAVE TEMPLES.

To face p. 154.

their monasteries and wandering monks. Asceticism and withdrawal from the world had always been an ideal of India from Vedic times. The more man withdrew himself from the objective side of existence the more he seemed, to those living in the world, to become spiritualized. The man of the world had many sins on his soul which no regrets could wash out; these sins exacted their full retribution in the dire penalty of the individual being reborn in degraded forms of human or animal life. A little charity to the mendicant monks might perchance redeem something of the past sins of the rich householder in the village.

For almost 1,000 years Buddhism swept into its monasteries, which arose all over India, much of the learning of the time, and gathered in from kings, princes, and lay members wealth sufficient to support the Buddhist monks. The Buddhist order of mendicant monks established by Buddha, "when it flourished in India, must have rivalled in wealth the most powerful orders of the Middle Ages; and in Buddhist countries of the present day the Church is often as wealthy as it is among ourselves."[1]

Buddhism, amid the gloom and pessimism of the time which first saw its birth, gave to the people at least a means whereby they might throw from off their saddened imaginations somewhat of their weary load of dread of an endless wandering of their soul through ceaseless

[1] Rhys Davids, "Buddhism," p. 167.

transmigrations, the sole reward of all their lifelong labour and good or evil actions, and it brought to India a respect for all animal and human life.

II. The Four Noble Truths

What is the good of this universe? This is a question to which Buddha gave no indecisive answer. To his disciples he said, "What think ye, disciples, whether is more, the water which is in the four great oceans, or the tears which have flown from you and have been shed by you while ye strayed and wandered on this long pilgrimage?"[1] Yet according to Buddha all these tears had been shed in vain. Not one tear need be shed if mankind had but knowledge of the Four Noble Truths. It was not ignorance of God and of the Soul that sent man through the weary pilgrimage of life and endless rebirths. It is ignorance that life is suffering arising out of desire, and that this suffering ceases on cessation of desire. This is the central and fundamental doctrine of Buddhism, contained in the ever repeated teachings of the Four Noble Truths:—

1. That life from birth to death is crowded in with suffering. Suffering is "the hankering after corporeal form, after sensations, perceptions, conformations, and after consciousness."[2]

[1] Oldenberg, op. cit. p. 216.
[2] Ibid., note, p. 211.

2. That desire or thirst for power, for pleasure, for being, leads from birth to rebirth with their sufferings.

3. That all sorrows cease when this desire or thirst is extinguished.

4. That there is a path which, if followed, leads to a cessation of suffering. This is an eightfold path of right belief or faith, right aspiration, right speech, right action, right living, right effort, right thought, and right meditation.

The Buddha essays in these Four Noble Truths no metaphysical speculations over the why or the wherefore of the universe. A fivefold craving after form, sensations, perceptions, conformations, and consciousness is all that Buddha's simple teachings set before his disciples. The Four Noble Truths held in themselves a code of ethics whereby all people, irrespective of caste or religious belief, could become free in this world from the pains and sorrows of life. It was ignorance of the cause of suffering and ignorance of the path to the cessation of suffering that the Buddha spent forty-five years of his lifetime in efforts to eradicate. To obtain freedom from desire and actions which attached themselves to desires, Buddha preached no doctrine of extreme asceticism so common in India from the earliest times. A monastic middle-life was ordained for those who sought freedom from ignorance, but who might find the allurements of the world too strong for a life of contemplation. By a life of intense concentration of thought and self-culture each man could find for himself the truth of Buddha's contention that when ignorance ceased actions would lose their potency by non-attachment to outside objects and pleasures. For those Buddhists who remained in the world, as lay members of the order, there was given a moral code by the observance of which they rose above the trammels of caste, above priestly superstitions. Further, the lower classes of the people, in accepting Buddhism, gained the proud position of belonging to a saintly, dignified, and widely revered order. The natural disposition of the lay members to store up merit by charity and good deeds was met to the full in the ample opportunities they had of giving of their alms for the support of the wandering Buddhist monks. Buddhism set before the people ideals of charity, chastity, and self-repression—ideals ever revered in the best of Indian belief and in the best of Indian literature. The question of the existence or non-existence of a Soul found no place in the primitive teachings of Buddhism. The question of the existence of a God was ignored, as were all questions of social rank or caste. None of these questions in any way affected the teachings of the Buddha.

To the simple teachings of the Buddha after ages added learned discussions on every conceivable cosmological, psychological, and even ontological problem that perplexed the thought of their times. The piety, or vanity, of these ages ascribed all their wordy disquisitions to the Buddha, and laid them as tributes of reverence at his feet. The Buddha had ever consistently refused to be drawn by his disciples into any definite statements or metaphysical discussions regarding the nature of the Ātman, or Soul, or even respecting the question of the existence or non-existence of a future life after death. It is even suggested that he was not responsible for the first annunciation of the principle underlying the grouping of the Four Noble Truths, for "these Four Noble Truths are nothing more than the four cardinal principles of Indian medical science applied to the spiritual healing of mankind." [1]

III. The Wheel of Life

The Wheel of Life gives the Buddhist conception of life as ever becoming, ever passing on like the rim of a moving wheel. The Four Noble Truths had taught that all the Suffering and Sorrow of the world arose from the Desire or Thirst for pleasures, existence, and prosperity. The Wheel of Life, or Chain of Causation, as it has been called, gives twelve divisions of life, or causes of existence (nidānas). Here Desire arises from Ignorance, which produces Karma, or deeds, necessitating a new existence for their reward or punishment. In this new life seven stages of early

[1] Kern, "Manual of Buddhism," p. 46.

development of life pass till Desire arises, which leads, through self-assertion, to married life, to family cares, thence to old age and death, ending again in Ignorance necessitating new existences. Thus, "Not to know suffering, not to know the cause of suffering, not to know the cessation of suffering, not to know the Path which leads to the cessation of suffering, this is called Ignorance." [1]

The twelve links in the Chain of Causation are usually represented in a pictorial manner on the rim of a revolving wheel, as painted in the caves of Ajanta of the sixth century of our era. In a picture from Tibet, of the eighth century of our era,[2] the wheel is seized by a demon, who represents the clinging to life.

Colonel Waddell states that the Lāmas of Tibet hold that there is a continuity of Being between death and rebirth, and that: "The Surviving thing, which is carried on with the new career of the individual, would indeed seem to be identical with what is now generally know to Occidentals as Hartmann's Absolute, 'the Unconscious Will.'" [3] He therefore interprets the sequence of the twelve links of life as follows, translating Avidyā, Ignorance, as Unconscious Will :—

[1] Vinaya texts, 1. 76.

[2] See Waddell, J.R.A.S., 1894, p. 371.

[3] Op. cit. p. 374.

THE BUDDHIST WHEEL OF LIFE.

To face p. 160.

CAUSAL CATEGORY.	SANSKRIT.	EVOLUTIONARY STAGE.
I. Unconscious Will	*Avidyā*	Stage of passing from Death to Rebirth.
II. Conformations.	*Sanskāra*	Shaping of formless physical and mental materials (in the Gāta).
III. Consciousness	*Vijñāna*	Rise of Conscious Experience.
IV. Self-consciousness	*Nāma-rūpa*	Rise of Individuality—distinction between self and not-self.
V. Sense-surfaces and Understanding	*Chadāyatana*	Realizes possession of Sense-surfaces and Understanding with reference to outside world.
VI. Contact	*Spars'a*	Exercise of Sense-organs on outer worlds.
VII. Feeling	*Vedanā*	Mental and physical sensations.
VIII. Desire	*Trishṇā*	Desire as experience of pain or delusive pleasure.
IX. Indulgence	*Upādāna*	Grasping greed as satisfying Desire, inducing clinging to Worldly Wealth and desire of heir to it.
X. Fuller Life	*Bhava*	Life in fuller form as enriched by satisfying desire of married life and as means of obtaining heir.
XI. Birth (of heir)	*Jāti*	Maturity by birth of heir (which affords rebirth to another spirit).
XII. Decay and Death	*Jarāmaraṇa*	Maturity leads to Decay and to Death.
I. Unconscious Will	*Avidyā*	Passing from Death to Rebirth.

The Wheel of Life does not assert that these links are results or causes one of the other in time; they arise or, generally, are sequences one of the other. Thus from Ignorance there arises, or ensues, conformations. The second link in the Wheel is forged when from these conformations arises consciousness (vijñāna). The next link in a new existence is when consciousness results in rebirth. The remaining links are then formed. The new birth passes into name and form—that is, mind and body; thence into the five organs of sense and the mind. From these come contact and sensations. From sensations arises Desire, the clinging to life, leading to suffering, decay, death. So life goes on: Ignorance, consciousness, rebirth, sensations, attachment to life and sorrow and ignorance working in an endless round.

This is the Chain of Causation, in which each effect presupposes a previous cause, but in which there is no originating cause. The only logical explanation of the Chain of Causation given by Western thought is that, if it be taken with the explanatory commentary of Buddha-Ghosa of the fifth century, "It implied as decided a negation of any absolute cause as did the doctrine of Demokritus and Leukippus, namely, that nothing happens save through a cause and of necessity."[1] It has also received an explanation, from another authority, to the effect that it expressed the idea that Ignorance produces present consciousness from previous experiences which further infect that consciousness.[2]

Buddhist commentators found the meaning of the Chain of Causation difficult to understand or to explain,

[1] "Buddhism," Mrs. Rhys Davids, p. 99.

[2] "La Formule Bouddhique," Paul Oltramare, 1909.

even with their intimate acquaintance with the connotation of the terms employed, and it has been said that: "It is utterly impossible for anyone who seeks to find out its meaning to trace from beginning to end a connected meaning in this formula." [1]

It seems clear, however, that the Chain of Causality merely expresses the primitive conception of causality, wherein effect can only be conceived as contained in the cause. Each effect in the chain is really contained in the previous effect, and so there is an endless circle of effect implied in the cause. The mind, therefore, never finds an absolute cause irrespective of the effect. Were the chain allowed to break down in any one of its links, the weakness of the link would involve the weakness of the whole chain. Thought would have to hold that the next link in the chain, if it was real, did not come out of cause but merely after the cause. The whole of the Buddhist chain of causality therefore ends in the immanence of cause throughout the course of existence, before and after birth. Therefore the cause must be the sole reality in which the effect is contained. All rational ideas of causality would mean interaction and imply that something was acted on. The Chain of Causality therefore escapes the difficulty of the times by refusing to work back on a cause such as Brahman, or, in the words of W. James, it refused to erect "an altar to an unknown God." Instead of following a regress from effect towards a

[1] "Buddha," Oldenberg, p. 226.

Self or final cause, it weaves a circle of existence in which the cause remains confined or immanent in the effect.

Buddha's essential teachings were contained in the Four Truths and in the Eightfold Path. He never entered on any metaphysical speculations respecting a final cause or respecting cause and effect, subjects dear to early Indian metaphysicians and illustrated in the Chain of Causation by later teachers. As for Buddha: "Il s'agissait non plus de faire la théorie de l'univers ou de la vie, mais d'enseigner que l'homme ne doit chercher en dehors de lui-même ni l'origine de sa misère morale, ni le moyen de s'en débarrasser." [1]

Ignorance is, however, the cause which starts the Chain of Causality into action. This ignorance is no cosmic force or potency. It is the ignorance of the Four Noble Truths which results in desires (samskāras). In later Buddhism the ignorance becomes a metaphysical ignorance that things "do not exist in truth. And inasmuch as they do not exist, they are called Avidyā (ignorance), that is, the non-existent, or ignorance." [2]

The later Buddhist metaphysicians, who framed the Buddhist Chain of Causation, seemed to have produced a metaphysical puzzle in which it is hopeless for the mind to do more than travel in a circle of cause and effect, and, "Ces gens-là paraissent avoir hérité d'un certain nombre de notions, ou plutôt de mots, et leur

[1] "La Formule Bouddhique," Oltramare, p. 31.

[2] Oldenberg, op. cit. p. 238.

sagesse consiste à varier les combinaisons à l'aide d'une subtile logomachie."[1]

S'ankara, in his Commentary to the Vēdānta Sūtras,[2] argues that the links of the Chain of Causality cannot hang together, because "those who maintain that everything has a momentary existence only admit that when *the thing existing in the second moment enters into being*, the thing existing in the first moment ceases to be. On this admission it is impossible to establish between the two things the relation of cause and effect, since the former momentary existence which ceases or has ceased to be, and so has *entered into the state of non-existence*, cannot be the cause of the later momentary existence." This argument of S'ankara is virtually an argument that time must be assumed as a factor in all perception.

The final result is that the causal chain on the one hand restored to matter its birthright, motion, but on the other hand left matter with no abiding or resting place in time or space.

Although the doctrine of universal flux of all things, wherein all phenomena are links in a chain of causality, was taught in Greece, about 500 B.C., by Heraclitus, still the practical mind of the Greek philosophers saw that such a principle, if left unqualified, would leave nothing abiding as an object of knowledge. Therefore, for Heraclitus, "Universal law stood unmoved and

[1] Professor de la Vallée Poussin, "Bouddhisme," p. 40.

[2] ii. 2. 20.

unshaken through all the changes of individual objects and all the vicissitudes of material forms, in defiance of the destruction on which the cosmic system hastened at regular intervals, and from which it was reconstructed anew; and under the vague mystic description of universal reason or universal godhead it took its place by the side of primary matter, endowing it with reason and soul, as *the one thing permanent* in the cyclic stream of occurrences, without beginning and without end."[1] True, there was a law or order, or norm (dhamma), and a formation (samkhāra) underlying the Buddhist formula of causality, still, "with both there is inseparably associated in the feeling of the Buddhist the thought that every order must give place to another order, and every formation to another formation . . . all that passes is a Dhamma, a Samkhāra."[2]

IV. Karma and Nirvāna

When a man dies, does anything, according to early Buddhist teachings, persist and remain to hand on his individuality and the result of his good or evil deeds to future generations? Buddha taught that on a man's death only his Karma, or deed, persisted, and this Karma passed into some new form of life in no way connected with the old life, except in so far as it was the recipient of the Karma of a once existent individual. The deeds a man does live after him. From this point of view of

[1] Gomperz, op. cit. p. 76. [2] Oldenberg, "Buddha," p. 250.

Buddhism, a man on his death is annihilated. There is, however, in man, according to Buddhist teaching, a principle termed Consciousness (vijñāna), which would seem to be an abiding principle not far removed from the current Indian conception of a soul. Consciousness is one of the four mental subjective qualities of man, who is composed of aggregates of ideal atoms forming five Skandhas. Of these five Skandhas what is termed form (rūpa) constitutes the material qualities. The four mental subjective qualities, termed name (nāma), are: (1) Sensations; (2) Perception; (3) Predispositions (samskāras); and (4) Consciousness. This Consciousness is held to be of a finer nature than the other elements of earth, water, fire, air, which are material attributes. In man there is, according to this analysis, no abiding principle such as an Ātman, Self or Soul. There is, however, the fine attenuated Consciousness (vijñāna), which is a link in the chain of causation, produced from ignorance (avidyā). From this consciousness comes name and form and rebirth, so that "consciousness forms, so long as the existent is bound in metempsychosis, the connecting link which connects the old existence with the new; not till the bourne of deliverance, the Nirvāna, is reached does the consciousness also of the dying perfect one vanish into nothing."[1]

The Buddhist conception of a series of transitory successions of momentary consciousnesses passing, as an attenuated substance, through a continuation of births

[1] Oldenberg, "Buddhism," pp. 228–9.

and rebirths, or becomings, approaches very closely to the Brāhmanic doctrine of a Soul passing through transmigrations. In fact, it has been pointed out,[1] "That since in place of soul the Buddhists substituted a protagonist who played the part of soul so uncommonly well, we must put in the background all their reiterated rejection of the Attā"[2] (Ātman, or Self or Soul). There can be no doubt that Buddhism constantly alludes to a person's past birth and *his* past deeds. It also so clearly alludes to the passing of this consciousness on birth that it has been authoritatively stated that "this highest of earthly elements, the consciousness-element, becomes at the moment when the old being dies the germ of a new being; this germ of consciousness seeks and finds in the womb the material stuffs from which it forms a new state of being coined in name and material form."[3] The seeming inconsistency between statements such as these and the ever repeated statements that Buddha denied the existence of the Ātman, Self or Soul, in man, can only be explained by holding that Buddha "was making a stand against priests and gods and sacrificial ritual. And where soul was believed in, there Oversouls and the claims of the soul's 'medicine man' could not be kept out. That belief he undermined by breaking up the notion of the person as consisting of two distinct homo-

[1] Professor de la Vallée Poussin, *J. Asiatique*, September–October, 1902.

[2] C. A. F. Rhys Davids, J.R.A.S., 1903, p. 588.

[3] Oldenberg, "Buddha," p. 229.

geneous substances, and by resolving him into a number of impermanent elements and activities—activities that were only potential till called into temporary actuality by natural law-governed antecedent causes. The path he hewed was inevitably rough and ill-guarded."[1] This explanation is amplified, by the able writer who gives it, by the statement that "the great mass of sober argument and positive exposition in the Piṭakas goes to show both that the Buddhists resolved soul entity into psychological process, and also that a future personal complex or self, like unto and the effect of, *yet not identical* with, the present self, would reap the Karma harvest sown here."[2] The Pāli Dictionary of Childers states that at the time of a man's death the Five Aggregates disappear, but that a new set are started into existence by the Karma or deeds of the deceased. A new individual then comes into existence possessing the new set of Aggregates, but this new individual "is in reality identical with the man just passed away, his Karma is the same." It follows, therefore, that the existence of an individual depends on the mysterious action of the Karma of some other individual whose past actions affect the misery or happiness of the new-born individual. This vicarious action of Karma is so inconceivable as almost to justify the remark that "the mode of action of *Karma* is an incomprehensible mystery (not, as the Buddhist thinks, because the Teacher said so, but simply

[1] C. A. F. Rhys Davids, J.R.A.S., 1903, p. 591.

[2] Op. cit. p. 590.

because the force itself is a non-existent fiction of the brain)."[1] In the action of Karma, therefore, "It must be remembered that, according to Buddhist belief, there is no propagation of species. Life is indivisible; hence the child is no relation to its parents, as the wandering individual finds its family through its own inherent Karma."[2]

Action or Karma, which includes the internal act of willing, determines, in some mysterious way, the life of every person. Apart from this activity of Karma there is no connection between the life of an individual and the life of the dead individual whose actions are transferred to the new individual. Huxley indicated how this doctrine of Karma might, in a more scientific age than that of Buddhism, have foreshadowed a principle of evolution, in which "the tendency of a germ to develope according to a certain specific type, e.g. of the kidney bean seed to grow into a plant having all the characters of *Phaseolus vulgaris,* is its 'Karma.' It is the 'last inheritor and the last result' of all the conditions that have affected a line of ancestry which goes back for many millions of years to the time when life first appeared on the earth."[3] Here the seed holds in itself the germ of life which produces all the subsequent changes

[1] Rhys Davids, "Buddhism," Twentieth Thousand Edition, 1903, p. 102.

[2] Waddell, J.R.A.S., 1894, p. 380.

[3] Huxley, "Evolution and Ethics," p. 43.

and differentiations of life. In Buddhism there is no principle with life-giving potentiality to affect in any way either the spiritual or physical life of a new individuality.

It has been stated that this Karma, "the very key-stone itself, the link between one life and another, is a mere word—this wonderful hypothesis, this airy nothing, this imaginary cause beyond the reach of reason—the individualized and individualizing force of Karma." [1]

The Buddhist conception of Karma, even if the individual's Karma persisted, would also seem to be opposed to modern scientific facts respecting the transmission by inheritance of acquired characteristics. There appears to be no evidence that such characteristics can be transmitted unless there be changes in the germ plasm. Conditions of life may produce changes in the germ plasm which may possibly be inherited.

The mass of the people who embraced the easy life of the mendicant monk, living on the willing charity of the lay members of the Order, never wearied themselves over metaphysical questions of the abiding or non-abidingness of consciousness. Sufficient for all, mendicant monks and lay members alike, that good deeds brought good results and evil deeds evil results. The greater the asceticism of the monks, the higher they were held in superstitious awe by the simple people.

[1] Rhys Davids, op. cit. p. 106.

All classes alike could take refuge in the Order, holding to the Noble Truths which set forth the sin and sorrow of the world, and so free themselves from the overweening social pretensions and exactions of the Brāhmans. The primitive psychology of the times sufficed as an explanation of any questions that might be raised respecting the real existence of things or their non-existence. In the case of external objects and the passing of conception to perception, it was sufficient to hold that consciousness sets the organs of sense—the eye, ear, nose, tongue, body—into action so that these organs obtained sensation by contact with the object of sense concerned. Thus in the case of the eye the sensation was held to arise from the actual contact of the eye with the external object. This mutual contact of the organ of sense and the object of sense was compared to two rams butting their heads together or to two cymbals clashing together. This contact is made by the potency of consciousness, a factor of ignorance, acting on the sense organ. All outside phenomena are merely the resisting medium, knowledge of which is gained by the contact sensation. From this contact arises the thirst for, and desire for, or clinging to, forms and sensations, the link binding to birth, sorrow, and death. Therefore the Buddhist held that it were well to free oneself from the senses, of which "the eye is like a serpent in an ant-hill; the ear is like an alligator lurking in a hole or cave filled with water; the nose is like a bird flying through the air to catch flies; the tongue, ready for all flavours that are presented to it, is like a dog watching for offal . . . and the body, gratified by that with which it comes in contact, is like a jackal feeding with delight on a putrid carcase."[1]

For Buddhism, the continuous series of consciousness, sensations, perceptions, desires, actions, and ensuing sorrows were only as the flowing of water or burning of a flame. All was transitory, and the individual condition in life depended on the good or evil deeds of some previously born individual. This doctrine of the transitory nature of all things and the abidingness of the result of man's good and evil deeds was no new doctrine in India. In the early Brihad Upanishad,[2] Yājñavalkya was asked by his pupil what remained of a man after his death, after he had gained knowledge of Brahman and the soul, for "when an enlightened man dies his dead body is consumed in the fire, his breath goes into the air, his eye into the sun, his mind into the moon, his hearing into space, his body to earth, *his Ātman into the ether* . . . where then is that man?"

The answer of Yājñavalkya shows that this teaching of the transitoriness of the body and virtual annihilation of the idea of a soul as an abiding principle had been well considered and discussed as a speculative

[1] Spence Hardy, "Manual of Buddhism," p. 401.

[2] iii. 2. 13.

doctrine even before the time of Buddhism, for "Yājñavalkya answered, 'Friend, give me your hand; we two alone must discuss the question, but not in public.' So they went apart and argued respecting Karma (deeds), and they lauded Karma, saying that a man becomes good by good deeds and bad by bad deeds."

Nirvāna to the perfected saint is the condition he reaches when his Karma produces no more effects here or hereafter. When the potentiality of Karma runs down the Buddhist rests in Nirvāna. Acts have no longer any operative power, and all deeds are done without attachment, and therefore without results. On death, the last form of life, the rūpa, breaks down and parinirvāna is reached, and man is no more.

Buddha never entered into discussions respecting the nature of Nirvāna, and even on the point "whether the perfected saint lives after death or not, the exalted Buddha has taught nothing."[1] For why, it is asked, should the exalted Buddha present "to the weak the keen edge of truth: the victor's prize of the delivered is Nothing."

It has, however, been authoritatively held that for the Buddhist "the sublimest aspiration is centred on a state of moral and intellectual purity, in this life, with which is bound up the blissful certainty that death, coming in the natural course of things, will, this time,

[1] "Buddha," Oldenberg, p. 274.

NIRVĀNA OF BUDDHA.

no more be the threshold of new life anywhere in time or space!" [1]

The Buddhist was therefore enjoined to practise self-culture, to perform deeds free from "covetousness, hatred, or infatuation," for deeds done otherwise produce new existences here and hereafter. For the mass of the people their old beliefs sufficed, wherein "evildoers go to hell, righteous people go to heaven."

Buddhism still lingers on in Ceylon, where "in practice the Ceylon Buddhist, among the masses, is both better and worse than his creed. Better, because, instead of a distant Nirvāna or a series of births, he has before him the next birth only, which he thinks will be in heaven if he is good and in hell if he is bad; because he calls on God in times of distress, and has a sort of faith in the One Creator, whom his priests would teach him to deny. Worse, because his real refuge is neither Buddha nor his Books, nor his Order, but devils, and devil-priests and charms, and astrology, and every form of grovelling superstition." [2]

V. Decay of Buddhism in India

Alexander the Great invaded India in 327 B.C., only to retire shortly afterwards, leaving colonists and

[1] "Buddhism," Mrs. Rhys Davids, p. 182.

[2] Reginald Stephen, Colombo, "Buddhism," *Nineteenth Century*, 1888.

rulers behind him in the Punjāb. On the death of the Macedonian monarch in 323 B.C., an unscrupulous adventurer, Chandragupta, chief of a hardy fighting clan known as the Mauryas, intrigued his way to power in North India. Tradition holds that a Brāhman, named Chānakya, had placed Chandragupta in power by slaying the last of the ruling royal line of Magadha. Chānakya remained Prime Minister of Chandragupta, and Brāhmanism thus asserted its right to sway the destiny of empire in India, claiming divine rank and knowledge of the ways of the gods to king and people. Buddhism took no part in the struggle for temporal dominion. Buddha had withdrawn from the cares of the world. He had counselled his followers to seek the seclusion of the monastic cell and there find refuge from the turmoil of the ceaseless struggle of life. The outside world was a world of sorrow and suffering. Buddha waged no war against caste nor against Brāhmanism, however foreign they may have been to his view of life. Buddhism was only one of the many sects of India, each seeking its own path of salvation. Of Buddhism itself it was recorded that "there does not exist a sect the followers of which do not perform the Vedic rites from birth to funeral—even though they regard them as having but a relative or tentative truth."

The Maurya Empire, founded by Chandragupta, passed in 272 B.C. to his grandson Asoka, who abandoned Brāhmanism and established Buddhism as the state

CAVE TEMPLE AT NĀSIK.

To face p. 177.

religion of India. The new Emperor Asoka, before he became a Buddhist, had extended the Maurya rule all over North India from sea to sea, and, by the conquest of Kalinga, as far south as Pulicat. In one of his inscriptions he has left a record that of the Kalingas, "one hundred and fifty thousand persons were thence carried away captive, one hundred thousand were there slain, and many times that number perished." [1]

The vast conquest and imperial spirit of Asoka may have made him intolerant of any divided authority between king and priest. Brāhmanism, on the other hand, has never compromised with territorial dominion striving to be independent of spiritual supremacy. The king, in Brāhmanic conception, ruled only through the divine power of the priest whose will could override even that of a king.

When Asoka in the eleventh year of his reign, after his conquest of Kalinga, abandoned the Brāhmanic alliance which had raised his grandfather Chandragupta to power, he appointed State Ministers to superintend the Buddhist faith of his subjects, and sent missionaries through the kingdom and abroad to preach the Buddhist doctrine. In his determination to rule his empire without Brāhmanic aid, he was careful not to alienate the power of Brāhmanism. Although he built and endowed Buddhist monasteries, he also carved out of solid rock homes for Brāhman mendicants.

[1] "Rulers of India, Asoka," by Vincent A. Smith, p. 16.

In his Rock Edict. IX, he announced to his subjects that, although Brāhmanic sacrifices were useless, they should be performed, for Buddhism is the ceremonial of true piety for all men, as "it includes kind treatment of slaves and servants, honour to teachers, respect for life, liberality to ascetics and Brāhmans."

In one of the Edicts of Asoka it is recorded that he was converted to Buddhism because "His Majesty feels remorse on account of the conquest of the Kalingas, because, during subjugation of a previously unconquered country, slaughter, death, and taking away captive of the people necessarily occur, whereat His Majesty feels profound sorrow and regret."

Buddhism wooed and won the favour of Asoka, but in doing so it sapped the sources of its own inherent vitality and vigour. The closer Buddhism clung to temporal power the weaker it grew. Brāhmanism was of the very nature of temporal sovereignty, and from time immemorial priest and king were one indivisible authority.

Even in Vedic times the S'atapatha Brāhmana[1] declared that "it is quite improper that a king should be without a Brāhman, for whatever deed he does, unsped by the priesthood, therein he succeeds not. Wherefore a Kshatriya who intends to do a deed ought by all means to resort to a Brāhman, for he verily succeeds only in the deed sped by the Brāhman."

The Purohita, who was originally the family priest

[1] 4. 1. 46.

of the king, "appears to have gradually raised himself to the dignity of, so to say, a minister of public worship and confidential adviser of the king. It is obvious that such a post was singularly favourable to the designs of a crafty and ambitious priest, and must have offered him exceptional opportunities for promoting the hierarchical aspirations of the priesthood."[1] As sacrificing priest, as a deity on earth, the Brāhman rose supreme in authority above the king, for the Brāhman by his magic spells and by his managing of the sacrifice could alone make the king all powerful and give him victory. If the Brāhman was slighted, or if he did not receive his due reward, he could bring ruin on the king and on his territories, and give the victory to the king's enemies.

Brāhmanism had ever grown stronger in proportion as sovereign power had spread further over India. Buddhism, in clinging to temporal sovereignty, was a parasite, and sapped the strength and warlike vigour of a conquering race. Asoka before he became a Buddhist deluged the land with the blood of those who opposed him. Surrounded by Buddhist monks, he wept over the blood shed, in the Brāhmanic sacrifices, to the gods. When the short-lived Maurya dynasty of Asoka ended with the slaughter of the last effete representative by the hero-usurper Pushyamitra (184 B.C.), the S'ungas rose to power over Magadha. To proclaim his right to universal sovereignty, Pushyamitra summoned to his

[1] S'at. Brāhmana, Int., p. xii.

side the power of Brāhmanism, and ordered the Vedic horse sacrifice to be performed, which challenged any power on earth to stay the wanderings of the horse released by the Brāhman priests. It is recorded that Pushyamitra, "not content with the peaceful revival of Hindu rites, indulged in a savage persecution of Buddhism, burning monasteries and slaying monks from Magadha to Jālandhar, in the Punjāb. Many monks who escaped his sword are said to have fled into the territories of other rulers. It would be rash to reject this tale as wholly baseless, although it may be exaggerated."[1]

India was drifting towards anarchy, and soon became the prey of Parthian, Turki, and, so-called, Scythian invaders. These half-Turki conquerors were little inclined to submit to Brāhmanic claims of social or spiritual supremacy. The monarch Kanishka (58 B.C. or 79 A.D.), who conquered India from the Punjāb to Benares, accepted Buddhism as the belief of his new-won subjects. Buddhism thus gained in royal favour, but it had to bow before the cravings of the people for gods and objects of worship. Buddha became a new god for North India, and in the doctrines of the Mahāyāna, or Great Vehicle, a new form of Buddhism spread to Nepal, Tibet, Japan, and China. The Nirvāna of Buddha approached the metaphysical conception of Brahman as the Unconscious Soul of the universe. In popular imagination Buddha became a

[1] "Early History of India," Vincent Smith, p. 190.

WORSHIP OF BUDDHA.

god of the Hindu pantheon, and Buddhist saints and Hindu deities became so mingled that "the relation is so close that even an expert often feels a difficulty in deciding to which system a particular image should be assigned."[1]

The Great Vehicle, or Mahāyāna form of Buddhism, has been held to have been established at a council held by Kaniskha in North India. It has, however, been pointed out that the Buddhist monks who were assembled together at this council were members of the Hīnayāna, or Little Vehicle of Ceylon. They were Vaibhāshikas, whose leading sect was that of the Sarvāstivādins, who asserted a belief in the reality of all things.[2]

The Mahāyāna, or Great Vehicle of North India, was itself divided into two sects. The first sect was that of the Mādhyamikas, whose doctrines were formulated by Nāgārjuna about 180 A.D. They held that the universe was a void, but they allowed a relative truth to the existence of things. This Middle Vehicle of Nāgārjuna accepted a relative or absolute truth of reality. The second sect of the Great Vehicle denied the existence of everything. This sect was known as Yogācāras; the only thing they would admit the reality of was a series of thoughts or consciousnesses, so they were styled Vijñānavādins or Thought Disputants. As Yogācāras, teachers of Yoga, they

[1] "Early History of India," Vincent Smith, p. 286.

[2] See Takakusu, J.R.A.S., 1905, p. 415.

adhered to a Yoga system of philosophy. The Little Vehicle was also divided into two disputant sects over the question of the reality of the universe.

One sect, that of the Vaibhāshikas, held that the reality of things was evidenced by their existence. A second sect, that of the Sautrāntikas, held that the reality of things was only known through the medium of images. Buddhism in its sectarian disputations over metaphysical abstractions was only hastening the doom which awaited her in consequence of her alliance with temporal power. Nāgārjuna, in declaring that everything was a void, but that there was a relative truth in the existence of things, arrived at a conclusion where "the erroneous truth (samvriti satya) of Nāgārjuna is really untruth. The practical truth of S'ankara is truth, provisory indeed, but truth *quand même*. Māyā *is*. S'ankara's magic play is caused by a magician, and this magician is a lord. Nāgārjuna's samvriti, the Buddhist counterpart of the Vedantic Māyā, is like the son of a barren woman: it is not, it cannot be."[1]

In South India the Buddhist doctrine of the Vijñānavādins, that all things were ceaseless flux and momentary flashpoints of consciousnesses, was attacked with bitter vehemence. It is recorded in the Purāna account entitled "The Victory over the Buddhists in Disputation" that the Buddhist monks came to the court of the reigning Choḷa king to defend their faith. They were even accused of murder, because, although they

[1] J.R.A.S., 1910, p. 130, de la Vallée Poussin.

assert that to kill anything is a great crime, they eat the flesh of animals killed by others. Again, it is urged against the Buddhists that although they allege the Buddha lived through many existences, yet they teach that when the five skandhas perish there remains only Nirvāna, or annihilation. The Vijñānavādin Buddhist doctrine that all is impermanent, and that thought even has no momentary continuity, is refuted by the words: "Thou hast told us that knowledge appears in an instant of time and then disappears; that all this is a ceaseless flux. If so, before thou didst finish uttering thy words and meanings, your understanding must have passed away. What revelation of truth or of virtue can there be in such teaching?"

The underlying current of thought in India, which had spread from Aryan and Vedic thought, reasserted itself. Brahman, the Supreme Soul of the universe, as abstract principle of consciousness usurps the place of Buddha in his highest form. In popular imagination Buddha became the divine Teacher, or Guru, to be worshipped in devotion and faith by his loving disciples. He became endowed with a visible body of a Trinity of Law, or the omnipresent principle of Righteousness, of Bliss, and of Illusory Form through which he is enabled to appear incarnate on earth. Other Buddhas dwell in heavens of their own, surrounded by potential Buddhas who in grace visit earth to aid humanity to gain salvation. Chief of these is Avalokites'vara, who enters not into Nirvāna, but allots a portion of his Karma for the benefit and salvation of those on earth. His spiritual form is worshipped as Amitābha, or an incarnation of the Body of the Law. Deities and innumerable sects spring into existence in bewildering confusion.

Supported by foreign rulers, Buddhism had aspired to become a temporal power on earth. Its living force was its conception of Karma, which in a more scientific age might have evolved into an ideal of a force throbbing through the ages for the amelioration of the common lot of humanity and not merely for the salvation of the individual through self-centred control. When India passed again under the control of its own native rulers during the Gupta dynasty (320–455 A.D.), Brāhmanism resumed its intellectual and spiritual sway over the destinies of the people.

A golden age of Sanskrit literature arose. India became a land of temples to Hindu deities, and from north to south and east to west the willing or forced labour of the people and wealth of ages was set to the sole purpose of glorifying the triumph of the Hindu gods over Buddhism. When the Chinese traveller Fa Hien visited India in the fifth century, 405–411 A.D., he left on record that Magadha, the ancient home of Buddhism, "was already a wilderness with very few inhabitants and full of ancient mounds and ruins."

When the Chinese traveller Hiuen Tsang visited India during the reign of the Emperor Harsha, 606–648 A.D., he found that the Hindu governor to the east, who

BODHI SATTVA.

To face p. 184.

worshipped S'iva, had razed all the Buddhist monasteries to the ground and dug up and scattered to the winds the long-buried relics of Buddha.

The two great intellectual champions of a revived Brāhmanism were Kumārila Bhaṭṭa, about 700 A.D., and S'ankarācārya, about 800 A.D. Kumārila systematized the doctrine of Vedic ritual and sacrifice, opposing all those who sought salvation through knowledge and not through works. S'ankara assailed Buddhism in his doctrine of the Spiritual, wherein the Supreme Soul of the universe and the Soul of man become the one and only reality. At the same time, for those who could not realize this intellectual conception of a universe, he allowed for ordinary knowledge the existence of a real world wherein were religious duties and over which presided a lord to be worshipped both by S'aivites and Vaishnavites. S'ankara preached his doctrines all over India, and restored the Hindu temples. To reclaim the Buddhist monks back into the folds of Hinduism he founded monastic orders and established four great monasteries. Buddhism has been held[1] to have "destroyed the very core of the Indian national beliefs, and as it also afforded no stable ground for a national existence based on morality and religion, it was pronounced heterodox."

The doctrine of Māyā, or Illusion, as taught by S'ankara, was accepted widely in South India, where, as the above account continues, "the great learning and the towering intellect, accompanied by the austere life

[1] Nallasvami Pillai, "Saiva Siddhanta," p. 123.

led by S'ankara, created a great following among the Brāhmans of the S'aiva faith, and it made great strides in the time of his illustrious follower Sāyana, who combined in himself both temporal and spiritual power." Sāyana was chief minister and spiritual guide to the King of Vijayanagara, near Bellary, and was the author of many commentaries on the Vedic scriptures. His brother Mādhava was also minister of State, but died as spiritual head of the monastery of Sringeri. He is renowned for his commentaries and his Sarvadars'anasamgraha, a "Compendium of all the Philosophical Systems," in which he treated of sixteen systems, including that of the Chārvākas, who held that:—

> "It is only as a means of livelihood that Brāhmans have established here all these ceremonies for the dead—there is no other fruit anywhere.
>
> "The three authors of the Vedas were buffoons, knaves, and demons.
>
> "While life remains, let a man live happily, let him feed on ghee (richly), even though he runs in debt.
>
> "When once the body becomes ashes, how can it ever return again?" [1]

Brāhmanism, freed from its blood sacrifices, emerged from its contest with Buddhism with renewed vigour and life. It had gathered into its own fold almost all of the

[1] "Sarvadars'anasamgraha," Cowell and Gough, p. 10.

REMAINS OF COLOSSAL BUDDHA STATUES.

To face p. 187.

vast heritage left to India by the gentle and long-suffering soul of the Buddha.

However much Brāhmanism and the keen wit of S'ankara were able to defeat Buddhism on all metaphysical speculations over the reality or illusion of the world and of consciousness, the final decay of Buddhism in India was due to more mundane reasons: "The Muhammadan invasions of the eleventh and following centuries were attended by persecutions and bloodshed on a large scale, and carried the fire and sword of religious fanaticism through the whole north of India. More pliant Brāhmanism bent to the storm and survived, to place itself at the service of the conqueror and to win its greater victories in the arts of peace. Buddhism, probably already decadent, could neither compromise nor resist, and was forced to retire from the field, leaving behind it only striking monuments of its former greatness."[1] Bihār, its last resting-place in India, was raided by the Mahommedans in 1193 A.D. The Buddhist monks were slaughtered or scattered abroad, so that there was not left a single soul to read a line of the vast literary treasures which Buddhism had gathered together and stored up in the Buddhist vihāras and monasteries.

[1] Geden, "Studies in the Religions of the East," p. 436.

CHAPTER X

HINDUISM

I. Government Proposals for a Hindu Faculty of Theology

Over 217 millions of people in India classify themselves as Hindus. A Hindu need not, necessarily, be interested in any theistic idea as to the nature of God. He may not even have heard of any metaphysical speculations concerning the nature of the first cause of creation. Nevertheless, a Hindu, if orthodox, acknowledges the supremacy of the Brāhmans and accepts their ministrations in his household concerns.

It has been stated that to be a Hindu one must belong to a caste, "which involves an admission, even at the present day, of the supremacy of the Brāhmans, yet this does not involve, or imply, a religious faith in such supremacy, any more than the admission of an aristocracy, either of birth or of wealth, would do in cases where such distinctions prevail." [1]

As the people join the ranks of Hinduism they may remain animistic, or worship their own local deities,

[1] Guru Prosad Sen, "Study of Hinduism," p. 190.

or none at all; they become Hindus if they observe the laws of caste and acknowledge the class supremacy of the Brāhmans. The Jains, who number a quarter of a million of people, worship their own deified saints and do not accept Vedic tradition. They nevertheless acknowledge the supremacy of Brāhmans, and they employ Brāhmans to officiate on all ceremonial occasions. They therefore claim to be classed as Hindus. They hold that if they waived their claim to be Hindus their social position and their laws of inheritance would be injuriously affected.

The consolidation of the people of India under the banner of Hinduism saw the fading away of the worship of the earlier Vedic deities. The Vedic Dyauspitar, the pre-Indo-Aryan Zeus Pater or Jupiter, and the Vedic Varuṇa no longer appeal to the imagination of the people. Even the worship of Brahmā, the Creator, has disappeared from Hinduism, there being now but two small temples, in all India, devoted to his worship.

A Hindu who is merely animistic in his beliefs may deem that his life is haunted by spirits of malign influences which spread cholera, plague, and famine, because of some neglected act of propitiation of these spirits. He may believe that the pen of a writer is guided by spiritual agency, and that spirits preside over the agricultural implements of the cultivator. To the vulgar mind ghostly fears fill the gloom of night. When the sun quickly sinks beneath the horizon the darkness of night wraps nature in silence after the heavy heat of the day. The slightest sound in the fields, or in the forests, sends a note of warning to the heart of the belated cultivator, or woodman, that night has let loose myriad phantom shapes which hover round the soul of man. The coolness of the night-air shrinks the heated sands, by the side of the running streams and the close-set boulders of mountain passes, until all nature groans and moans as though ghostly bands of headless horsemen and phantom armies had come forth to strike awe to the peaceful villagers.

Still lives in more remote tracts the memory of human sacrifices offered to appease the earth-goddess. The mass of the agricultural population have their own tribal or local deities in whose protecting power, against disease and evil influences, they place a simple faith. All of these deities have their own legends telling of their protecting aid and power and of their miraculous deeds. In order to enrol the mass of the people into the folds of Hinduism these deities and legends were given, under Brāhmanic guidance, a literary record of their past history. On the decay of Buddhism, voluminous Purānas, or legendary histories, were composed, telling of the deeds and miracles of the deities, so that they might form a sacred record for the use of those people and women to whom the sacred scriptures of the Brāhmans were a closed book. Each Purāna glorified some local deity as greater than all other gods. Every grove, every wayside shrine, every village in India had its own legend of the power and deeds of its local deity.

From the fourth to the eleventh century of our era vast sums of money were spent, and armies of forced and paid labour employed, in erecting Hindu temples all over India as the abodes of gods and deified saints. These temples grew in size and magnificence, and as local and tribal deities increased in importance, in the imagination of the people, each temple added to itself wealth and fame. Brāhmanism, true to its intellectual heritage, held aloof, and still holds aloof, from the worship of the gods in the temples. The Law Book of Manu [1] shows how the sacerdotal, social, and intellectual power of Brāhmanism rose above all popular forms of temple worship, where it says: "Temple priests must be avoided at sacrifices offered to the gods or to the *manes*," and again,[2] "Food given to a temple priest is lost."

The Hindu gods and idols in the Hindu temples may be as countless as the grains of sand on a sea shore, yet "the higher Brāhmans would probably agree that the popular polytheism is not much more than a pious mystery-play, exhibiting under various masks and costumes the marvellous drama of Nature, in which the divine power is immanent, and with which it is identical. They would say that the deities themselves are but signs and shadows of the Incomprehensible." [3]

[1] 111. 152. [2] 111. 180.

[3] "Natural Religion in India," Sir A. C. Lyall, p. 58.

The population of India is virtually an agricultural population, and the beliefs of an agricultural people change but slowly. The patient toiler on the soil may bow before rude-cut idols at the village shrine, or worship strangely shaped fossil shells, but such images only send to his simple mind some vague message of the complexity and mystery of creative force throughout the universe.

On the hot plains of India, the patient serf drawing water for his withering crops from the deep-sunk well, with the fire of a fierce sun on his head and the fire of hunger in his body, sings his refrain that life is as frail as the dewdrop on the trembling lotus leaf, but that God has framed the dewdrop with as much care as He has framed the life of man. For the cultivator the rainfall wards off want, famine, disease, and pestilence, but the rainfall often fluctuates between extreme drought and devastating floods. Over the cultivator ever hangs the demand to pay his land-tax, for his fate was written at birth on his forehead.

A recent Ten Years' Official Return of the Material and Moral Progress of India states that "as regards the prevalence of indebtedness there are few parts of India in which it is not found to a greater or less extent among the agricultural population." The reason is not far to seek, for, as the same report states : "Here we are face to face with one of the tendencies of the present system which must lead to serious trouble if it were to become widely prevalent. Hitherto, as it appears, the increased value given to the produce of the land by the peaceful development of the resources of the country that has been in progress for the last generation or two has largely redounded to the advantage of the producer, but it has also awakened the cupidity of the trader, who, by means of advances in cash or kind at high rates of interest, is naturally anxious to extend his influence over the landed classes, so that what now goes into their pocket may be diverted into his: that is, to sweat down to the living-wage and to take advantage of the railways to dispose of the rest as may be most lucrative to himself."

The patient cultivator has still left to him his worship at the village altar or in the sacred temple. He still can drone to himself his treasured ethical stanzas, which form his rules of life from the day he picked them up in the village school or from some wandering minstrel. The gods are very near to him, and he hears with pride how his piety and faith can bring him very close to the side of S'iva or Vishṇu, gracious gods loved from of old. He listens in the eventime, beneath the village tree, to the bard who recites from learned books, and explains in the simple vernacular, past traditions of the strife and struggles of heroes and saints and of the long-strained devotion and chastity of the heroines of the Mahābhārata and Rāmāyana. He looks forward with joy to the days of festival, when the village will be gay with streaming flags as the gods are carried forth from the temples amid the songs of the minstrels telling of a salvation for all men from the toils of life and from rebirth. Over all this glamour of popular Hinduism, "the dominant idea of intellectual Hinduism, the belief which overhangs all the jungle of superstitions, is the Unity of Spirit under a plurality of forms. Every religion must be in accord with the common experiences and needs of the people; but if it is to keep its hold on the higher minds it must rest somewhere on a philosophic basis."[1]

Western civilization has introduced into the midst of the jungle of the superstitions of Hinduism new views of the universe. Hinduism, however, claims that it is established on a basis of philosophic reasoning which has not been shaken by any modern system of Western metaphysical thought.

It would be impossible for anyone to state exactly what is the most universally accepted philosophic thought of India to-day, but it has been asserted that "75 per cent. of Brāhman thinkers adhere to the monistic teachings of S'ankarācārya and that fifteen out of every hundred adhere to the so-called dualism of Rāmānuja."[2] Western civilization and English education frequently in India have the result of shaking the indigenous beliefs of the people. The restrictions of caste become irksome, and the very basis on which it was founded, as a divinely ordained division between different classes, tends to receive no longer the superstitious respect of the

[1] Lyall, op. cit. p. 56.

[2] "Hinduism," L. B. Nath, p. 89.

educated. The highest caste, that of the Brāhmans, thus loses its guiding and restraining influence over the home-life of the people. The tendency is to reject the conception of the divine as incarnate in any one caste, or class, of the people. With the weakening of the fundamental conceptions on which caste restrictions were founded, there arises a vague ideal of a brotherhood of mankind, to culminate in nationality. This ideal inspires an increasing pride in past traditions and in the literary record of the past ages. Western scholarship and the work of well-known Indians, on the other hand, has established much of the past history of India and its literature on a reliable historical basis. The evidences of numismatics, and those of epigraphy, have led to the abandonment by many of much of the fabulous chronology of the past. Literary records, once considered as existent from before all time, and therefore too sacred to be printed, are now poured forth in profusion from the press. Few such printed texts are unaccompanied by commentaries and criticisms, often endeavouring to ascertain, on linguistic and accepted evidence, the era of their composition. A new spirit of toleration, freed from sectarian bias, gradually tends to become developed. As the last Census Report states: "The Hindu has no fanatical opposition to Christianity. So long as he is not asked to abandon his own religion he is quite ready to appreciate what is good in Christianity and to listen to the teachings of missionaries." The reaction against a Western system of education which necessarily remained neutral to all forms of religious belief has lately become manifest among leading Indians of different sectarian schools of belief, as well as among Western educational reformers.

A Bill is now before the Legislative Council in India to establish at Benares a Hindu University with a Hindu faculty of theology. The Hon. Sir Harcourt Butler, Member of the Legislative Council, as Minister of Education, on introducing the Bill, on the 22nd of March, 1915, stated that: "We are watching to-day the birth of a new and, many hope, a better type of university in India. The main features of this university which distinguish it from existing universities will be, first, that it will be a teaching and residential university; secondly, that while it will be open to all castes and creeds, it will insist upon religious instruction for Hindus; and, thirdly, that it will be conducted and managed by the Hindu community, and almost entirely by non-officials."

This Hindu University is to have five faculties: Arts, Sciences, Law, Oriental Studies, and Theology. The Governor-General is to be the Lord Rector of this proposed Hindu College, and the Lieutenant-Governor of the United Provinces of Agra and Oudh to be the Visitor. The degrees of the university are to be accepted as equivalent to the degrees of existing universities, but the Government, as stated by Sir Harcourt Butler, "must in the public interest, in the interests of the rising generation . . . have powers to interfere should things go wrong. We could not contemplate the existence of a university or recognize its degrees on any other terms." Sir Harcourt Butler stated, in conclusion, on introducing the Bill: "I confess that the other day, when I was standing opposite Ramnagar, on the site where your university buildings will, I hope, soon be rising in stately array, and looking down the river Ganges to the ghats at Kāsi . . . I felt that if I was a Hindu I should be proud indeed of the achievement of my people, and at the same time I felt some pride myself that I was a member of a Government which has joined in one more large endeavour to combine the ancient and honoured culture of India with the culture of the modern Western world."

The Hon. Dr. Sundar Lal, in support of the Bill, said that the Government of India had, by reason of its principle of strict neutrality in all religious matters, been unable to include in its examinations for degrees "any subjects connected with religious belief." "Nevertheless," he continued, "there has been a widespread feeling that a system of education which makes no provision for religious teaching is essentially imperfect and incomplete."

It was stated by the Pandit Madan Mohan Malaviya that the university would "teach the Vēdas, the religious scriptures, and impart instruction even in rituals and other religious ceremonies which are practised by Hindus."

It was urged by the Hon. Mr. Justice Sankaran Nair, in a letter which appeared in the *Madras Weekly Mail*, November 1911, that "a sectarian university in India is bound to widen the gulf between its own community and the other religious communities, including Christians." He further urged, in opposition to the proposed university, that "Hinduism is opposed to liberty of thought and action, which is essential to progress. Orthodox opposition has been uncompromising in regard to every step hitherto taken by Government in favour of such liberty. Such being the case, the progress of India is dependent upon the emancipation of its thought from spiritual bondage."

It must be remembered that in South India, where Mr. Sankaran Nair wrote, the Brāhman caste leads in the statistics for education, according to the last Census Report, but that in the United Provinces and other Provinces the writer castes, such as the Kāyastha and Karan, and the trading classes outnumber the Brāhmans. Some of Sūdra and lower castes of Bengal are more literate than the Brāhmans of the United Provinces or of the Punjāb. The Brāhman does not necessarily follow the traditional occupation of his caste; less than one-fifth of the Brāhmans now follow religious callings.

There therefore may be no danger, as many anticipate, that the new proposed Hindu University at Benares may revive the dominion of Brāhmanism and lead to efforts to regain temporal supremacy. A properly equipped faculty of Oriental Studies in a new Hindu University must have the warmest support of all those to whom the welfare of India is entrusted. As for a faculty of Hindu Theology, it must suffice to quote the words of Dr. Geden, a distinguished Oriental scholar and Vice-President of the British and Foreign Bible Society, that: "It is worth while to note briefly how profound and universal a change has come upon the attitude of thinkers in general, and Christian thinkers in particular, towards the alien faiths and the religious postulates of the outside world during the last half century. The change has been wholly in the direction of sympathy and intelligent appreciation. Where too frequently in former years was a mere denunciation of error, or a tacit assumption that strange creeds were not worth investigation, there is keen interest and a genuine attempt to understand the mind that works in religious ways other than our own."

Dr. Geden therefore says that: "Those who maintain most firmly the unique position and rights of the Christian faith concede freely to-day that in all the more important systems of religion there is a measure of truth—some aspect or detail of truth seized and emphasized, which has been the salt of the system and in spite of all accretions of error has made it *live*, a vital force in the hearts and lives of its professors."

In Hinduism, and in the establishment of a faculty of Theology in a Hindu University, it may be found that: "The consciousness of mankind, in all its varied development, has not gone wholly and hopelessly out of the way in its search after God." [1]

Benares is still the sacred home of Hinduism, and in

[1] Geden, "Studies in the Religions of the East," p. 9.

Benares, as depicted by Pierre Loti: "The morning prayer ascends from all the rafts and landing-places, but I have no place among the faithful, who look scornfully at me or feign to ignore my presence."[1]

Western civilization looks with wonder at the myriad temples of Benares, and the passing stranger knows not that the worship of Vishṇu has inspired lyric poets to compose poems of deep religious rapture, which live in the literature of India as indelibly as do the creative works of Chaucer and Shakespeare in English literature. The worship of S'iva, which predominates at Benares, had its own mediæval and modern poets, whose hymns of faith in, and devotion to, God, and in the saving grace of God, have been claimed to be merely an echo of Christian teaching, so reminiscent are they of the mystic raptures of Santa Teresa and other saints of mediæval times in the West.

II. Christ and Krishṇa

Vishṇu first emerged from the mists of the past as a Solar deity, the Sun-god of Vedic times, the cherished guide and friend of Indra. All over India Vishṇu is now worshipped mainly in the forms of Rāma or Krishṇa. Vishṇu is held to have descended (avatāra) to earth in the forms of the deities Rāma and Krishṇa or Vāsudeva, the Bhagavat, the Adorable One. Vāsudeva first emerges from the mists of the past in

[1] "India," p. 275.

the lands beyond the Kuruksetra, the Midland, the ancestral home of the Brāhmanic sacrifice. Buddha had proclaimed in the east that the mystery of the sorrows of life could only be solved by turning from life to find peace in a monastic cell as emblematic of the peace that awaited mankind in a long-hoped-for Nirvāna.

To the west, in the last quarter of the fourth century B.C., Vāsudeva-Krishṇa was worshipped as the One Deity who was infinite and eternal, willing to save those who were devoted to Him. It was not in Vedic sacrifices nor in Buddhist renunciation of the world that the soul could shake off the stain and burden of past deeds, and thus hope for its freedom from transmigrations.

Vishṇu, the Vedic deity, became identified with the Bhagavat, the adorable Vāsudeva, who had descended on earth to teach the Ekāntika Dharma, the One Rule, that God was to be worshipped in faith and devotion and was ready, in grace, to give rest to all His loving and beloved worshippers.

This is a belief which permeates the after Hindu worship of Krishṇa-Vāsudeva, or Vishṇu, as well as that of Rudra-S'iva, two beliefs now known as Vaishṇavism and S'aivism.

The traditions respecting Krishṇa appear in the early epic poetry of India,[1] which centres round the Mahābhārata, the record of a great internecine feud between the contending tribes of Kurus and Bharatas. The epic

[1] See Keith, J.R.A.S., 1915, p. 548.

in its earliest form was compiled in the fifth or sixth century B.C. Some time later, about the fourth century B.C., it was enlarged by the addition of five Pāṇḍava brothers with one common wife, Draupadi. In this new redaction Vishṇu rises supreme as the One God incarnate in Krishṇa. Some few centuries later the Song of the Lord, or Bhagavad Gītā, was grafted on to the Mahābhārata. In the Gītā the deity, Krishṇa, appears disguised as the charioteer of Arjuna, who was one of the five Pāṇḍava brothers. Arjuna shrinks from the coming contest, and asks Kishṇa to teach him why man, in this world, should be called upon to slay his own fellow-men and kinsmen. Kishṇa instructs Arjuna that God has allotted to all men a duty to do in this world. The duty of the warrior is to fight, without considering the divine purport of the world. God gives salvation to all who do their duty, not driven to it by their own Self, but trusting in the decrees of God, which have allotted duties to be done on earth as leading to a final purpose. Krishṇa then urges Arjuna to engage in war, for if he thinks only of his own Self, he will determine not to fight, but "this thy resolve is vain; nature will compel thee." Therefore Krishṇa, as the Lord or Adorable One, teaches Arjuna to do his duty in this world, and in doing so, "Have thy mind on Me, thy devotion towards Me, thy sacrifice to Me. To Me thou shalt come. I make thee a truthful promise; thou art dear to Me."[1]

[1] Barnett, "Bhagavad Gītā," 18. 65.

YOUTH OF KRISHṆA AMONG THE COWHERDS.

To face p. 205.

Tradition represents Krishṇa as of the Yādava tribe and eighth son of Vāsudeva and Devakī, and as born at Mathura, a place still sacred to all Hindus. A prophecy foretold that he would slay his uncle and take possession of the Yādu country. His uncle, hearing of this prophecy, sought to slay Krishṇa, who was removed by his friends and placed as an unknown child in the charge of a cowherd. The tenth book of the Bhāgavata Purāna is dear to all Hindus, as it narrates the cowherd life of the god Krishṇa and tells of his intrigues and amours amid the cowherd maidens. He is generally called Gōvinda, or Gōpāla, protector of cows, from having lived a shepherd life. In after-life he slew his uncle and became king of the Yādu tribe. A connection between the words Krishṇa and Christ has been often assumed and as often denied. It has been recently held[1] that this identification of the names of Christ and Krishṇa arose from the fact that a powerful race of nomad cowherds, called the Ābhīras, migrated into the Mathura country about 180 A.D. These Ābhīras are now represented in India by the Āhirs. They brought with them, on their migration, the story of a boy-god, of his humble birth, and the massacre of the innocents, and "it is possible that they brought with them the name Christ also, and this name probably led to the identification of the boy-god with Vāsudeva-Krishṇa. The Goanese and the Bengalis often pronounce the name Krishṇa as Kuṣṭo or Kriṣṭo, and so

[1] See R. G. Bhandarkar, "Religious Systems," p. 38, 1913.

the Christ of the Ābhīras was recognized as the Sanskrit Krishṇa."

In the Purānic period, following and continuing the epic traditions, Krishṇa appears, not only as a tribal deity but as the child Krishṇa, whose birthday is the holy festival of his Hindu worshippers, who hold that Krishṇa was born on the eighth day of the month Bhādra (August-September).

It has been said that this birth-festival of the child Krishṇa was borrowed from Christianity, which had been introduced into the north-west of India and into the south during the early centuries of the Christian era.

Figures of the seven divine mothers, with one of the mothers holding her child to her breast, are to be seen in the sculptures in the rock-cut cave temples at Elura, which date from the eighth century of our era. The worship of the infant Krishṇa, and his mother nursing him, has been connected by scholars with representations of the *Madonna lactans*. It has, however, been pointed out that "the earliest undoubted Christian example of a Madonna suckling her child is of the twelfth century, and from the well-known church of S. Maria Trastavere in Rome."[1]

The worship of the Krishṇa-child, instead of the earlier worship of a tribal deity, Krishṇa-Vāsudeva, combined with the worship of the divine Mother of Krishṇa, holding to her breast the infant deity, has been held to be based on the worship of the Virgin

[1] J. Kennedy, J.R.A.S., 1907, p. 483.

and the *Madonna lactans.* This view is expressed by Professor Hopkins, of Yale University, in the words: "So decided is the alteration and so direct is the connection between this later phase of Krishṇaism and the Christianity of the early centuries of our era, that it is no expression of extravagant fancy but a sober historical statement to say that in all probability the Hindus, in this cult of the Madonna and Child, have in reality, though unwittingly, been worshipping the Christ-child for fully a thousand years."[1]

In the Mahābhārata, in the S'ānti-parvan, it is told that the Supreme Lord, Nārāyana, declared that his true nature, as the original source of all things, could only be learned in the northern mountain Meru. Three saints, Ekata, Dvita, and Trita, declare that they had seen the original form (Prakriti) of the Supreme Lord, for: "On one occasion we went to the north, for the attainment of eternal bliss, near the milky ocean, and practised austerities for four thousand years, and at the end a voice in the air declared, 'Well, how can you see that great Lord? In the milky ocean there is a White Island, where there are men with the lustre of the moon, who are the devotees of the god and possess no senses, do not eat anything, and being devoted solely to the god (Ekānton or monotheistic) are absorbed in him, who is bright like the sun. Go to that island; there shines my soul.'"

When the saints arrived at this mysterious continent

[1] "India Old and New," p. 167.

they found the inhabitants possessing "every mark of blessedness. The faces of some were turned to the north and of others to the east, all with hands clasped in prayer, silently, with unuttered words, meditating on the Supreme. . . . All the inhabitants were perfectly equal in glory, there was no superiority or inferiority among them. We then suddenly beheld a light arise that seemed to be the concentrated effulgence of a thousand suns. The inhabitants, assembling together, ran towards that light, with hands clasped, full of joy, and uttering the words 'We bow to Thee.' We then heard a very loud noise uttered by them all together. It seemed that those men were employed in offering a sacrifice to the Great God. . . . The sound said, 'Victory to Thee, O Thou of eyes like lotus-petals. Salutations to Thee, O Creator of the universe . . . O Lord of the organs of sense—O Foremost of Beings. Thou who art the First-born.' This is what we heard, uttered distinctly and melodiously. . . . Without doubt God appeared in that place whence the sound arose, but as regards ourselves, stupefied by His Illusion, we could not see Him."[1]

This account in the Mahābhārata further states that the deity worshipped in the White Island can only be seen by those who possess Bhakti, or faith. It has therefore been urged[2] that the above account, in the

[1] Mahābhārata, xii. 237 ff.

[2] "Modern Hinduism and its Debt to the Nestorians," J.R.A.S., 1907, p. 311, Grierson.

S'ānti-parvan of the Mahābhārata, of the worship of One God is: "Just the account that would be given by a devoutly disposed stranger of the gorgeous ceremonies of some of the ancient Eastern Christian congregations: the universal equality; the proclamation of monotheism, the necessity of pureness of heart for seeing God; the great Church into which God, visible only to the eye of faith, Himself descended; the adoration of the First-born, the silent prayer, the bursting forth of the loud *Gloria in excelsis*; the melodious chant of the eucharistic ritual."

Professor E. Washburn Hopkins[1] is, however, of opinion that the account in the Mahābhārata is a recasting of the S'aiva faith of Kashmir into Vishṇuite form, for: "The sea to which the pilgrims come is merely the mythical milk-sea of the Himalayas, and Kashmere men are almost white as compared with Hindus. The doctrine taught shows no trace of Christianity, but only a belief in One God." He says, however, that as the account refers to a visit to a White Continent and "is very likely not earlier than the fourth or fifth century of our era, a pilgrimage may have been made to Herat or Merv, where there were already at that time Christian bishops."

The underlying didactic and epic basis of the Mahābhārata dates at least two centuries before the Christian era. Brāhmanic enterprise and learning utilized the moving dramatic framework of the early epic to build

[1] "India Old and New," 1901, p. 161.

therein the details of the Hindu deities and their doings. Such later redactions and enlargements of the epic were probably the work of some centuries after the Christian era, perhaps as late as 900 A.D. There is therefore no inherent impossibility of Christian ideals having been incorporated into the Mahābhārata.

In the Nārāyaṇīya section of the S'ānti-parvan of the Mahābhārata there are two clear accounts given of this Supreme Being and the Gospel of Grace or Bhāgavata doctrine. In the first account, which is held to be the earlier one,[1] "the worship of Vāsudeva and his three other forms is not known. The Supreme God is named Hari, and his worship has not thoroughly emancipated itself from the religion of sacrifices." The second account is a later one, and gives the origins of a reformed Hinduism, wherein devotion to a personal God is "identical with that taught in the Bhagavad Gītā."

The present religious thought of India finds its resting-place in the worship of S'iva, or Vishṇu, as Gods who in their grace await the salvation of those who serve with loving faith and devotion. This religious phase of thought has been the abiding faith of India from even before the Christian era. In this later account in the Mahābhārata the reform is associated with Vāsudeva, and his brother, his son, and grandson. This reformed Hinduism was taught for all India in the Bhagavad Gītā, the Song of the Lord, as Ekāntika, or One-Pointed. Its doctrines were that, "The cherishing of desires which

[1] Bhandarkar, op. cit. p. 8.

the sacrificial rites encouraged is considered harmful, and the fruit attained by means of them is perishable. It was because this Ekāntika religion was so conservative, that it gradually made its way into Hindu society in general, though it did not succeed in uprooting the religion of sacrifices. Still it always retained its character as a religion for women and for all castes, Sūdras included, and in its later development it was associated with such Vedic rites as then remained when it was professed by the Brāhmans, but not so associated when its followers were of lower castes, among whom it continued to exercise great influence."[1]

Brāhmanism had taught from Vedic times a Path of Knowledge and a Path of Works based on sacrifices to the Gods wherein the Soul might find salvation. The mass of the people had no part in Vedic sacrifices. They were excluded from participation in the mysteries of Brāhmanic metaphysical speculations, which were enshrined in a literature only open to the Aryan twice born. The agricultural population of the plains, and the wild aborigines of the hillsides and mountains, had their own gods whom they worshipped as personal gods able to bestow favours on those who propitiated them.

Brāhmanism, in order to ensure its traditional supremacy over all India, had to recognize the local deities of the people. In the Epics and Purānas the legendary lore of the times was given a Vedic heritage so that the current beliefs of all Hindus could flow from one common

[1] Bhandarkar, op. cit. p. 30.

Brāhmanic source. Brāhmanism, in thus gathering within its own fold all the varied religious beliefs and deities of outlying people, "incorporated within the system such of the ideas as each of these new religious systems had to impart, and as suited themselves to the genius of the Hindu races and the surrounding circumstances of their position."[1] The result was that Hinduism gained as a basis for its Vaishṇava faith the two merged phases of thought flowing from the worship of the Vedic Vishṇu and the outlying Sātvata tribal deity Vāsudeva. The Bhagavad Gītā, in order to recommend itself to the hearts of the people, had to reconcile the Sānkhya-Yoga system with the worship of a personal God and, later, to reconcile itself with the Vēdāntic conception of the Absolute as abstract subject of thought. In this mingling of conflicting doctrines the Soul of man had to seek a solution for its final salvation, either through the Sānkhya-Yoga system of asceticism, the Vēdāntic path of knowledge, or through the Vāsudevik teachings of love and devotion to a personal God, which gained for the soul a place in the heaven of Vāsudeva-Krishṇa.

The Sānkhya-Yoga had taught that from Prakriti, or Primal Matter, there was derived Buddhi or intelligence, then Ahamkāra or egoism, and Manas, mind. The Vēdānta of S'ankara taught spiritual monism. In the Bhāgavata teachings the Supreme is pure spirit, and therefore it rests on a monistic basis. Sir George

[1] Guru Prosad Sen, "Study of Hinduism," p. 5.

Grierson, in his articles on the Bhakta-Māla,[1] the leading text-book of Vaishṇavism, of the seventeenth century, states, "that the Bhāgavata theology, although philosophically allied to the Sānkhya-Yoga is monist. Prakriti, or indiscrete primal matter, does not exist independently but proceeds from the Supreme."

The Bhagavad Gītā teaches Sānkhya doctrines when Krishṇa reveals himself as the five elements, ether or space, air, fire, water, earth and mind, will and egoity. This is his cosmic form as Prakriti, subtler than his soul-form as living-being (jīva-bhūta) the psychic principle of the universe. The primitive atheism of the Sānkhya is, however, avoided, for Krishṇa teaches[2] that he who sees God equally in all things attains the highest good, while others see the Self by the Sānkhya, or by the Yoga, or by the doctrine of works.

Therefore, as a modern text-book—the Bhakta-Kalpadruma—states, "Now the Holy One is imperishable, everlasting and indestructible, and for this reason those fruits which have been dedicated to Him without any ulterior object also become themselves imperishable, everlasting and indestructible. Then, in His mercy the Holy One manifesteth His nature in the heart of man, or, in other words, begetteth therein a love and devotion for His gracious feet."[3]

The worship of Krishṇa-Vāsudeva was the worship of a personal God to be loved in adoring faith by his

[1] J.R.A.S., July 1909, note p. 624. [2] 13. 24. 27.

[3] Translation by Grierson, J.R.A.S., 1908, p. 345.

disciples. Vāsudeva was a deity infinite and eternal and full of grace. To those who adored him in faith without any hope of reward or recompense for their deeds, there awaited a salvation of eternal bliss in heaven *very near* to the Lord. Through the adoring faith, love, or Bhakti, of His worshippers the grace of God flowed down on them, so that they might rest assured of a final beatitude of joy hereafter.

This devotion to God was an intense and fervent meditation (upāsanā) on the Supreme as immanent in the universe and in man. It then passed into a Bhakti, or devotional love, or faith in God, a belief which has been held to find its commentary in the words of Augustine: "Quid est credere in Deum? Credendo amare, credendo diligere, credendo in Eum ire, et ejus membris incorporari"[1]—"What is it to have faith in God? By faith to love Him, by faith to be devoted to Him, by faith to enter into Him, and by personal union to become one with Him." The word *bhakti* is derived from the Sanskrit verbal root "bhaj," which means to serve or adore. It was used by the grammarian Pānini, of the fourth century B.C., in the sense of "love directed to the deity."

In the Rig Vēda, the Goddess of Speech, Vāc, was said to choose him whom she loves and to make him mighty. Here the grace of the Goddess is bestowed on those she loves and who love her. The idea of the grace (prasāda) of a loving God towards those who

[1] "Sāndilya Aphorisms," Cowell, p. viii.

KRISHṆA INSTRUCTS ARJUNA.

To face p. 213.

have faith (Bhakti) in Him rises to prominence in the last chapter of the Bhagavad Gītā. Here Krishṇa teaches that:—[1]

> "By devotion (bhakti) he recognizes in verity who and what I am; then, knowing Me in verity, he speedily enters into Me.
>
> "Doing always my work, making his home in Me, one attains by my grace to the everlasting changing region. . . .
>
> "If thou hast thy thought on Me, thou shalt by my grace pass over all hard ways."

The translation by Mrs. Annie Besant[2] of the next few verses of this last chapter of the Bhagavad Gītā, keeps very close to the original Sanskrit: "Abandoning all duties (dharma) come unto Me alone for shelter, sorrow not, I will deliver thee from all sin. Never is this to be spoken by thee to any one who is without asceticism nor without devotion, nor to one who desireth not to listen, nor yet to him who speaketh evil of Me." In this last stanza the original Sanskrit for asceticism is Tapas, that for devotion is Bhakti.

Here the doctrine of devotion to a personal God as a means towards salvation usurps the place of the doctrine of salvation through the Vedic sacrifices and Brāhmanic ritual. The full development of this

[1] "Bhagavad Gīta," Barnett, translation, p. 172.

[2] Madras, 1913, pp. 402–3.

doctrine of salvation by faith, as it rose to eminence in the religious thought of India after the eleventh century, has been held to be due to Christian influences.

These Christian influences are said, on doubtful authority, to have asserted themselves at a very early date in India. The Acts of St. Thomas, in the Syriac version, which dates back probably to the middle of the third century, states that when the Apostles cast lots, as to which country they should preach in, the lot fell to St. Thomas to go to India, and he objected, saying to the Lord, who pleaded with him: "Wheresoever else Thou wishest me to go, send me, for to the Indians I am not going." It is then told that one Habbān, a merchant, had been sent by Gūdnaphar, King of India, to find a fitting carpenter to erect a palace for the King. So Habbān bought St. Thomas from our Lord for twenty pieces of silver. St. Thomas is then recorded to have gone to the East and to have built the palace for the King Gūdnaphar, and to have preached throughout "all India." At the court of a King called Mazdai he converted the King's wife Tertia. The King being enraged ordered his soldiers to slay Thomas, and they took him to the top of a hill and "the soldiers then came and struck him altogether."

In the year 1857 an inscription was found in North-West India, at Takht-i-Bahi, which is held to give evidence, coupled with that afforded by coins, that a King Guduphara, or Gondophernēs, commenced to reign in A.D. 20 or 21, and to establish the fact that "in A.D. 46 his dominions included, in India itself, at any rate the territory round Peshāwar."[1]

Tradition tells that St. Thomas in his travels visited South India, having landed on the Malabar coast, and that he suffered martyrdom at Madras on the mount now known as St. Thomas's Mount.

The Persian Church holds St. Thomas to have been its founder, and by the sixth century there was a branch of the Persian Church on the Malabar coast. Here also, as early as A.D. 68, there was settled a colony of Jews from Palestine, 10,000 in number. In A.D. 190, in the time of Pataenus, the Christian Church on the Malabar coast is said to have been in existence. When Cosmas Indicopleustes visited India in or about A.D. 525, the Christians on the west coast of Malabar had a Persian bishop. It must, however, be remembered that "these communities were few in number; and that their clergy and most of their members were foreigners. This was the case even as late as the eighth century—witness the signatures to a well-known copper-plate grant which the Malabar Christians regard as their charter."[2]

Faith and belief in a personal God, who by His grace granted salvation to those who believed in Him and loved Him through devotion, have been held to have spread over India through the Christian teachings

[1] Fleet, J.R.A.S., April 1905, p. 235.

[2] J.R.A.S., Kennedy, 1907, p. 479.

of the Church in South India. Early Tamil literature of South India was moulded under Jain and Buddhist influences. An early collection of versified Tamil ethical maxims, assigned to 80 A.D.,[1] has been held to show the first evidences of Christian teachings in South India. The reputed author, Tiru Vaḷḷuvar, has been claimed to be a Jain—in fact all Hindu sects claim that he taught these doctrines. The author is said to have lived at Mayilapuram, now a suburb of Madras. The Kural treats of three of the ordinary subjects of Sanskrit ethical treatises: Virtue, Wealth, and Love. According to all rules of classical composition no poetical treatise is complete unless it treats of four subjects: Virtue, Wealth, Love, and Salvation or Release. The last topic on Release of the Soul—Moksha, or Salvation—is omitted. Dr. Pope, who would fain see Christian teachings in early South India, explained the lack of this topic because the author, who he assigns to between 800 and 1000 A.D., perhaps "was not satisfied with the glimpses he had obtained of man's future and waited for light, or, perhaps, he thought his people not prepared for higher teaching." He however stated that, "Of *Bhakti*—that compound of Πίστις and ἀγαπη, the introduction of which into India I still think (with Weber) is mainly due to the influence of Christianity—the first chapter of the Kural is a beautiful exposition."[2]

[1] "Tamil Studies," p. 248.

[2] Pope, G. U., "The Sacred Kurral," p. vi.

Dr. Pope also stated of the author, in a footnote to his translation of the first chapter: "Though his first chapter is 'The Praise of God,' theology is no part of his general subject, and he hardly alludes to a Divine Being in the remaining chapters." The following is after the translation of the first chapter, as given by the Rev. J. Lazarus.[1] In the original Tamil there is no mention of bhakti or faith; the translation here given is very close to the original:—

1. As all the letters have A for their first, so the world has the eternal God for its first.

2. What profit have those derived from learning who worship not the good feet of Him who is possessed of true knowledge?

3. They who are united to the glorious feet of Him who occupies swiftly the flower of the mind shall flourish in the highest of worlds.

4. To those who reach the feet of Him who is void of desire or aversion, evil shall never come.

5. The two-fold deeds that spring from darkness shall not adhere to those who delight in the true praise of God.

6. Those shall prosper long who abide in the faultless way of Him who has destroyed the five desires of the senses.

7. Anxiety of mind cannot be removed, except

[1] Edition, Madras, 1885.

from those who are united to the feet of Him who is incomparable.

8. None can swim the sea of vice, but those who are united to the feet of that gracious Being who is a sea of virtue.

9. The head that worships not the feet of Him who is possessed of eight attributes is as useless as a sense without the power of sensation.

10. None can swim the great sea of births but those who are united to the feet of God.

In the original Tamil the word for God is Lord or Ruler, and in the first couplet is Bhagavan. The author is held to have been of the weaver caste, and Mr. Lazarus writes, in his introduction to the Kural: "It is difficult to judge from the tenor of his Kural to what sect he belonged, for he has entirely avoided in the work everything that savours of sectarianism."

That the last chapter on Salvation, or Release, was never written seems evident from a stanza by a Tamil poet, Toḍi Talai, who lived at or about the time of Tiru Vaḷḷuvar, and explains this want of classical proportion in the Kural, its lack of the chapter on Moksha or Release, by stating in a laudatory stanza: "The great poet has in his Kural divided the topic Virtue into four sections; the topic Wealth into seven sections; and the topic Pleasure into three sections; including in them the fourth topic, Eternal Happiness, a happiness difficult to attain. Therefore the work comprises everything."

SUNDARAR.

To face p. 219.

The Tamil poets from the fifth century to the eleventh century of our era had but one consistent purpose, and that was to glorify the worship of the Hindu gods, S'iva and Vishṇu and thereby to defeat Jainism and Buddhism.

The Vēda for the S'aivites of South India is the Devāram which includes the revival hymns of Sambandhar, Appar a converted Jain, and Sundarar. The first of these Dravidian saints was a Brāhman, and as such particularly vehement in his denunciation of Buddhists and Jains. Every tenth stanza of his poems ends in imprecations against the Jains, whom he reviles as Vultures and Demons. He lived in the seventh century of our era, and is traditionally held to have instigated the slaughter of 8,000 Jains, by crushing them to death in oil-mills. The memory of this slaughter lives to-day in Madura, and pictures still appear depicting the impaling on stakes of Jain men and women. The bitter contest against Jainism and Buddhism in South India did not close until the ninth century. The memory of Sambandhar is still revered in South India, and his image is worshipped in every S'aivite temple. In the temple of Rājarājes'vara, at Tanjore, there was set up an inscription stating that the King Rājarājadeva, who reigned at the close of the tenth century, decreed that there should be a daily allowance made to all reciters of the sacred S'aiva lyrics of the most renowned and worshipped Saint and Sage, Sambandhar, known as the Hammer of the Buddhists and revered as Tirujñāna Sambandhar. In early times, in South India, Aryan Brāhmans and Dravidian people alike joined in the worship of Vishṇu and S'iva, to found thereon a new Hinduism: "And to ensure its stability in the Tamil country and elsewhere, the Brāhmans caused hundreds of temples to S'iva and Vishṇu to be erected all over the land. Small bands of Brāhmans from Upper India were induced by Tamil kings to settle in the south. Endowments of tax-free lands were made for their maintenance and worship in temples."[1]

In order to obtain funds to enlarge the temple at Srirangam one Vaishṇava saint, the Āḷvar, Tirumankai, is said to have broken up a golden image of Buddha at Negapatam. In the Pallava, Chola, Chera, and Pāndya kingdoms of the south, the Āḷvars sung their songs of praise to Krishṇa and Rāma, so that by the early half of the seventh century Buddhism was on its decline.

The sectarian zeal of one Āḷvar, who lived towards the close of the eighth century or beginning of the ninth century A.D.,[2] named Toṇḍaraḍi-poḍi, was so great that, as it has been recorded, his "pure love, fervid faith, undivided heart," was so wrapped in Vishṇu, in the form of Ranga Nātha, that he composed a Holy Garland, or Tiru Mālai, of which the following verses are given as translations:—[3]

[1] Srinivasa Aiyangar, "Tamil Studies," p. 218.

[2] "Tamil Studies," p. 308. [3] *Visishtādvaitin*, April–May, 1906.

"If they the luckless Buddhas, Jains and those
That follow Rudra's feet in poignant words,
Do hateful talk of Thee, O Lord, Thy slaves
With anguish keen pierced, sure sick'ning die.
Hence Thou, that dwellest in Rangam huge, pray list.
If chance e'er throws athwart my furious path
Such God-denying souls, but righteous work
I ween, I then and there, their heads lay low."

The following verse by the same poet is typical of much of the poetry of the period. The snares alluded to are described in such a manner as to obliterate any impression they might convey of Christian influences:—

"Truth have I forsworn! Caught in the snares
Of wily dames of flowing locks, come I
An erring soul. Refuge for all the sins
That teem the world, O gracious Lord Ranga!
'Tis but my certain hope Thy grace will save
Which makes me bold to come to Thee and wait;
Yea, Lord, my heart doth harbour nought but lies
In thought, in word, yet knowing Thou art wise."

The following verse is addressed to Vishṇu, who in his descent as Vāmana, a dwarf, made his foe, Bali, promise to give him as much land as he could cover in two strides. In one stride the dwarf covered Heaven and in another Earth, and then shone forth as Vishṇu Tri Vikrama, "He of Three Strides."

The poet first cries: "Thy shadowing Grace shelters even sinners like me," and then addresses Vishṇu:—

"O Thou of lore, infinite, growing vast
Measured the world, and pressed Thy Sacred Foot
On all creation's head. Grace Incarnate!
O, who but Thou my heart shall own, sweet Love!
My life! Ambrosia! The dearest King
That rules my being. To none but Thee
My homage deep I pay; to none but Thee
My mind I give. Oh, sinner rank am I."[1]

The mystic devotion and love of these early Tamil saints for S'iva and Vishṇu is mingled throughout with visions of realistic love for the dancing-girls in the temples. The Holy Garland or Tiru Mālai gives one of many instances of this mingling of the spiritual and real found throughout the whole range of mysticism:—

"Is not Rangam the glorious shrine of Him
Who gracious oped my darkened heart and there
Enthroned, forced the current of my love
To Him, what time with heretics and thieves
Of souls, and those bound in snares of lust,
Enmeshed of women gazelle eyed, alas!
I suffered vast, sunk deep in pits of vice!"[2]

[1] *Visishtādvaitin*, 1906, p. 21.
[2] Ibid., April–May 1906, p. 16.

The whole literature of South India down to the time of Rāmānuja had thus but one object, and that was to re-establish Brāhmanism, S'aivism, and Vaishnavism as against the waning influence of Jainism and Buddhism. Brāhmanism had found its champion in about A.D. 700 in Kumārila, who had resuscitated the Vedic ritual of the sacrifice. The second great champion of Brāhmanism, S'ankarācārya, at the end of the eighth century intellectually overthrew the last remnants of Buddhism by his doctrines of illusion and unreality of the world. From a philosophic point of view, India may claim that the teachings of S'ankara are not illogical, but the religious life of India could not rest on a basis of illusion. The enquiring mind of India demanded a philosophic basis on which to rest its worship of a personal God, and its love and devotion and faith in the saving grace of that God. Brāhmanism therefore found in South India its third great champion in the eleventh century in Rāmānuja, who, inspired by a continuous current of thought from Vedic times, sought to establish a doctrine of dualism to satisfy the cravings of the people for rest for their souls in the saving grace of a loved and loving God.

Even S'ankarācārya, in his philosophic reasonings, never lost sight of the fact that devotion, or intense meditation, directed to the object of faith, had been the traditional belief of India from scriptural times.

In his Commentary[1] on the Vedānta Sūtras, he contends

[1] ii. 2. 42.

against the doctrines of the Bhāgavatas, who hold that the Bhagavat Vāsudeva, "whose nature is pure knowledge, is what really exists, and that he, dividing himself fourfold appears in four forms (vyūha)," and that of the four forms "Vāsudeva constitutes the ultimate causal essence, of which the three others are the effects." He continues however: "Nor do we object to the inculcation of unceasing concentration of mind on the Highest Being, which appears in the Bhāgavata doctrine under the forms of reverential approach; for that we are to meditate on the Lord we know full well from Smriti and Scripture."

III. Vishṇu the Adorable.

The worship of a personal God, such as Vishṇu, could only be justified to thinking enquirers when it had been proved to be established on a philosophic reasoning which was consistent with the true purport and meaning of the Vēdānta. The adoration of, and love for, Vishṇu, were the means whereby all worshippers of Vishṇu, or Vaishnavas, could obtain release from transmigrations of their souls. The metaphysical monistic idealism of S'ankara had therefore to be refuted, and efforts had to be made to show that it did not set forth the true purport of the Vēdānta and Vedic scriptures.

In South India an adoring faith in a personal God and in His saving grace had inspired the religious enthusiasm of Aryans and Dravidians alike. From A.D. 500 to A.D.

VISHṆU.

THE CHILD-KRISHṆA, CARVED IN GREEN CHLORITE.

To face p. 221.

900 sixty-three S'aiva Nayanmars, or revival poets, had sung the praises of S'iva throughout all the temples of the land, while the twelve Vaishṇava Āḷvars had rivalled them in proclaiming the majesty and might of Vishṇu. All the sacred poetry of the S'aivites was collected together, about A.D. 1026, by Nambi Āṇḍār Nambi, in the eleven Holy Utterances or Tiru Murai. The lyric songs of the twelve Vaishṇava Āḷvars were, about the same time, grouped together by S'rī Nātha Muni as the "Book of 4,000 Psalms," or the Nālāyira Prabandham.

It was during this period that the great rival and opponent of S'ankarācārya, and his doctrine of illusion, or Māyā, arose. He was a Brāhman of South India known as Rāmānuja Ācārya, born at Perambūr. He had been inspired by the songs of the Āḷvars to undertake the defence of their faith. He is said to have converted the Jain King Vishṇu Vardhana in or about A.D. 1098, by whose aid he reconstructed in A.D. 1099 the temple of Nārāyana at Mēlukōte, near French Rocks in the Mysore district.

He studied the sacred Sanskrit literature at Conjeeveram near Madras. In his Commentary on the Vēdānta sūtras, which is known as the S'rī Bhāshya, he undertook to refute the whole of the Māyā doctrines of S'ankara. He held that the Vēdas, the Upanishads and all valid scriptural texts had but one consistent purport in view, and that was to reveal the Supreme, or Lord, as all-pervading and all-knowing. This Lord, or highest Self, possessed all intelligence as his highest attribute, and so was able by a mere act of volition to create the universe. This doctrine of Dualism is sometimes termed a doctrine of qualified Dualism, from the idea that the Lord is self-existent and yet pervades all things and the soul of man.

Rāmānuja in his Commentary drives back the signification of the term "bhakti" to its source in the Vedic scriptures. In his first definition of bhakti he says[1]: "He who possesses remembrance marked by the character of immediate presentation (Sākshātkāra) and which is dear itself above all things . . . he, we say, is chosen by the highest Self and by him the highest Self is gained. Steady remembrance of this kind is designated by the word 'devotion' (bhakti), for this word has the same meaning as meditation (upāsanā). For this reason Smriti and Scripture agree in making the following declarations: 'A man knowing him passes over death'[2] 'Knowing him thus he here becomes immortal'[3] 'Neither by the Vēdas, nor by austerities, nor by gifts, nor by sacrifice, can I be so seen as thou hast seen me. But by devotion exclusive I may in this form be known, and seen in truth, O Arjuna, and also be entered into'[4] 'That highest Person may be obtained by exclusive devotion.'[5]

Rāmānuja[6] further states that, as all knowledge is founded on the knowledge of Brahman, it must be understood that two kinds of knowledge must be

[1] p. 16. [2] S'vet. Up., iii. 8. [3] Taitt. Ar., iii. 12, 7.
[4] Bha. Gī., xi. 53, 54. [5] viii. 22. [6] Commentary on i. 2. 23.

acquired: one from the study of the Scriptures, and a direct knowledge which "springs from concentrated meditation (yoga)." This latter knowledge, he explains, is "of the nature of devout meditation (bhakti) as characterized in the text: He whom the Self chooses, by Him the Self can be gained." The means to gain this knowledge are "sacred tradition, assisted by abstention, and the other six auxiliary means."

Rāmānuja then proceeds to show, from Upanishad teaching, that "The highest Brahman which is imperishable and higher than the soul, which itself is higher than the unevolved; which dwells in the highest Heaven; which is of the nature of supreme bliss, is to be meditated upon as within the hollow of the heart." This meditation has the character of bhakti, devout love, and the devotee, freeing himself from nescience obtains for his reward intuition of Brahman which renders him like Brahman. Finally, Rāmānuja teaches[1] that the highest Brahman, or Vishṇu, is only to be attained through this meditation, which is of the nature of bhakti, or devotion, and that by this meditation the devotee "reaches the highest abode of Vishṇu."

To gain this knowledge there are four requisites. The seeker after knowledge of God must distinguish between things which are permanent and not permanent, he must have calmness of mind, self restraint, he must renounce all enjoyment of the fruit of deeds here and hereafter, and have a desire for final release.

[1] Commentary, i. 4, 6.

Rāmānuja in his teachings of a real world and of a personal God to be worshipped by faith and devotion relies on the Upanishad texts, which declare that the Self or Ātman is the inward controller or ruler (antaryāmin) of all things, and of the soul of man. Thus it is said,[1] that the Supreme Self of the universe is "Thy Self, that immortal, that ruler within, all else is sorrow."

Rāmānuja contended that this Brahman, the inner Ruler of all things, withdraws within himself matter (a cit) and individual souls (cit) at the time of dissolution of the Universe at the end of each period, or Kalpa, of creation. Brahman is then, before a new creation ensues, in his causal condition (kāraṇa), and matter abides in him in a subtle (sūkshma) condition. When creation again takes place (Kārya avastha) the Lord wills that individual souls and matter shall become manifest (sthula). The Lord, or Brahman, is there qualified (vis'ishṭa) by matter and individual souls in a manifest state. Before Creation was willed by the Lord both matter and individual souls qualified Brahman by residing in him in their subtle or imperceptible forms. The dualism taught by Rāmānuja is generally termed qualified monism, or Vis'ishṭa-advaita.

The term, however, refers to the twofold states of Brahman, when Brahman exists with souls and matter in a subtle condition, and when they become manifest in the causal condition. Brahman is in both states the same as qualified (vis'ishṭa) by the subtle and causal, or

[1] Bri. Up., 3. 7, 23.

perceptible, condition of soul and matter. Therefore, instead of the teachings of Rāmānuja being qualified monism or qualified duality they essentially teach that the two qualified (vis'ishṭa) conditions of Brahman are one and the same in both conditions. Brahman thus always remains vis'ishṭa-advaita, or not Dual, by his qualified conditions or vis'ishṭas.

Rāmānuja held that all Vedic texts which declared Brahman to be One only without a Second (ēkam ēva advitīyam) merely expressed that Brahman was in the beginning One only (ēkam ēva), and that there is no Second (advitīyam), meaning[1] "the denial of a further operative cause implied in the further qualification advitīyam, which is, without a Second." To an idealist, following the teachings of S'ankara, the phrase would mean that there is One only and nothing else—pure monism of spiritual Brahman. To a follower of Rāmānuja the phrase would mean that Vāsudeva is One only, and that He contains in Himself full operative powers to evolve a universe of reality, and consequently there is no necessity to postulate the existence of anything Second or associated with Vāsudeva as an agency or source for creation.

S'ankara argued that it is not possible that from Vāsudeva, i.e. the highest Self, "there should originate Samkarshaṇa, which is the individual soul; for if such were the case there would attach to the soul non-permanency, and all the other imperfections which belong to things

[1] i. 4. 23.

originated. And thence release, which consists in reaching the highest Being could not take place; for the effect is absorbed only by entering into its cause."[1] Here S'ankara agrees that intense concentration of the mind, meditation in devotion, which is the later bhakti, is necessary for release. He, however, held that no possible element of duality can be assigned for the creation of a material world, and for the soul, as there exists, in the Beginning, only a spiritual Being whose nature is merely abstract perfect knowledge.

Speculative Brāhmanism closed the door to any who might endeavour to prove the existence of a deity capable of appearing in forms, for as S'ankara urges, if Vāsudeva appears in forms, these forms "cannot properly be limited to four, as the whole world from Brahman, down to a blade of grass, is understood to be a manifestation of the Supreme Being."

Rāmānuja[2] answered the attack of S'ankara by stating that the theory of the Bhāgavatas is that from Vāsudeva, who is the highest Brahman and the highest cause, originates individual souls, or Samkarshaṇa, from Samkarshaṇa the internal organ or mind called Pradyumna, and from Pradyumna the principle of egoity called Aniruddha. Rāmānuja continues by stating that this system of the Bhāgavatas has been attacked because it implies the origination of individual souls, which is a doctrine contrary to Scripture which declares

[1] Commentary on ii. 2. 42.

[2] Vēdānta Sūtras, S.B.E., vol. xlviii. pp. 524–57.

souls to be without a beginning. His reply is: "The criticism that the Bhāgavatas teach an inadmissible origination of the individual souls is made by people who do not understand that system. What it teaches is that the highest Brahman, there called Vāsudeva, from kindness to those devoted to it, voluntarily abides in a fourfold form, so as to render itself accessible to its devotees."

Rāmānuja replies to a further argument that was brought against the Bhāgavatas, and their doctrine of salvation by devotion, because it implied a lack of belief in efficacy of Vedic scriptures and of the sacrifice. His answer is that: "This objection, we reply, springs from nothing else but the mere unreasoning faith of men who do not possess the faintest knowledge of the teachings of the Vēdas, and have never considered the hosts of arguments which confirm that teaching." He therefore held that Vāsudeva, seeing that mankind follows different teaching, and, "recognising that the Vēdas, which teach the truth about his own nature, his glorious manifestations, the means of rendering him propitious and the fruits of such endeavour, are difficult to fathom by beings other than himself, whether gods or men, since those Vēdas are divided into Rig, Yajus, Sāman, and Atharvan, and being animated by infinite pity, tenderness, and magnanimity, with a view to enable his devotees to grasp the true meaning of the Vēdas himself composed the Pancarātra S'astras." He finally concludes that all the teachings of the

Vēdas, Upanishads, Sānkhya, and Yoga philosophies find their full consummation in the Bhāgavata, for "the mental concentration enjoined in the Yoga is a mode of meditation on Brahman, and the rites and works which are set forth in the Vēda are means to win the favour of Brahman—thus giving instruction as to Brahman's nature."

The followers of Rāmānuja divide themselves into two schools, one that of the Vaḍa-kalai which clings to the northern Sanskrit Vēda, the other the Ten-kalai, or Southern school, who used the hymns of the Āḷvars. The Vaḍa-kalai school holds to an Arminian doctrine of "free will," which they term the Markaṭa nyāya, or Monkey theory. In this the Soul clings to the Supreme Being, as a young monkey does to its mother. The South school holds a Calvinistic doctrine, which they term Mārjāra nyāya, or Cat theory. Here the Soul remains passive, awaiting in faith that the Supreme Being will uplift it just as a cat does its kitten without any effort on the part of the kitten.

The chief temple of the Ten-kalais is at S'rīrangam, near Trichinopoly, which is a supposed replica of Vaikuntha, the heaven of Vishṇu. In a judgment over a dispute between the two Vaishṇava sects, the South Indian Deputy Magistrate, in 1894, recorded, "That the Temple with all its endowments and enormous revenue appears to have been specially created for the benefit of Iyengars, who are the chief residents of S'rīrangam." These Iyengars are divided into two sects: the Ten-

SRĪRANGAM TEMPLE.

To face p. 232.

kalai and Vaḍa-kalai, or as Europeans understand them as the Ụ marked and U marked Brāhmans respectively. The Ten-kalai bears the Ụ mark on his forehead, the Vaḍa-kalai has no end sign to his U mark. The Deputy Magistrate held that the evidence proved that the Vaḍa-kalai defendants entered the temple at night time and chiselled off the Ten-kalai end sign of the Ụ from the mark on the forehead of the figures of Vishṇu in the temple. The defendants were convicted, and the Magistrate in his judgment said: "The moment the slightest controversy or dispute regarding these particular sects arises, they are only too ready to take up sides and to counter-swear and fight as hard as circumstances may require. When the religious frenzy or fanaticism is excited, their weapon of fight is not the sword, as they are a very intelligent class of people, but unlawful assemblies and riots and subsequent scenes in courts of law, with all their low cunning, trickery, and hard swearing." The Indian Magistrate concluded his judgment by asserting that, "Such disputes have existed in almost every Vishṇu temple of South India."

The foremost of living exponents of Southern Vaishnavism is Govindācārya Svāmin of Mysore. In his recent edition of the Yatīndra-mata-dīpikā, or Light of the School of S'rī Rāmānuja, a work of S'rinivāsa of the beginning of the seventeenth century, he gives an account of the Vaishṇava doctrines. God, he says in his notes to the text, is "He who is possessed of all Holy Graces, Perfections, Glories, who is distinct from matter (prakriti) and soul (purusha), who is constituted of these, the Supreme Brahman, viz. Nārāyaṇa, is the cause of the Kosmos."

He also shows that the Path of Works, or the Karma Yoga, is the path by which "through holy teaching one acquires true knowledge regarding Soul and God, and according to the best of his abilities performs, without regard to fruit, diverse actions of virtue." This Path of Works "engenders" Jñāna-Yoga, or the Path of Knowledge, and "this contemplation is useful to love (Bhakti). Whether these ways or Paths are independent ways to Salvation, or ancillary to Love, depends upon the several authorities presenting such views."

It is, however, elsewhere stated[1] that in the system of Rāmānuja, "what are necessary for the efficacy of the method of Bhakti are Karma Yoga, or the performance of actions, and Jñāna Yoga, or the acquisition of knowledge," and that Karma Yoga, "purifies the Soul and leads to Jñāna Yoga or acquisition of knowledge. This knowledge consists in seeing oneself as distinct from Prakriti, or matter, and as an attribute of God himself. This Jñāna Yoga leads to Bhakti. Bhakti Yoga, or the method of Bhakti, consists in continuous meditation accompanied by the eight Yoga processes,[2] Yama, Niyama, etc." In fact, as is stated in the preface to the translation of the Vēdānta

[1] "Vais'ṇavism, Saivism," etc., Bhandarkar, p. 54.

[2] See *ante*, p. 135.

Sūtras:[1] "The only sectarian feature of the S'rī-bhāshya is that it identifies Brahman with Vishṇu or Nārāyana . . . Nārāyana is in fact nothing but another name of Brahman."

Govindācārya Svāmin holds[2] that "the conflict that seems to exist between the dualistic and monistic texts in Vēdas and Upanishads is reconcilable by means of the reconciling (or arbitration, ghaṭaka) texts; the texts that seem to import non-differentiation (or quality-lessness) are interpretable as meaning absence of evil qualities."

Surrender (prapatti) to God is of two kinds: the first kind is One-pointed (ekānti), the second is One-only-pointed. The first addresses itself to God for the grant of worldly boons as well as for salvation. The second craves only for knowledge and love of God. The second is also of two kinds, the patient and the impatient. The patient bows before the fruit of deeds done. "The impatient is he who feels his presence in worldliness unbearable, as if he were placed in the midst of raging flames and pants for deliverance (or redemption) immediately on craving God."[3] On death of the Freed, or saved, his soul passes along the rays of the sun to the world of Fire, thence by stages to the City of Vaikuṇṭha, onward to the Divine Seat. Finally, the absolved soul is "for evermore installed in the joy of the Lord," but, "its equality with the Lord (Brahman)

[1] Thibaut, "Vēdānta Sūtras," Part I, p. xxxi.

[2] "Yatīndra-mata-Dīpikā," p. 145. [3] Op. cit. p. 131.

is as respects the bliss alone thereof," for "the Absolved Soul ever in harmony with the Will of the Lord Bhagavān freely everywhere tours."[1]

God's appearances in "Vibhava, or Incarnate Manifestation (or objectification), is the assumption by God of Forms resembling those of the order of Creation in which he wills to appear. Ten of them are reckoned as the most renowned."[2]

The ten chief incarnations as known in the Purāṇas are the Matsya or Fish, the Kūrma or Tortoise, the Varāha or Boar, the Narasinha or Man Lion, the Vāmana or Dwarf, Paras'urama, for the purpose of exterminating the Kshatriyas, Rāma, to establish the Law of Righteousness or Dharma, Balabhadra, Krishṇa, and Kalki, the last to put an end to the irreligious.

All these Descents are of God's own Will, to protect the good and destroy the wicked. The condition of the Lord as Immanent in the universe "is that of abiding in the regions of the heart of the Soul through all its states of experience in heavens or hells, even as the Soul's constant Friend and realizable by Yogis. Though co-dwelling with the Soul He is intact of taints affecting it."[3]

The Lord in "the Image incarnation is the species of Forms presented for worship in homes, hamlets, cities, selected hills, etc., devoid of distances interposed by space and time; deigning to descend with His immaterial or spiritual Person into any material substance as may lovingly be chosen by the votary; lending Himself to

[1] Op. cit. pp. 135–6. [2] Ibid., p. 152. [3] Ibid., p. 154.

the sweet will of His worshipper in all details of bath, food, place, and rest; all-forgiving; the all-sufficient God. Four phases of this aspect exist, viz. Self-manifest, Superhuman or Celestial, Saint-made, and Man-made." [1]

In an earlier publication [2] the same writer, Govindācārya, states that the Lord thinks that "time is ripe for sacrificing Himself for love: and this thought realized is the great fact of Incarnation—a fact demonstrating the link between Heaven and Earth. This the mystery and rationale of Incarnations. God takes on flesh. He becomes Rāna, becomes Krishṇa, and becomes countless other forms in every order of His creation, so as to encompass the runaway souls—millions by one embrace —and rescue them from the wrong way."

Early in the twelfth century Nimbārka, a Tailanga Brāhman of Bellary, in South India, taught that God was pure existence, intelligence, and joy—Sadcid-ānanda —and is as such developed throughout the whole universe. He set forth His teachings in ten stanzas, known as the Das'as'lokī, or Siddhānta-ratna, of which the eighth and ninth stanzas are:—

"There appears no way to salvation except the lotus-like feet of Krishṇa . . . who, at the desire of a devotee, assumes a form easy of meditation and whose power is unthinkable, and whose essence cannot be comprehended. His grace extends itself to those who have a feeling of helplessness and other qualifications, and by that grace is

[1] Op. cit. pp. 154–5.

[2] "The Holy Lives of the Azhvars," p. xviii.

generated Bhakti, or devotion, consisting of special love for him, who has no superior lord."[1]

Rāmānuja had turned away the thoughts of the people from a realistic love as typified in the worship of the Krishṇa and Rādhā. Nimbārka found love idealized in the conjugal union of Rāma and his spouse Sītā.

The so-called qualified duality of Rāmānuja was in turn refuted by Mādhava, or Ānandatīrtha, a Brāhman, said to have been born in South Kanara about the middle of the thirteenth century. He held that the Upanishads and the Vēdānta Sūtras of Bādārayana consistently taught the supremacy of Vishṇu as Supreme Being. This Supreme Being remains ever distinct from individual souls and from the material world.

This Lord, or Supreme Soul, is omniscient, made of all benign qualities, joy, knowledge, bliss, manifesting Himself in many incarnations. He can be known to all by meditation, love, and faith.

Rāmānuja had taught a theistic doctrine in which God was of composite nature, holding a so-called modified dualistic essence. Mādhava conceived God as Supreme beyond all conceptions of materiality. God remains for ever distinct from the soul of man and from the inanimate world. His grace alone enables the soul of man to free itself from attachment to the world, and to seek in faith salvation (moksha) in a knowledge of the Supreme God known as Hari or Vishṇu. Lakshmī, the consort of Vishṇu, is held also to have no material body,

[1] Sir R. G. Bhandarkar, op. cit. p. 65.

but to be eternal as a form of highest ideal love. The Supreme Soul disturbs the equilibrium of prakriti, and creates, protects, dissolves the world, and controls all things. The Supreme bestows knowledge and, manifesting himself as Vishṇu, gives salvation of eternal bliss to those who gain knowledge of Him by detachment (vairāgya) from the world (s'ama), self-control (dama), and self-surrender. He is to be meditated on as Being (sat), knowledge (cit), joy (ānanda), and spirit (ātman).

The Bhāgavata doctrines of Vāsudeva, and of the Vyūhas, were replaced in the system of Mādhava by the principles of Vais'ēshika, while Vishṇu became the sole object of worship, sometimes in his incarnations as Rāma and Krishṇa.

The worship of Krishṇa and his beloved Rādhā was eclipsed at the beginning of the fourteenth century in Central and Northern India by the fervent preaching and songs of Rāmānanda, a Brāhman of Prayāga, who glorified the god Rāma and his long-suffering spouse Sītā.

In order to gather together the mass of the people towards the worship of Rāma, the teachings of Rāmānanda were given in the common vernacular of the time, and not, as was usual, in the Classical Sanskrit.

He admitted all men to his religion irrespective of caste, for his precept was "Let no man ask a man's caste or sect; whosoever adores God is God's own." Sir George Grierson[1] holds that he had in South India "drank afresh at the well of Christian influence," and

[1] J.R.A.S., 1907, p. 319.

states, as corroborative of Christian influence, that "He had twelve apostles (note the number) and these included, besides Brāhmans, a Mussulman weaver, a leather worker (one of the very lowest castes), a Rājput, a Jat, and a barber. Nay, one of them was a woman."

The danger point of a service of love and devotion and self-surrender to a deity personified not only in images but even in the person of priests, or spiritual preceptors, was reached in the fifteenth century by the teachings of Vallabhācārya, a teacher of South India. His doctrine of a surrender to Krishṇa of all that man held sacred and dear on earth spread among the trading classes of Guzarat and Rājputāna, until his followers held as their ideal that "all their belongings shall be dedicated to their Gurus, and this doctrine is, not seldom, carried to an extreme." [1]

Vallabhācārya taught a doctrine of idealistic evolution of the universe. God, as supreme controller, manifests himself first in the inanimate world with his attributes of joy and intelligence concealed. In the soul intelligence is made manifest by the power of God, but His joy is for a time concealed.

Vallabha was held to be a descent or embodiment of a portion of Krishṇa, and although he studied under Vishṇu-svāmi he is said to have himself revealed his own religion. His commentary on the 10th Book of the Bhāgavata Purāṇa, which gives the boy life of Krishṇa, is authoritative among his followers who follow his Pushṭi

[1] Bhandarkar, op. cit. p. 82.

Mārga, or path of enjoyment, in which human love is only symbolical of the love of the soul for Krishṇa.

Happily these doctrines did not spread to Bengal, where towards the end of the fifteenth century the songs and mystic raptures of Chaitanya over devotion and service to Krishṇa and Rādhā roused the feelings of the people to the deepest religious fervour.

Chaitanya denounced not only ceremonial ritual but the restrictions of caste, and preached faith and devotion as the only means to salvation. He taught an ideal of spiritual love as symbolized in the love of the hero-deity Krishṇa for Rādhā, but too often, as with the followers of Vallabhācārya, the symbolism drifted into a realistic human love of the cow-herd Krishṇa for the amorous Rādhā. The danger of such symbolism is reached when the worship of a god such as Vishṇu, or Krishṇa, is lost sight of in replacing the spiritual and ideal love of Rāma for his spouse Sītā by that where the emotions become centered on the love of Krishṇa for his mistress Rādhā.

Much of the later worship of Krishṇa tends towards a Sūfiism: "a strange combination of the pantheism of the Aryan race and of the severe monotheism of their Semitic conquerors, and aims at leading men to the contemplation of the spiritual by appealing to their emotions. The keynote of the system is that the human soul is an emanation from God, and that it is always seeking and yearning to rejoin the source from which it sprung. Ecstacy is the means by which a nearer intercourse is obtained, and absorption in the divinity is the ultimate object to be attained."[1]

The work of Rāmānanda was carried on by Kabīr, a weaver, who died in A.D. 1518. He preached the equality of all men before God, who was to be worshipped by devout faith (bhakti) and fervent meditation, so that the Māyā, or illusion, of a transient separation from God may fade away. Kabīr is claimed by Hindus and Muhammadans alike as their patron saint, and "His apothegms are on the lips of the educated man, whether Hindu or Musalmān, and have been largely incorporated into the Granth, or Sikh Scripture."[2]

Kabīr was an illegitimate son of a Brāhman widow, and was adopted into the household of a Muhammadan weaver. He afterwards adopted the Hindu faith and claimed Rāmānanda as his guru, or spiritual preceptor. It is stated that at his death his body appeared as a heap of flowers, half of which were claimed by the Muhammadans, who erected a tomb over them, the remaining half being taken by the Hindus to be burnt at Benares. The basis of his teaching has been said "to be purely Hindu, though Kabīr was a bold and uncompromising reformer, and hurled anathemas at the Pandits, the Brāhmans proud of their caste, and the teachers of the existing sects of the Hindus, and thus appears to have come under the influence of Mahomedanism."[3] In his teachings he says: "Nobody knows the secret of misery,

[1] "Gazetteer of India," chap. viii. p. 437, quoting Prof. Palmer.
[2] Ibid., p. 425. [3] Sir R. G. Bhandarkar, op. cit. p. 69.

and the world has become made in a variety of ways. Everybody is a fool or a sage in himself, and nobody knows Rāma who dwells in the heart." And again: "If you want me (God) give up your desire for every other thing and become mine, and then everything will be yours. He has entered into every body and remains there fully watchful." [1]

It was not until the fifteenth century that there came "the greatest religious revolution that India has ever seen, a revolution the effects of which are still the moving force of the spiritual life of millions upon millions of Hindus." On the crest of the wave of this spiritual revolution there appear, not the Brāhman, as God on earth and dictator of all earthly and divine affairs, but spirits akin, "in sympathy with Bernard of Clairvaux, with Thomas à Kempis, with Eckhart, and with St. Theresa." [2]

Tulasī Dāsa, born in 1532, was a disciple of Rāmānanda, and has been held by Sir George Grierson to be "the greatest poet India has produced." [3] The words of Sir George Grierson, in his description of the teachings of Tulasī Dāsa, might almost apply to some phases of Christian thought of to-day.

"There is one God, says Tulasī, inconceivable, unknowable, and absolutely pure. The world is very wicked. Out of pity for the miseries of this world this

[1] Op. cit. p. 72.

[2] "Modern Hinduism," J.R.A.S, April, 1907, p. 319.

[3] Op. cit. p. 322.

Supreme Being became personal, i.e. He became incarnate in the person of Rāma, the Redeemer of the world. He is now in heaven, still a personal deity, full of love, and, with all His experience of man's weakness, full of compassion. Knowing by actual experience how great are man's infirmities and temptations, and Himself incapable of sin, He is ever ready to extend His help to the sinful being that calls upon Him. 'Although,' he cries, 'my every word is foul and false, yet, O Lord, with Thee do I hold the close kinship of a perfect love.' Sin is no longer considered merely as an impediment to ultimate salvation. It is far more than that, for it is hateful in itself as being incompatible with the pure nature of the incarnate God. Finally, the belief in the universal brotherhood of man was not a duty, the brotherhood itself was a fact, for every man or woman was the child of the infinitely loving All-Father."

The two chief doctrines of Kabīr were the Unity of God and the Brotherhood of Man, two doctrines which, under the guidance of Guru Nānak,[1] and his follower Guru Govind Singh[2] welded the Sikhs into a body of militant warriors. The Sikhs disdain all caste distinctions, and therefore, in theory at least, do not acknowledge Brāhmanic supremacy. They hold themselves aloof from other Hindus, bearing the marks of Sikhism, the five Ka—Kes, Kachh, Kara, Khanda, and Kangha, that is, hair uncut, short trouserings, an iron bangle, their steel knife, and a comb. The Japji is the morning prayer of

[1] 1469–1558, A.D. [2] 1675–1708, A.D.

all true Sikhs, and of the Japji two verses give the key to the eclectic teaching of the early Gurus. The full translation[1] was made by the late Mr. Macauliffe after consulting many learned Sikhs :—

Then what can we offer Him whereby His court may be seen?
What words shall we utter with our lips, on hearing which He may love us?
At the ambrosial hour of *morning* meditate on the true name and *God's* greatness.
The Kind One will give us a robe of honour, and by His favour we shall reach the gate of salvation.
Nanak, we shall thus know that God is altogether true.

V.

He is not established, nor is He created.
The pure one existeth by Himself.
They who worshipped Him have obtained honour.
Nanak, sing *the praises* of Him, who is the Treasury of excellencies.
Sing and hear and put His love in your hearts.
Thus shall your sorrows be removed, and you shall be absorbed in Him who is the abode of happiness.
Under the Guru's instruction God's word *is heard*; under the Guru's instruction its knowledge is acquired; under the Guru's instruction man *learns that God* is everywhere contained.

[1] See J.R.A.S., January, 1900.

The Guru is Shiva: the Guru is Vishnu and Brahma; the Guru is Parbati, Lakhshmi, and Saraswati.
Make continence Thy furnace, forbearance Thy goldsmith,
Understanding Thine anvil, divine knowledge Thy tools,
The fear *of God* Thy bellows, austerities Thy fire,
Divine love Thy crucible, and melt God's name therein.
In such a true mint the Word shall be coined.
This is the practice of those on whom God looketh with an eye of favour.
Nanak, the Kind One, by a glance maketh them happy."

The teaching of the period which culminated in the poetic raptures of the mediaeval mystics was dualism, which always tended to merge into spiritual monism. The thought of India seemed inevitably to lead to the spiritual conception of the Universe as first taught in the Upanishads[1] by Yājñavalkya: "From death to death he goes who sees here plurality, as it were (nānā iva)."

S'ankara had carried the speculations of the earlier thought of India to its logical conclusion, and held that they taught the metaphysical unreality of all things in a transcendental conception of the universe. In the twelfth century, the popular beliefs of the time in reality and in more or less anthromorphic gods necessitated that Rāmānuja should give a philosophic theory for the conception of God as idealistically qualified

[1] Bri. Up. iv. 4, 19.

in his own nature by material and spiritual essences. One century later Mādhava conceived God as free from all taint of the material in an idealistic duality of Supreme Soul and individual souls. Two centuries later Vallabhācārya taught that God was spiritually supreme, evolving his spirituality throughout existence as intelligence and final joy.

Theism and realism in India has always wavered in giving a final monotheistic answer to the early question of the Vēda: "Does anyone know who created the Universe and how it was created?" Religious thought in the West holds that the First Cause is to be sought through the words of Genesis: that in the Beginning "earth was without form and void, and darkness was upon the face of the deep. And the spirit of God moved upon the face of the waters." When the "Descent of Man," by Darwin, appeared in the West, it was held that it was "putting God further off." India in the past sought to bring an intuitive conception and perception of God nearer in beliefs free from the spiritual monism of S'ankara. India still holds that Brahman was revealed in the Vedic scriptures as the First Cause, in the Beginning, of all things. Her more spiritual and thoughtful classes fear that western realism and scientific research only tend to put "God further off." They count realism and scientific truths of but small gain when Brahman is not known, and that when Brahman is known all things are known.

IV. S'iva as Love

In the extreme North of India, and in the South, S'aivism, or the worship of S'iva has been the faith of the people from time immemorial. S'iva is said to be the son-in-law of Daksha—a name always associated with the Dakshaṇa, or south—and of the Himālayas, and it is in the Himālayas that S'iva is now enthroned in his heaven. The earliest and most primitive conception of S'iva was that of a personified agency of wrath, fierceness, and destruction, and as such his origin can be traced in the savage rites of human sacrifice of early aboriginal folk.

Amongst the wild tribes of the Khonds, who live in the hill-tracts of Ganjam, in South India, human sacrifices were, within the memory of man, offered to the earth-goddess. The victims were kidnapped from the lowland plains, or bought for a price, and when sacrificed their flesh was sown in the fields, with the idea that the sacrifice would gain the good-will of the earth-goddess and make the land fertile. The practice was forbidden by the British Government, and the intended victims, who had lived among the Khonds until the time arrived for them to be sacrificed, were placed under Government protection. The present author, when in charge of part of these hill-tracts during the Rumpa rebellion, some thirty-five years ago, had periodically to have these rescued victims brought before him to see that none of them had been sacrificed. They were

KAILĀSA ROCK-CUT TEMPLE—"HEAVEN OF S'IVA."

To face p. 248.

summoned in from surrounding Khond villages, and slight presents made to them when they answered to the roll-call. It is certain that none of these intended victims was missing, nevertheless there was full evidence that the practice of human sacrifices had not ceased in the Khond country at that period of only a little over thirty years ago. These facts fully justify the statement that in early times "Hinduism owes, to the earlier Indian races, Kolarian or Dravidian, the human sacrifice which is admittedly a constant feature of the worship of S'iva and Durgā from the times of the Epic downwards. In this ritual it can hardly be doubted that S'iva appears as a vegetation spirit, and Durgā or Kālī as the earth-goddess, and the nature of the sacrifice as a spell to secure good crops appears clearly in the practice among the Khonds of scattering pieces of the victim's flesh over the fields."[1]

S'iva, in his more benign form as Creator and Preserver of the world, emerges into history with a lineage and tradition dating back to Vedic times. Rudra was the fierce deity of the early Rig Vēda, who went roaming through the heavens with his marauding and howling sons, the Maruts. He and the fierce mountain-born god S'iva became identified as the benign god S'iva, or as the supreme deity Rudra-S'iva.

In early Indian thought the Supreme Being was held to pervade all nature as resting in the five primary elements—ether, fire, air, water, and earth. S'iva

[1] Keith, J.R.A.S., 1907, p. 948.

pervades all these elements, and also the soul of man and the moon. There S'iva is known everywhere as the Eight-Form god (ashṭa-mūrti). As symbols, marks, or lingas of the eight-forms S'iva is worshipped as (1) Earth, in the S'aiva temple at Conjeeveram; as (2) Water at Trichinopoly; as (3) Air, at Kālahasti; as (4) Fire, at Tiruvannāmalai; as (5) Ether, or Ākāśa, at Chidambaran; as (6) the Sun, when salutation is made in homage to the Sun; as (7) the Moon, at Somnāth; and finally as (8) the Soul, the Ātman or Pas'u, at the Pas'upati Temple in Nepaul.[1]

The Linga is the symbol of the creative power of S'iva, ever present in the universe. It has been held that, "of all the forms to be met with in our temples, from Mount Everest to Cape Comorin and beyond, and from the caves of Elephanta to Mahabalipuram, the form of the Linga is the most universal and frequent, and not only so, it is, in fact, the most ancient form of worship."[2]

S'iva, in popular worship, is represented by many other symbols or emblems.

In the second century before our era the grammarian Patanjali mentions images of S'iva as then existing; but he does not refer to any emblems or symbols of the god. Greek writers thought that S'iva represented Herakles, because both carried a club. The club as a thunderbolt was the symbol of Zeus, wherewith he

[1] "Studies in Saiva-Siddhanta," Nallasvami Pillai, p. 103.

[2] S'ivajnana Bodham," Nallasvami Pillai, p. 116.

conquered the Titans. The coins of Huvishka, the Scythian Emperor in North India at the beginning of the Christian era, represent S'iva bearing a club. The coins of Kadphises II, A.D. 85, bear the figure of S'iva, as half-man and half-woman, wearing a solar nimbus, his hand resting on the bull, Nandi, always associated with S'iva as creative power.

The worship of Apollo had, in Persia, been mingled with the worship of the Sun-God Mithra. This Persia Sun-worship had spread to India, where there were temples to the Sun and priests known as the Magas or Magi. This worship in India had, further, become merged into that of Apollo, identified as S'iva, during the time of the Indo-Scythian rulers of North India. The coins of Kanishka, at the beginning of the Christian era, have figures of Artemis, twin sister of Apollo, with the trident of S'iva.

S'iva has always been represented in popular worship as wearing a necklace of skulls of the gods whose worship he dethroned. He is the typical Yogi, or ascetic, with begging bowl in his hand, ash-besmeared. He has matted hair, rising to a pinnacle as though it were the dark smoke wafted upward from the sacrificial altar. His symbol of creative power is the bull Nandi, on which he rides throughout the universe. He has five faces and three eyes to denote his omnipotence and omniscience. His throat is stained dark from drinking the poison which threatened to destroy the world; his face gleams red above the dark stain, like as the red lightning gleams along the edge of the dark cloud. He bears in his hand the Assyro-Chaldean trident, emblem of the branching lightning, an emblem "which the Hindus borrowed from the West or else imagined themselves spontaneously."[1] He holds in his hand a drum, or hour glass with which he counts the hours of man's life. His chief consort is Umā, known as Kālī, Pārvatī, Durgā, or Bhavānī. The eldest son of S'iva is Ganēs'a, the deity of wisdom, and his emblem is the rat, which also accompanies figures of the Grecian Apollo. Like Apollo, the Indian deity S'iva is a healer, a famed physician, and like Apollo the pastoral lord of flocks and cattle. In his usual forms he is shown as blended together as man and woman, neither he, she, nor it of the universe, but as Soul of all.

In the S'vetas'vatara Upanishad, Rudra-S'iva is God, the One and only God whom sages hold as sole existent, there being no second. He is said to rule the spheres by his will and power, and to stand behind and within all things. He creates and preserves all things, and retracts them into himself at the end of each period of creation. He is addressed as dwelling in the mountains, as of fearful aspect, still as auspicious. He is prayed to reveal himself as holiness and as most blessed. He is said to be the multiform creator of the universe, yet as the One Soul dwelling and living in all things. He is a dweller in a chaos of

[1] "Migration of Symbols," D'Alviella, tr. by Birdwood, p. 98.

illusion, yet as being Supreme Soul, those who know the soul as S'iva pass into peace for ever.

In the Mahābhārata a Brāhman instructs Arjuna, who came seeking knowledge of all weapons: "When thou art able to behold the three-eyed, trident-bearing S'iva, the Lord of all creatures, it is then, O child, that I will give thee all the celestial weapons. Therefore strive to obtain the sight of the highest of gods; for it is only after thou hast seen him, O son of Kunti, thou wilt obtain all thy wishes."[1]

The story then tells how, in the Himālayas, S'iva took on the form of a Kirāta—a low caste hunter—and accompanied by his wife Umā, in the guise of a Kirāta woman, met Arjuna, who engaged with S'iva in a fierce conflict until Arjuna, recognizing his foe as S'iva, bowed down and worshipped him, saying: "O chief of all gods, O destroyer of the eyes of Bhaga, O god of gods, O Mahādeva, O thou of blue throat, O thou of matted locks, I know thee for the Cause of all causes, O thou of three eyes, O Lord of all. . . . Thou art S'iva in the form of Vishṇu, and Vishṇu in the form of S'iva. . . . O Hari, O Rudra, I bow to thee. . . . It was even to obtain a sight of thee that I came to this great mountain which is dear to thee, which is the excellent abode of ascetics. Thou art worshipped of all the world; O Lord I worship thee to obtain thy grace."

In North India, in Kashmir, the worship of S'iva is said to have come down (āgama) from before all time

[1] "Vana parva," p. 117, tr. by Protab Chandra Roy.

and to have been revealed to mankind. Kashmir doctrine held that the Universe existed eternally in the "unuttered thought of the Supreme Deity in the form of the all-transcending Word." [1]

In the mind of the Creator, S'iva, there arose in the Beginning the thought of the whole Universe which is to be, "as it were in a Mighty vision." The whole Universe is therefore held in this primeval Mighty Vision, arising from Thought and the All-transcending Word, from which the form of the Thought arose. Therefore, in the Universe there is "the essential unity and identity of all that appears as many."

In South India the early S'aiva commentator, Nīlakaṇṭha, held by S'aivas to have been a contemporary of S'ankara, wrote his Commentary on the Vēdānta sūtras, interpreting them as setting forth S'iva as the Supreme Soul. S'iva as the Supreme Soul here retains his Vedantic non-duality, and never undergoes any change of condition. The explanation given by Nīlakaṇṭha for the evolution of a universe, is that mind and matter exist in S'iva before the creation in a subtle form of Darkness. When the universe is evolved it is through the action of an "Illumining Power," which is dormant in S'iva, but flares up and illumines the subtle inward form of Darkness. This "Illumining Power" of S'iva, "which cannot be separated from the Lord, appears and vanishes in Him as a rainbow would appear and vanish in the sky. The Lord is the material Cause of the universe, in that the

[1] "Kashmir S'aivism," Chatterji, Kashmir, 1914.

stuff of which the universe is made remained originally in a state of subtle involution within the boundless bosom of His Absolute Being. He is the efficient cause because He made the Illumining Power to go forth from him and animate the universe." [1]

S'aivism is based, both in North India and in South India, on S'iva-sūtras, or strings of short stanzas, said to have been revelations from S'iva setting forth his true nature and the nature of the Universe. They are held to have been engraved by S'iva on a rock on the mountain Mahādēva-giri in the Himālayas, in the eighth or ninth century, and to have been revealed to Vasugupta so that he might lead the people back from Buddhism to the orthodox, traditional, spiritual idealism of India.

The S'iva-sūtras of Kashmir were expounded in the Spanda doctrines, in the ninth century, by Kallaṭa, a pupil of Vasugupta. Later, in the same century, the northern S'aivism was systematized into a formal school of philosophic thought by Siddha Somānanda in the Pratyabhijña s'āstra, and by Abhinavagupta in commentaries thereon. The Pratyabhijña school held that the supreme Lord produced the world by his own mere will. S'iva, in his grace, created a material world so as to give "manifestation, in the mirror of one's own soul, to all entities, as if they were images reflected upon it. Thus, looking upon recognition as a new method for the attainment of ends, and of the highest end, available to all men

[1] "S'aiva Bhāshya," tr. by V. V. Ramanan, p. 48.

alike, without any the slightest trouble and exertion, such as external and internal worship, suppression of the breath, and the like, these Mahes'varas[1] set forth the system of recognition (pratyabhijña) "[2] This recognition of the soul of man as identical with the Supreme Soul, which is full of good qualities such as omniscience and omnipotence, is aided by the instruction of a spiritual preceptor. The Recognitive System compares the Supreme Soul to a lover, and man's soul to a wooed maid, for:[3] "As the gallant standing before the damsel is disdained, as like all other men, so long as he is unrecognized, though he humble himself before her with all manner of importunities: In like manner the personal self of mankind, though it be the Universal Soul in which there is nothing perfect unrealized, attains not its own glorious nature, and therefore this recognition must come into play."

The realization of S'iva as Supreme Soul, and the awakening of man's soul to the full knowledge of S'iva and love for S'iva, is thus likened to the awakening of uncontrollable love in the heart of a woman who realizes in a lover her ideal vision of love. This realization of S'iva finds expression in the worship of S'iva in South India in the ever repeated words of Tamil poets: God is Love.

The worship of S'iva in South India is based on the

[1] Great lords.

[2] "Sarva-dars'ana-Samgraha," Cowell, p. 128.

[3] Op. cit. p. 136.

doctrines set forth in what is known as the S'aiva Siddhānta. These doctrines are founded on twelve S'iva-sūtras, said to be part of the S'aiva Āgama known as the Raurava Āgama. These S'iva-sūtras were expounded by Meykandar in his S'iva-jñāna-bodham, in the beginning of the thirteenth century.

The S'aiva system, or Siddhānta, of South India accepts as revealed books the 28 Āgamas, held to date from soon after the time of Buddha. These Āgamas are said to teach Mysticism of the highest order, but only few are available for reference, and search is now being made to discover if there still exists copies of the older Āgamic literature. The authoritative text-book explaining the Āgama S'iva-sūtras of South India, the S'iva-jñāna-bodham of Meykandar, teaches that the Universe, spoken of as he, she, and it, undergoes changes of original creation and development leading to decay. Therefore there must be some First Cause, known as S'iva or Hara. With S'iva is associated an eternal principle of elemental matter, called pure, or s'uddha, māyā. Souls of men are associated with impure elemental matter, which surrounds the souls of men with impurities of actions (karma), and with Ignorance and the state of limitation of the Soul as an atom (aṇu), instead of its appearing in its true state of oneness with S'iva. Past deeds of mankind necessitate the creation of a world wherein those deeds may be expiated, so the S'akti (power, or light) of S'iva creates the world from elemental Māyā.

The First Cause of Creation is therefore S'iva, from

whom the Universe emanates, and into S'iva it is again, at the end of each period of Creation, retracted. The souls of men, which are one with S'iva, and yet different from S'iva, emanate from S'iva at the time of creation in conditions of life, good or evil, in accordance with their former good or evil deeds. The souls of men when attracted by the objects of the senses do not recognize their own true nature, nor their true relationship to God. S'iva in his grace, however, continually draws the soul of man nearer to Himself, just as a magnet acts on iron. Finally, "The Lord appearing as Guru to the Soul which had advanced in Virtue and Knowledge instructs the Soul that it is wasting itself by living among the roaming senses, and the Soul, realizing its own self, abandons all attractions of the senses, and knowing its oneness with S'iva becomes united to the feet of S'iva."

The Soul thus "having thrown off all the defilement of the world, and of matter, should ever mingle his thoughts with visions of saints who have been made perfect, and he should worship their images in the temples as though S'iva himself were in those forms. Therefore all men should worship and fix their thoughts on holy images, so that in doing so they worship S'iva and come closer to full knowledge of the essential non-duality of S'iva and their own souls."

The authoritative work of Umāpati, of the early fourteenth century, entitled Tiru Aruḷ Payan, or Fruit of Divine Grace, teaches that Emancipation of the Soul, the final Moksha, Mutti, or Vīṭu arises "when the Soul

HINDU TEMPLE—S'IVA.

To face p. 258.

finally set free from the influence of threefold defilement, through the grace of S'iva, obtains divine wisdom and so rises to live eternally in the conscious full enjoyment of S'iva's presence in full bliss." Again, the same authority says that, "If the Supreme Soul and the Soul of man are one, then there is no union in Moksha (salvation). If they are two then there is no Moksha. Therefore they are neither one nor two."[1] Sometimes the soul is said to be identical with the highest subjective Brahman as S'iva. The S'iva-prakāsam of Umāpati teaches that the soul, on receiving the grace of S'iva, rests in S'iva as air rests in space or as salt dissolves in water. The S'iva-jñāna-bodham holds that the soul, instructed by S'iva, knows its true nature and "not being different from Him becomes united to His feet."

In order to attain this union with, or nearness to, S'iva the Soul must await the grace of God. It must, however, prepare itself for this consummation by becoming daily more contemplative and more habituated to seek after spiritual things. The individual should therefore practise charity and altruism (caryā), perform the ordained ritual of worship (kriyā), and practise Yoga. All these three—caryā, kriyā, and yoga—can only gain for the soul rewards in its future transmigrations. All these aids add to the karma, or deeds, which necessitate rebirths.

Above caryā, kriyā, and yoga lies the San-Marga, or path of knowledge, wherein the soul finds its oneness

[1] "Light of Grace," Madras, 1896.

with S'iva. The grace of S'iva, which is the highest power, or S'akti of universal pure abstract knowledge, can alone reveal Knowledge to the soul of its true nature, so that it may "unite to the divine feet of S'iva."

S'iva, the Lord or Pati, in His grace gives knowledge to His flock (pas'u) of souls, severs all their ignorance or fetters (pās'am), casts off from them their burden of good and evil actions. The threefold mystery of Pati-pas'u-pās'am absorbs the faith of all devout S'aivites in contemplative thought.

As with the Vaishṇavas, two contending doctrines of S'aiva faith arose. The Northern school held that the soul could aid and aspire to its own salvation by faith, co-operating with the grace of S'iva just as a baby monkey clings to its mother: this is known as monkey like, or Markaṭa, faith. The Southern school held that the soul remains passive, awaiting in faith the uplifting aid, through grace, of S'iva, just as a kitten awaits being uplifted by its mother: this is the cat like, or Mārjāra, doctrine of faith. Both schools agree that it is S'iva alone who, by infinite love and grace, can free the soul from its heavy burden of good and evil deeds, from the delusions of this world and from its inherent bondage to matter. Dravidian early poetry is full of ecstatic outbursts of emotional faith in S'iva. S'aivite hymns exhaust the phraseology of human love in expressing a mystic love for the deity. They only differ from similar mystic raptures of the West in that the love of the East is deeper, more passionate, and less reticent than that of the West. Tamil poetry is often untranslateable when it expresses the sinner's frequent lapses from virtue, and enumerates in profusion and in detail the attractions of a damsel who led him astray—attractions which he renounces in terms of loathing, as he seeks safety at the feet of S'iva. Such Tamil poetry, in passages, lacks the restraint of the West, and therefore is often stigmatized as erotic. Tamil poetry was, however, composed to be recited to a musical accompaniment. The melody of the words often overpowers the thought. The western mind analyses and seizes hold of the thought, and pictures therefrom concrete ideas which would never arise in the mind of one who reads such poetry in the flowing cadence of the original.

Much in India that attracts the wondering gaze of the West passes without notice before the subdued thought of the East, which broods more over the spiritual symbolism of things than over their reality. Eastern poetry revels more in the music of words than in realization of the thought conveyed by the words. Most eastern poets can improvise words at will to harmonize with music which incites words to flow melodiously without any mental effort to weigh the thought.

Tamil verse was composed to be intoned to the music of the Yāl, an instrument of which the form is not now even known or recognizable from the descriptions given of it in early writings. Rhyming alliterations, sequences of sounds, and succession of rhythmic melodies are some of the demands of Tamil verse, and renders it impossible of translation into any form of western poetry. The following gives but a faint echo, so faint and crude that it demands an apology to the memory of the composer, the sweetest singer of Tamil land, Tāyumānavar, who lived about 150 years ago. In the original the sound rules over the thought, and is far divided from any western forms of verse :—

"Eyebrows arched as crescent moon,
Soft dimples, silken robes, sweet scents, and shapely feet,
Glowing breasts, and gliding gait,
From there I tear away my throbbing thoughts,
Seeking self-restraint with S'iva's saints,
Longed-for love and life at S'iva's feet,
Such love as Umā, maid of mountain mists,
Sought for her soul at S'iva's side."

The Tiru Vācakam or "Holy Utterances" of the most typical of Dravidian lyric poets, Māṇikka Vācakar, who lived not later than the ninth century A.D., are inspired by faith in the saving grace of S'iva. S'iva is "the one deity who despised heaven and entered on earth to receive mankind." He is "the Holy One who, despising the body, entered my soul and filled all my thoughts." S'iva is hailed as "Highest Understanding," as "transcending all thoughts and speech." It is S'iva who "with love makes glad all my body and soul and bestows sweet grace far beyond my merit."

S'IVA AS NAṬARĀJA.

The Dance of Life.

To face p. 263.

S'iva is addressed as "Unknown even to those in the highest heavens: when the heavens and earth have passed away shall I see thy face." In one lyric outburst a maiden sings to her mother the glories of S'iva: "Our Lord is one boundless sea of compassion. He has entered and melted my heart. He abides there and fills it with tears of ceaseless joy." In these translations no effort has been made to distort the original; they only lack the deep, wailing melody and heavy alliteration of the original.

The following are translations from the Tiru Vācakam, following as far as possible the original Tamil, word for word, of verses where the term Salvation, or Release (vīṭu or mutti = Sanskrit mukti), is used: O Truth, having seen thy golden feet this day I gained Release; O Truth, that abides within me, save me, O spotless One, Lord of the Bull, Lord of the Vēdas.[1] Both the beginning and the end he transcends: Behold. Both the bond and the Release he creates: Behold.[2] All false I must quit, Hail! O, Grace, that gives Release! Hail! To your true ones, True One![3] Have you heard, dear one, how One who makes deceit, the Southern One, the Lord of Perunturrai, set round with strong walls, things not seen before He showed, glory showed, the lotus foot He showed honey of His grace (Karuṇai) he showed, simple ones to laugh he made, heavenly Release to gain he made us his.[4] The following is a trans-

[1] 1. 32. [2] 3. 52. [3] 5. 400. [4] 8. 30–36.

lation by Dr. Pope from the song "The Merging of the Soul in Rapture." Dr. Pope states that: "In the Vātha Ūrār Purāṇam we are told that the Sage when in Tillai saw women pounding the gold dust which, mixed with perfumes, is strewn on the heads of distinguished visitors to the shrine, and on great occasions is lavishly thrown over all things and persons connected with the worship. As they pounded, they sang foolish songs: and he composed these twenty verses, in a somewhat loose metre, to be sung in time with the pestles. The song is much admired, but is a little obscure and almost colloquial. I have tried to preserve the rhythm—five principal accents in each half line." The verse is the last in Dr. Pope's translation, and alludes to the Bond (bandha) and the Release (vīṭu):—

"For Him Who is the Vēdam and the Sacrifice; for Him Who is the Falsehood and the Truth;
For Him Who is the Splendour and the Gloom; for Him Who is Affliction and Delight;
For Him Who is the Half, Who is the Whole; for Him Who is the Bond and the Release;
For Him Who is the First, Who is the Last; dancing, pound we the sacred dust of Gold!"

The word Bhakti (or Tamil—Ṛatti), Faith or Love, is used in the Tiru Vācakam as follows:—

"Becoming Lord of the ancient Pāndya land He

raised to Highest state us His servants who make Faith." [1]

"To me, who know not the path of Release, He taught the path of Faith." [2]

"Behold Him the First! Behold Him the All! Behold Him adorned with the ancient tusk of the wild boar. Behold Him girdled with the forest-tiger's skin. Behold Him Ash besmeared. Behold, I dread each thought. Alas! I perish. Behold! He sounds in the sweet Vīṇā. . . . Behold! He is seized in the net of Faith." [3]

"Param Jōti, Highest Light, sunk in the sea of devotion, to the elephant He gave grace." [4] (This refers to a legend of a miracle which S'iva performed in causing a stone elephant to eat sugar-cane.)

The following is the translation by Dr. Pope of a stanza in Tiru Vaḷḷuvar's Devout Musings, where the word "piety" is in the original Tamil, patti, or bhakti :—

"Of piety I am void, nor bow at vision of Thy Golden Feet;
My heart is dead, my lips are seal'd; yet cause this birth to cease, our Lord!
Pearl like Thou art, gem like Thou art! First One, I utter my complaint:
So oft I've follow'd Thee, henceforth apart from Thee I bear not life!"

[1] 2. 119. [2] 51. 1. [3] 3. 28–42. [4] 11. 47.

The unreality of all things in the higher reality of nearness to S'iva is expressed in the following verse:—

"To each his own kin. To each his own path of right, or law. Who are we? What is ours? These things are all Māyā, illusions. Let all these things go, and with the ancient devotees of the King, each his own Will as guide, shaking off the false, serve (or follow) the path by which he goes, to the golden feet of Bhuaṇgan, the Lord." [1]

The S'aiva system of South India has been held to be "a system of dualism, it is also a system of non-dualism, but it differs from the other schools of dualism and non-dualism," for "what was the purest and most transcendent monotheism degenerated into a most crude anthropomorphism and blatant pantheism." [2]

This "transcendent monotheism" is, as described by the same writer, "the Highest conception that we can ever reach of God, describing as it does His inmost nature, and of course the only way we can know Him is that God is Love and Blessedness, S'ivam."

S'iva has been defined as "not material nor enveloped in matter . . . ever blissful and All Love, and all His acts, such as creation, are prompted by such Love. S'iva is neither He, She, nor It, nor has S'iva any material Rūpa (form) or Arūpa (not form), and S'iva can reveal His grace and majesty to those who

[1] Stanza from "The Pilgrim Song" of Tiru Vaḷḷuvar.

[2] "Studies in S'aiva-Siddhānta," p. 128.

APPAR.

MĀṆIKKA VĀCAKAR.

To face]

love Him. He cannot be born, nor can He die, and as such He is the Pure and Absolute and Infinite Being." [1]

The S'aivite poet Appar, ascribed to the seventh century of our era, in one hymn describes S'iva as "The Lord with the braided hair, He and His fair-eyed Umā dwell in Kāñci. He has no stain. He has no peer; He is of no mortal form. He abides in no one place, His grace alone we may seek to know. This way alone His form and nature He may show."

A later saint and poet, Tirumūlar, ascribed to the first century, whose mystic poems were included in the Tiru Murai, or S'aiva Veda, of the eleventh century, in one hymn of praise to S'iva says: "To those who know not, Love and S'iva are different. Those who know view S'iva and Love as One. If all men knew that God and Love are One, they would abide in S'iva as Love."

A modern S'aiva poet, Ellappa Nāvalar, has given the account of why S'iva is often represented as half-man and half-woman. It is from the fifth canto of the Aruṇācala Purāṇam, a favourite legendary history in Tamil of the Aruṇācala S'aiva shrine:—

"When He who was in the Beginning before Creation, Great beyond measure over all the Vedas, appeared seated on his Bull, then She, the chaste Pārvatī, bowed down to his feet. The Great God cried, 'You are not you and I not I, you and I are one, the Linga and the Yoni, united as the inner and outer of the tree.

[1] "Studies in S'aiva-Siddhānta," Madras, 1911.

From us united all creation flows. For me thou hast come to the mount Hima, quitting thy body; therefore take half of mine.' So S'iva and Pārvatī united and became one, she on his left side."

S'iva is thus he, she, and it, combining all elements that pervade the universe. Half the Hindus of India are S'aktas, worshipping the ideal of womanhood and motherhood as symbolized in the half-man, half-woman form of S'iva.

One Tamil poet, S'iva Vākyar, who lived after the Muhammadan invasion of the south, sung hymns in which he taught a pure monotheism, and attacked Hinduism in its worship of idols. He refers to Muhammadans in his verses, and may have been influenced by their creed or by Christianity. The following adapted from a translation by F. W. Ellis, shows how S'iva Vākyar had abandoned the worship of S'iva and of the idols in the temples :—

> "Many flowers I gathered and scattered.
> Many prayers I repeated in vain,
> As I knelt at the holy places of S'iva.
> Now I know the true God, the Lord of heavenly beings.
> And I believe not the idol in the temple to be God,
> I lift not my hands to the idol in prayer,
> I lift not up water in my hand and pour it in vain;

To the god in the temple, to the idol of S'iva
The dead leaf and faded flower fall to the ground.
So a man once he dies is not born again."

The following are from Gover's Folk-songs of Southern India, which is in itself a treasure store of balanced information regarding Dravidian poetry. S'iva Vākyar sings:—

"There is but One in all the world, none else.
That one is God, the Lord of all that is,
He never had beginning, never hath an end.
O, God! I once knew nought of what Thou art,
And wandered far astray. But when Thy light
Pierced through the dark, I woke to know my God.
O Lord! I long for Thee alone. I long
For none but Thee to dwell within my Soul."

A popular folk-song by S'iva Vākyar approaches near to the same idea:—

"Even if you read the Vēda
The Sāma and the Rik
And know the S'āstras six
You still may never know
The great divine S'ivam.
Yet if you will but turn
From flesh and its desires,
Suppressing lust and shame,
Your eyes and heart may see
The Being that is God."

Indian Thought

The idea of S'iva as Love was expressed by the poet Appar :—[1]

> " What though ye be great doctors wise?
> What though ye hear the S'astras read?
> What though the duty ye assume
> Of doling out cooked food and gifts?
> It boots him naught who does not feel
> The noble truth that God is love."

[1] Tr. of Nallasvāmi Pillai, Madras, 1910.

NUR MAHAL.

To face p. 271.

CHAPTER XI

PAST AND PRESENT POSITION OF WOMAN IN INDIA.

THE position of woman in India still remains based on status, from which it has not yet commenced to pass towards a condition of contract. In India the family is still a joint-family. On marriage the new wife goes to the home of her husband's father. The husband remains under the control of the eldest male head of the family, and the wife under the control of the husband in a common family household, where the property is a joint-property. The husband's duty in life is to have a son to perform his funeral ceremonies when he dies, and afterwards to present the periodic offerings to the manes and gods for the welfare of those departed.

Marriage is therefore "the most ancient, sacred, and inviolable of all Hindu institutions, and its due performance the most complicated of all religious acts. It involves intricate questions of caste, creed, property, family usage, consanguinity, and age. To remodel the institution of marriage is to reorganize the whole constitution of Indian society, and to create, so to speak, an entirely new social atmosphere." [1]

For all orthodox Hindus marriage is a sacred union, and no woman can be divorced. She may be turned out of caste and thus lose all social status. As long as she remains within the caste the marriage bond, if performed between Hindus, is binding as a sacrament. Thus, an orthodox Hindu must marry, for a valid marriage, within his own caste or sub-caste, but he cannot marry within his own family group. Under the first condition he is endogamous, and in the latter, not marrying within his family group, he is exogamous. The Census Report of 1913 points out that an orthodox Hindu may not, in North India, marry within seven degrees of relationship, while in South India the restrictions are not so severe, or, at least, not usually observed. The one ideal of marriage, the one duty of husband and wife, is to look forward to the birth of a son who will perform his father's funeral rites, and make periodic sacrificial offerings to the spirits of the fathers and forefathers for their progress through the future life. The joint-family and the joint-property are thus held together and sanctified by the status of woman in the duty allotted to her of having a son.

The joint-family is a seven-fold sacramental bond [2] uniting the living Pater-familias with the father,

[1] Monier Williams, "Indian Theistic Reformers," J.R.A.S., 1881, p. 23.

[2] Manu, v. 60.

grandfather, and great-grandfather, and with the son, grandson, and great-grandson.

The S'rāddha ceremonies are the periodic offerings of water (udaka) and funeral cake (piṇḍa) to the deceased father, grandfather, and great-grandfather. Therefore "all who offer the funeral cake and water together are Sapiṇḍas and Samānodakas to each other, and a kind of intercommunication and interdependence is thus continually maintained between the dead and living members of a family—between past, present, and future generations." [1]

Thence came, in old days, the fanciful derivation of the word Putra, son, from tra, to protect from Pu, or hell. In theory every Hindu has a right to take a second wife if his first wife has no sons, although in practice the Hindu adheres to monogamy. A custom still existing of the wife eating apart from her husband dates back to the earliest Aryan times. The S'atapatha Brāhmana [2] decreed: "Whenever women eat they do so apart from men"; and again: [3] "The husband should not eat food in the presence of his wife, for from him who does not do so a vigorous son is born, and she in whose presence the husband does not eat food bears a vigorous son."

Temple worship stands open to men and women of the four castes alike, but no women should read the

[1] Monier Williams, "Indian Wisdom," 3rd ed., p. 254.

[2] i. 9. 2. 15.

[3] x. 5. 2. 9.

Vēdas, or sacred law books: S'ankarācārya definitely excluded them from the knowledge, of the Vēdānta, that all the world was a delusion; a knowledge, it might be thought, they specially needed. India is a museum filled with specimens of every conceivable mode of marriage rites, from the still surviving relics of primeval capture of the bride, to polygamy and even to the polyandry of the present ancestors of the pre-Aryan aborigines, down to the latest product of man's ingenuity—the Niyoga.

The most primitive relic of bygone days is to be found among the Todas, a small group of about eight hundred pastoral folk settled near Ootacamund, in the Nīlgiri hills of South India. They are still polyandrous. A woman marries several husbands, as a rule all the brothers in one family. The first-born child belongs to the eldest brother, the second to the next brother, and so on, till they are all supplied with children.

Dr. Rivers[1] states that for all social and legal purposes the father of a child is the man who presents the wife with an imitation bow and arrow before the child is born, and "when the husbands are brothers, the eldest brother usually gives the bow and arrow and is the father of the child, though so long as the brothers live together, the other brothers are also regarded as fathers. It is in the case in which the husbands are not own brothers that the ceremony becomes of real social importance. In these cases it

[1] "The Todas," 1906.

is arranged that one of the husbands shall give the bow and arrow, and this man is the father not only of the child born shortly afterwards but also of all succeeding children till another husband presents a bow and arrow. Fatherhood is determined so essentially by this ceremony that a man who has been dead for several years is regarded as the father of any children born by his widow, if no other man has given the bow and arrow."

Kinship through the female line does not, however, hold among the Todas as might be expected. The children are supposed to belong to the father's family, and inheritance runs only through the males. The marriage rites are simple. The bride is led to the home of her future husband or husbands. She then bows down, the eldest brother places his foot on the fore part of her head, and each brother does the same in turn. She is then told to engage herself in some household duty—to cook or to fetch water—and if she obeys the marriage ceremonies are at an end. If the husband does not approve of his wife, or if he dislikes her, he returns her to her parents. If the wife gets tired of her husband she can leave him and seek some other household.

The Juangs of the Tributary States of Orissa until recently wore only leaves for clothing. If a Juang desires a wife he sends the chosen girl some rice through a friend; if she accepts it the friend leads her to the house of the waiting bridegroom.

The Lepchas are a pure Mongoloid tribe dwelling on the southern slopes of the Himālayas, in a tract of country about 120 miles long. The women do most of the work, and are purchased by the bridegrooms from the parents of the women. Sometimes a Lepcha serves in the house of his proposed father-in-law until the price for the bride is worked out in labour.

Among the Khonds of Ganjam, Vizagapatam, and Orissa, there is a survival of the ancient custom of marriage by capture. Before the marriage there is always a mock fight which ends in the bridegroom and his friends carrying off the bride. The price paid for a bride is in part contributed by the tribe. Intermarriage between persons of the same tribal clan is punishable by death; the capture is supposed to take place from an outside tribe. There is further a survival of a saturnalia. When the boys and girls come towards marriage age they are taken from the homes of their parents. The boys are brought up together in a bachelors' hall at one end of the village, and the girls in a similar hall at the other end of the village under the charge of a matron. In due time, in the days of spring, they are let free, boys and girls, to wander into the jungles, whence they return having made their selections.

All property descends to the sons, the eldest son always receiving the largest share. If there be no sons the property goes to the nearest male relation, but if there be no male relations the property reverts back to the village community.

Half-way between these survivals of marriage customs of primeval times among the non-Aryan primitive tribes, and the more advanced forms of marriage which grew up under the Aryan law-makers, lie the marriage customs of the Nāyars. Among the Nāyars who live along the Malabar coast, on the west of India, the Matriarchal system survives. Descent is traced through the female. The married woman is absolutely free, freer probably than she is anywhere in the world. If she accepts a present from a man that in itself is marriage. She lives independent, and if she no longer likes or approves of her husband she dismisses him and selects another.

Among the Nāyars "polyandry may now be said to be dead, and, although the issue of a Nāyar marriage are still children of their mother, rather than of their father, marriage may be defined as a contract based on mutual consent and dissoluble at will. It may be well said that nowhere is the marriage tie, albeit informal, more rigidly observed or respected than it is in Malabar; nowhere is it more jealously guarded, or its neglect more savagely avenged."[1]

The Malabar Marriage Act of 1896 sought to legalize the marriage, or sambandham, of the Nāyars nevertheless: "the total number of sambandhams registered under the Act has, however, been infinitesimal, and the reason for this is, admittedly, the reluctance of the men to fetter their liberty to terminate sambandham at will by such restrictions as the necessity for formal

[1] "Malabar Law and Custom," 1882.

divorce, or to undertake the burdensome responsibility of a legal obligation to maintain their wife and offspring."[1]

It seems impossible to ascertain if the Aryans, who entered India, had in their ancestral homes any marriage customs similar to those of the Nāyars. Max Müller held that the question "whether in unknown times the Aryans ever passed through the stage in which the children and all family property belong to the mother, and fathers have no recognized position, is one we can neither assert nor deny." Schrader, in his "Prehistoric Antiquities of the Aryan People," held that "the power of the husband over the wife among Indo-European people was a hard and cruel reality against which our modern sentiment rises in revolt." He further held, quoting Strabo, that "they marry many wives, purchased from the parent, giving a yoke of oxen in exchange," and that "the wife belonged to the man, body and soul, and her children are his property as much as the calf of his cow and crop of his field."

It may be that during the long journey towards India the women became few in number, so that they received a consideration which would not otherwise be granted them. There is evidence from the Rig Vēda that women in Vedic times occupied a far higher position than they did in their ancestral homes, or

[1] Thurston, "Castes and Tribes of South India," vol. v, p. 338, Nāyar.

even in later days in India. The old Indo-European custom of widows burning themselves on the death of their husbands seems to have died out, for there is no mention of it in the Vēda. There is one verse [1] which was at one time interpreted to sanction widow-burning, a practice which became common in later India, especially in Lower Bengal. This verse says: "Without tears, without sorrow, decked with jewels, let the wives go up to the altar first." This was held to be an injunction for the widow of the deceased to burn herself on the funeral pyre. The word "first" is "agre," but a slight misreading might make it appear as "agne," which means "in the fire," so that the verse tells the widow to go up into the fire. The result was "that thousands over thousands of deluded women, in the moment of their greatest grief, have been sent to the blazing pyre with this miserable passport to heaven." [2] The interpretation of "agre" as "agne" was, in the words of Max Müller, "the most flagrant instance of what can be done by an unscrupulous priesthood. Here have thousands of lives been sacrificed and a fanatical rebellion threatened on the authority of a passage which was mangled, mistranslated, and misapplied."

There seems no doubt that re-marriage of widows was an established custom of Vedic times. There are verses which refer to a son of a woman by her

[1] x. 18. 7.

[2] "Indo-Aryans," Rajendra Lal Mitra, vol. ii, p. 147.

second husband, and to a woman (parapurvā) who has taken a second husband, as well as to a man who has married a widow. None of the later Law-books of Gautama, Apastamba, or Manu refers to such a custom as widow-burning. The Code of Vishṇu, which is late third or fourth century A.D., however, says that "after the death of her husband a widow should either lead a virtuous life or ascend the funeral pyre of her husband."

One verse of the Rig Vēda says that, in certain cases, a woman can choose her own husband, for "happy is the woman who is handsome, she chooses her husband among the people."

One entire hymn is ascribed to a woman, Vishvavārā, of the family of Atri. It would appear that wives and husbands performed religious sacrifices together, for one verse[1] tells how "from olden times the matron goes to feast and general sacrifice." Other verses give pictures "of the Dawn shining forth with sun-beams, like women trooping to the festal meeting"; of how "maidens deck themselves with gay adornment to join the bridal feast," and of "women at a gathering, gently smiling and fair to look on."

Polygamy, when it existed, seems to have been confined to chiefs and heads of tribes. One verse[2] says: "For like a king among his wives thou, Indra, dwellest"; and another verse declares that "Indra hath taken and possessed all castles as one common husband

[1] x. 86. 10. [2] vii. 18. 2.

does his spouses." One verse[1] gives an instance of a husband gambling with dice for his wife, a habit which became the motive for many subsequent tragedies told of in the dramas and epics. Here, in the Vedic verse, the husband laments the loss of his wager, his wife, for: "she never vexed me, nor was angry with me, but for the sake of the die, whose single throw is final, mine own devoted wife I alienated."

The sayings of some of the Vedic poets give a more realistic view of the position women held in ancient India than the poetic similes of other hymns. One poet declares that Indra himself hath said: "the mind of woman brooks no discipline, her intellect hath little weight." Another poet[2] seems to have considered himself particularly badly treated in some love episode, for he says: "with women there can be no lasting friendship: hearts of hyenas have the hearts of women."

As the Brāhmans consolidated their power in India they compiled, for the guidance of the Aryan races, long treatises called Kalpa Sūtras and S'rauta Sūtras, giving elaborate details and instructions respecting the numerous sacrifices that had to be duly performed under the Vedic ritual. They also compiled Grihya Sūtras, giving injunctions respecting the duly carrying on of the domestic life of the joint-family. Finally, there were the Dharma Sūtras, giving a full account of the sacred laws, customs, and manners of the time. The most important of the Dharma Sūtras was that of Manu, which is now long

[1] x. 34. 2. [2] x. 95. 15.

lost. There is, however, a later redaction of it known as the Law Book of Manu, dating somewhere between the second century B.C., and the second century A.D. From these sources can be traced the position of India as it became hemmed in, from about the seventh century B.C., by the authority of the Brāhmans. Life was reduced to a stereotyped system formulated by a priesthood claiming divine heritage and divine powers, the so-called divine ordinances of the Brāhmans. A woman's sole longing in life was directed towards the birth of a son, who could carry on the sacrificial rites of the household. A son could alone sacrifice and perform the obligatory periodic offerings to the souls of his father and forefathers, to ensure their progress through endless transmigrations.

To perpetuate the sacrificial system sons were married before they were even boys. Girls were hastened in their infancy to the homes of their husbands, there to deem as a dread calamity, inflicted on them for misdeeds in this or in previous births, the not having a son. If a wife had no son it was imperative that she pray her husband to seek out a new wife. When her husband died there was only the safe refuge of the funeral pyre, else she must mourn alone all the remaining days of her life, forsaken by the gods and a portent of unlucky omen to all around her. If she remained a widow, one lapse from virtue would be met by death from poison, or in the village well, or from the sting of a snake, no one except her own people knowing how that death came. In India the time had come when, as Westermarck says in his History of Human Marriage, "a man's happiness in the next world depended upon his having a continuous line of male descendants, whose duty it would be to make the periodic offerings for the repose of his soul." As for woman, as Jolly remarks, "all respect man had for woman was not grounded on any ideal motive, but because she fulfilled the religious necessity for continuing the race."

The woman's duty is clearly defined in the Law Books. It is to please her husband, rejoice in all that he does, worship him as a god, consider herself an outcast if she has no son, and to die in the only hope that she may have a reward hereafter as having worshipped her husband as a god here on earth, and not through any other merit of her own. The Law Book, known as that of Manu, says:[1] "the father protects her in childhood, her husband in youth, her sons in old age, a woman is never fit for independence"; and further, "nothing must be done by her independently in her own house." Manu also declares[2] that "though destitute of virtue or seeking pleasure or devoid of good qualities, a husband must be constantly worshipped as a god by a faithful wife"; and again:[3] "If a wife obeys her husband she will for that reason alone be exalted to heaven." The Law Book of Vishṇu, which closely follows Manu, decrees[4] that: "No sacri-

[1] ix. 3. [2] v. 154. [3] v. 155. [4] xxv. 15.

fice, no penance, and no fasting is allowed to women apart from their husbands. To pay obedience to her lord is the only means for a woman to obtain bliss in heaven."

An earlier legislator, Brihaspati, of the sixth or seventh century B.C., states that the duties of a wife are: "Rising before the others, paying reverence to the elders of the family, preparing food and condiments, and using a low seat." He also says that: "The wife is declared to be devoted to her husband who is afflicted when he is afflicted, pleased when he is happy, squalid and languid when he is absent, and who dies when he dies." Manu[1] decreed that: "A wife, a son, and a slave, these three are declared to have no property, the wealth which they earn, or acquire, is for him to whom they belong."

A wife might be superseded for specific reasons. Āpastamba, the law-giver of the sixth or seventh century B.C., held that: "If a husband who has a wife who is willing and able to perform her share of the religious duties and who has a son, he shall not take a second." He also decreed that: "He who has unjustly forsaken his wife shall put on an ass's skin with the hair turned outside, and beg in seven houses, saying, 'give alms to him who forsook his wife.' That shall be his livelihood for six months."

Manu, legislating a few centuries later, is much more specific, for he ordained: "For one year let a husband bear with a wife who hates him, but after the lapse of

[1] viii. 416.

one year let him deprive her of her property and turn her out." He extends this law of supersession by another injunction that: "If a woman indulges in intoxicating liquor, or does sinful things, or opposes her husband, or annoys him, or wastes his money she may be superseded by a second wife."

The general rule respecting the abandoning of a wife was declared, by Manu, to be that: "If she has no children she may be superseded in the eighth year. If her children all die in the tenth year, if she has only daughters in the eleventh year, but instantly if she says disagreeable things." Nevertheless he says:[1] "Neither by sale nor by repudiation is a wife released from her husband."

The same teaching is followed by the law-giver Baudhāyana,[2] who decreed: "Let him abandon a wife who has no children in the tenth year, one who bears daughters only in the twelfth, one whose children all die in the fifteenth, but one who is quarrelsome without delay."

With respect to this abandonment it has been held that it "Probably only meant that the husband took another wife, but still maintained his own wife as a member of the family, and this is the practice which is still observed. To send a virtuous wife adrift in the world because she is incapable of bearing male issue, is a practice unknown in India, and would bring disgrace and dishonour on the family."[3]

[1] i. 46. [2] ii. 2, 4, 6.

[3] R. C. Dutt, "History of Civilization in India," vol. ii, p. 91.

In India marriage is spiritual as well as a bond of human love. Therefore the Law-Book of Vas'ishṭa decreed that: "The teacher (ācārya) is ten times more venerable than the learned exponent of the scriptures (upādhyāya), a father a hundred times more than the teacher, and the mother a thousand times more than the father."

The earliest Upanishads of about the sixth century show women taking their part in controversies with men, probably due to the fact that the Upanishads contain the free thought of Kshatriyas and outlying clans not inclined or accustomed to submit to Brāhmanic guidance. In the Brihad Āranyaka Upanishad the renowned priest Yājñavalkya and his wife, Maitreyī, engage freely in discussing philosophical speculations. That this was an exception seems clear from the fact that the priest had a second wife, Kātyāyanī, and that she "possessed only such knowledge as women possess."

The same priest, when too closely pressed by questions respecting the nature of Brahman, in public assembly, by a woman named Gārgī Vācakanavī, gently rebuked her, saying: "O Gārgī, thou askest too much about a deity about which we are not to ask too much."

Under Buddhism women were allowed to enter the Order on the entreaties of Mahāprajāpatī, the foster-mother of Buddha.

In the Culla Vagga we are told how Buddha was approached by his foster-mother, who pleaded that "it would be well, O Lord, if women should be allowed to

AJANTA CAVE TEMPLE. BUDDHIST.

To face p. 287.

renounce their homes and enter the homeless state under the doctrine and discipline explained by Tathāgata." Buddha consented, but he said: "Under whatsoever doctrine and discipline women are allowed to go forth from the household life into the homeless state that religion will not last."

Five hundred women were at one time admitted by Buddha to the Order, and, according to the Culla Vagga "thus the order of Nuns was firmly established and waxed in numbers in one place and another, in village, town, country, and royal city. Matrons, daughters-in-law, and maidens hearing the wisdom of Buddha, the Law and the Order rejoiced at his system, and feeling terror at the prospect of continuous rebirth joined the Order."

Mrs. Rhys Davids has held that under Buddhism "the bereaved mother, the childless widow, are emancipated from grief and contumely, the Magdalen from remorse, the wife of rajah or rich man from the ennui of an idle life of luxury, the poor man's wife from care and drudgery, the young girl from the humiliation of being handed over to the suitor who bids highest, the thoughtful woman from the ban imposed upon her intellectual development by conventional tradition." [1]

As a natural result of this admission of women the Buddhist monks made love to the new comers, who were on several occasions indignant. Matters came to a crisis when one woman of the clan of the Mallas "seeing a weakly Bikshu on the road struck up against him with

[1] *Buddhist Review*, July, 1909.

the edge of her shoulder and knocked him over." This case and other cases were brought before Buddha, who directed that for the future the Buddhist men should not make love to the women, and that the women should get out of the way and make room for the men.

Although women were tolerated in the Buddhist Church, nevertheless "we find the women of India all the more zealously engaged as fellow-labourers through charity, assistance, and service in those practical spheres which the young Church opened up for religious usefulness. The stupendous munificence which met the Buddhist Order at every step, proceeded in great measure, perhaps in the greatest measure, from women."[1]

Mrs. Manning, in her valuable book on Ancient India, wrote that in India "women in poems appear as forest trees flowering in wild luxuriance, whilst women in real life resemble flowering pears and peaches nailed against the wall." Certainly women in the epic and dramatic poetry of India stand out vividly in the wild luxuriance of free and unfettered action. They choose their lovers from those who have done heroic deeds in brilliant scenes of contest between rival wooers. They place garlands on the victor's neck, and thus freely choose him as a husband. Arrian, writing from the accounts of Nearchus and of Megasthenes, who was Greek Ambassador at the Court of Chandra Gupta from 306 to 298 B.C., gives the account of real life in describing these contests: "As many of their young women as

[1] "Buddha," Oldenberg, p. 167.

they deem marriageable are brought forth by their parents into a public place, where he who wins the prize at wrestling, boxing, or running, or any proposed exercise, chooses her for bride who pleases him best."

Still, the poets of the epics and dramas of India must have woven from a synthesis of reality their ideal pictures of the periods they depict. The epic Mahābhārata tells the story, so often mistranslated into English verse, of Draupadī, the common wife of five Pāndava brothers. The eldest brother of the five staked Draupadī as a wager on a single throw of the dice. He lost the wager, and Draupadī. The other brothers exclaimed in wrath, "O, elder brother, gamblers have in their houses many slave women, they do not stake these women having kindness for them." Draupadī is then dragged away by her captor, and subjected to indescribable insults.

The story of the gentle, long-suffering Sītā, the wife of Rāma, is told in the second great epic of India, the Rāmāyana. The story is one that has aroused the love and pity of many generations of Indian women, as they listen to the moving sound of the stately Sanskrit telling how Sītā was carried off by the deceit of the fierce demon, Rāvana, and of all her sufferings in the demon's stronghold in Lanka, or Ceylon, and of her gentle resignation under the loss of the love of her husband, Rāma.

In the well-known drama of S'akuntalā, by India's greatest poet, Kālidāsa, the King Dushyanta fails to recognize his wife, S'akuntalā, after she had lost the token of recognition, a ring he had given her. The words of S'akuntalā, in her sorrow at not being recognized by her husband, give the ideal picture of a faithful Hindu wife. She pleads that: "The wife is man's half. The wife is the first of friends. The wife is the root of virtue, wealth, and pleasure. The wife is the root of salvation. Sweet-speeched wives are ever near in times of joy. They are ministering helps in hours of sickness and sorrow. . . . A wife, therefore, is man's most treasured wealth. No man, even in his anger, should do aught that is displeasing to his wife, for on her depends happiness, joy, and virtue." To relieve the tenseness of the situation, and to quench the tears of the spectators when the drama is acted, the usual poetic device of a relief is immediately introduced by the King's words: "Women generally speak untruths. Who shall believe in thy words?"

The wave of Mughal and Muhammadan invasions of India had a deep-felt influence on the position of woman in India. A widespread system of polygamy was introduced as well as the Zenana system, which reacted on the Hindu population so as to lead to a custom of seclusion of women, partly in self-defence, partly in imitation of the alien conquerors. The Emperor Akbar, who reigned from 1556 to 1605, is said to have inculcated monogamy, but as his Vizier, Abul Fazl, wrote: "There is a great inconvenience arising from the number of his Majesty's wives, but his Majesty,

THE TAJ MAHAL.

To face p. 291.

out of the abundance of his wisdom and prudence, has made it subservient to public advantage; for by contracting marriages with the daughters of the princes of Hindustan and of other countries, he secures himself against insurrection at home and from powerful alliances abroad." He is said to have held that "a man should marry four wives. A Persian woman to have some one to talk to, a Khorasani woman to do the house work, a Hindu woman for nursing the children, and a Turkistan woman to have some one to whip as a warning to the other three."

Sir Thomas Roe was Ambassador from James I to the Court of Jahāngīr, who reigned from 1605 to 1607. He wrote of Nur Jahān, the wife of the Emperor, that "coins were struck bearing her name, as did also the great seal affixed to the Imperial patents. By degrees she became supreme in the empire. The Emperor used to say that she was capable of conducting all affairs, and that all he wanted was a joint and a bottle of wine to keep him merry." When Jahāngīr was captured by a rebel, the Empress Nūr Jahān, known as Nūr Mahāl, took the field and fought until three elephant drivers were killed in front of her and her elephant wounded; she retreated firing arrows into the enemy and encouraging her troops. The most wondrous tomb the world has ever seen—the Taj Mahal—was erected by the Emperor Shah Jahān for his wife, Arjamund Banu Begum Most of the Muhammadans of the present day have only one wife, and it has been held that 95 per cent.

of Muhammadans are now monogamists, and that "it is earnestly to be hoped that before long a general synod of Moslem doctors will authoritatively declare that polygamy, like slavery, is abhorrent to the laws of Islam." [1]

Under Muhammadanism a wife's property and possessions are her own. The Prophet declared: "May the curse of God rest on him who repudiates his wife capriciously."

Sir Lepel Griffin was of opinion that "it may fairly be asserted that the position of a married Muhammadan woman to-day is socially and legally more secure and protected against arbitrary violence either to person or property than that of an Englishwoman, whose disabilities until the last few years were a reproach to our civilization." [2]

As regards the Zenana system, which was adopted by respectable Hindus as a necessity, on the Muhammadan invasions, or copied as a sign of respectability, it has been held to be: "the last downward step, fatefully possible because of all that had gone before it, was the acceptance of the custom of secluding women of the upper castes in the women's apartments and cutting them off from all participation in public life." [3] Lady Dufferin, who in India had unique opportunities of forming an opinion on the matter, wrote that: "The

[1] See "Life and Teachings of Mohammed," Syed Ameer Ali.

[2] See Introduction, "Woman's Influence in the East," Poole.

[3] "The Crown of Hinduism," Farquhar, p. 101.

impressions I carried away from my visit to India were invariably pleasant ones. I have never seen women more sympathetic, more full of grace and dignity, more courteous or more successful in the art of giving a really cordial reception to a stranger than those I met behind the purdah." Her conclusion was: "I for my part consider that under the present condition of eastern life the Zenana system affords many undoubted advantages." The mass of the ordinary female population of Hindu India move about as freely as in the west. Nevertheless, "the first pretension to gentility consists in making the females of one's family *purdahnashins*." [1]

There can be no doubt, however, that the Zenana system has some practical disadvantages, as it prevents women from establishing their own individuality in the ordinary concerns of life. The risk a woman runs in being fraudulently represented by some one else in a purdahnashin system, where she cannot unveil her face, is illustrated in a case reported in *The Times* of June 3, 1915. The case was an appeal to the Judicial Committee of the Priory Council, and "Sir John Edge, in delivering judgment, said that the suit was brought to enforce, by sale of certain villages, payment of money due under a mortgage deed executed in 1892. The appellants alleged that the mortgage had not been properly attested. The mortgagors were two *purdahnashin* ladies who did not appear before the attesting witnesses, and consequently their faces were not seen

[1] Guru Prosad Sen, "The Study of Hinduism," p. 109.

by them. The latter were, however, well acquainted with their voices, and their Lordships were satisfied that they did identify the mortgagors when the deed was executed. The mortgagors on that occasion were brought from the *zenana* of the house in which they were to an ante-room to execute the deed. In the ante-room the ladies seated themselves on the floor, and between them and the two attesting witnesses there was a *chick*, or bamboo screen, which was not lined with cloth, hanging in the doorway. Those witnesses recognized the ladies by their voices, and said that they saw each lady execute the deed with her own hand, although owing to the *chick* they were unable to see their faces. On the other side an attempt was made to prove that a *tat*, through which nothing could be seen, was hanging in the doorway. Their Lordships accepted the evidence of these witnesses as true, and held it proved that the mortgage deed was duly attested within the meaning of the Transfer of Property Act, 1882. It was not disputed that the mortgage deed was in fact the deed of the two *purdahnashin* ladies."

The later Hindu period teems with women of commanding genius and ability. The Maratha widowed Queen, Ahalyā Baī, who died in 1795, was a woman who stands out alone in India as supreme for wisdom, piety, and incessant labour and good work. She raised Indore from a group of hovels to a wealthy city and in Mālwā she is still worshipped as a deity.

The custom of the seclusion of women has always

been relaxed in the case of ruling princesses. The Begum of Bhopal, Shah Jahān, before her marriage, always attended durbar in open court and administered justice. Her mother, the Sikandar Begum, ruled with inflexible will and skill. Sir Lepel Griffin was of opinion that "it would almost appear that the Phulkian chiefs excluded, by direct enactment, all women from any share of power from the suspicion that they were able to use it far more wisely than themselves."

Under British rule in India many problems respecting women have presented themselves for solution. In all cases in which reforms have been carried out they have been in accordance with the general concensus of educated opinion in India. It would be futile to assert that suicide under the strain of overwhelming calamities can be averted. In India the suicide of widows on their husband's death has been prohibited by law in conformity with not only Western but Indian demands. The suicide of a widow on the death of her husband may be explicable on the grounds of poignant grief, or in hopes of joining the departed in a future life. Mr. Farquhar has fairly stated this side of the question in saying of a Hindu widow: "Overwhelmed with grief, she does not want to live. The hard asceticism and lonely misery of widowhood make the outlook all the darker. On the other hand, she has only to endure the pyre, and she will immediately have a rapturous reunion with her lord in heaven."[1] The first two questions which present

[1] "The Crown of Hinduism," p. 99.

themselves are: who reduces her to a hard asceticism and to a lonely widowhood? The only answer given is that it was the Brāhmanic lawmakers. The dire fate of a widow depends on the Brāhmanic soul doctrine. Under Brāhmanic ritual the widow on the death of her husband has herself passed out of life, all her prayers and all her tears can no longer bring aught to her soul but the bitter memory that she can no longer be of service to one she loved. She is brushed aside, and the care of the future progress of the deceased's soul is left, under Brāhmanic-made laws, to her infant son or to the nearest male relative. Here comes in the bitterness of the struggle for the widow, and there are many devout and noble souls of women in India of to-day who believe firmly that in quitting life they follow the course Brāhmanic tradition has laid down for them. Mr. Farquhar has recorded that, "Quite recently, near Calcutta, a bereaved wife, in the exaltation of her anguish, determinedly burned herself in her own room at the very time when the body of her husband was being consumed on the pyre. When such a case occurs, the Hindu community thrills with sympathy and reverence. The old religious ideas have by no means lost all their force."[1]

"Sati," means the woman who is, who exists, as perfect woman; therefore it has been said that: "She who dies for her husband is also called Sati in a more special sense. . . . It is this last proof of the perfect unity of

[1] Op. cit. p. 99.

body and soul, this devotion beyond the grave, which Western critics have chosen as our reproach. They were right in attaching so much importance to it; we only differ from them in thinking of our Satis with unchangeable respect and love, rather than pity."[1]

The same spirit lives in the stories of Sir Rabindranath Tagore, where "the devotion and the heroism of the Hindu wife he paints are of a kind to explain to us that though the mortal rite of Sati is ended, the spirit that led to it is not at all extinct. It lies re-embodied in a thousand acts of sacrifice, and in many a delivering up of the creature-self, and its pride of life and womanly desire."[2]

In India of to-day 17 per cent. of the total female population are widows, and of these one-third of a million are under fifteen years of age. Under orthodox Hindu custom marriage is a religious sacrament, and accordingly 48 per cent. of the total female population is married of which 7 per cent. are classed, in the Census Report, as widows.

The Indian point of view holds that under the forced Western stress of life, "In actual fact some 75 per cent. of Western graduate women do not marry; and certainly, industrial conditions on the one hand, and devotion to social pleasures (or duties) on the other, more and more unfit a majority of women for efficient motherhood." [3]

[1] "Sati: A Vindication of Hindu Women," by A. K. Coomaraswamy, Paper, Sociological Society, London, 1912, p. 7.

[2] "Rabindranath Tagore," Ernest Rhys, p. 57.

[3] Coomaraswamy, op. cit. p. 6.

The problem of existence was solved for woman in India by Brāhmanism, which asserted that she has no individuality apart from her husband, and that on his death she had best blot herself out of existence and be applauded for so doing. No human being could maintain that this is a reasoned view of life, or that it is one which could appeal to any intuitive feelings of human nature. A solution has been given for this sad lot of a Hindu widow which dooms her to a perpetual loneliness of widowhood, if not to death. The most renowned lawgiver, after Manu, is Yājñavalkya, with the authoritative commentary thereon, the Mitākshara, by Vignēsvara, of the eleventh or twelfth century. This law book rules supreme in Bengal, Mithila, and in West, and even in parts of South, India. It decrees "that the wealth of a regenerate man is designed for religious purposes and a woman's succession to such property is unfit, because she is not competent for the performance of religious rites." The widow, however, under the decrees of another authority, Kātyāyana, could "enjoy with moderation the property of her deceased husband until her death. After her death let the heirs take it. But she has not property therein to the extent of gift, mortgage, or sale." In order to prevent the retention of the property in the hands of the widow, it was held that she must, under the authority of the Vedic text, go into the fire and commit suicide. The property then passed to the male heirs, who had fuller discretion to expend it on religious sacrifices for the supposed benefit of the soul of the deceased and for the real benefit of the officiating Brāhman priests. If this be the real explanation of the unnatural crime of widow-burning, and one can only hope that it is not, it is the most tragic instance of the woes which a priesthood can inflict, not only on women but on mankind. Other more practical reasons have been suggested for the practice of widow-burning. A French traveller, Bernier, who gives a vivid description of his life in India from 1656 to 1668, stated that: "Many persons whom I consulted on the subject would fain have persuaded me that an excess of affection was the cause why these women burn themselves with their deceased husbands, but I soon found out that this abominable practice is the effect of early and deep-rooted prejudices. Every girl is taught by her mother that it is virtuous and laudable in a wife to mingle her ashes with those of her husband. . . . These opinions men have always inculcated as an easy mode of keeping women in subjection, of securing their attention in times of sickness and of deterring them from administering poison to their husbands." Referring to the Brāhman priests who performed the funeral rites, Bernier wrote: "I have not yet mentioned all the barbarity or atrocity of these monsters. In some parts, instead of burning the women the Brāhmans bury the widows alive by slow degrees."

Many efforts were made under Muhammadan rule to prohibit the custom of widow-burning. No woman was allowed to sacrifice herself without permission from the ruler of the province where the widow resided, and unless the widow insisted on receiving permission it was always refused.

Under the Portuguese administration of their territories more decisive steps were taken to prohibit the custom. In the Commentaries of Affonso De Albuquerque, which were copied from despatches sent to King Dom Emmanuel, it is narrated that: "If any Hindu died his wife had to burn herself of her own freewill, and when she was proceeding to this self-sacrifice it was with great merry-making and blowing of music, saying that she desired to accompany her husband to the other world. . . . However, when Affonso De Albuquerque took the city of Goa he forbade from that time forth that any more women should be burned, and though to change one's custom is equal to death itself, nevertheless they were happy to save their lives, and spoke very highly of him because he had ordered that there should be no more burning."

The feeling against widow-burning had grown so universal, especially after it had been vigorously denounced by Ram Mohan Roy, that in 1829, under the government of Lord Bentinck, it was declared to be illegal in British India. Public opinion had advanced so far in favour of the remarriage of widows, an opinion that was swayed much by the learned advocacy of the Sanskrit scholar Chandra Vidyāsāgara, that the Act XV of 1856 was passed, declaring that: "No marriage contracted with Hindus shall be invalid (and no issue of such marriage shall be illegitimate) by reason of the woman having been previously married or betrothed." Girls in Hindu India are betrothed at the age of three or four, but this is imperfect and revocable until the real ceremony of marriage takes place by the bride and bridegroom taking seven steps together, the last step marking the marriage. On marriage, the bride enters the joint-family of her husband, and on her husband's death—and in higher castes even if he die between the betrothal and marriage—her status becomes that of a widow. Her hair then cut off, the bracelet on her arm broken, she is viewed as an omen of ill luck, to be avoided on all festive occasions. Public opinion revolted against the early age at which a bride was taken to her husband's house, and the custom was denounced publicly by Keshab Chandra Sen, with the result that in 1891 the Government of Lord Lawrence passed a Marriage Act, that the age of marriage for a bride should be raised to twelve.

Education—in the Western use of the term "education" —of women in India can hardly be said to be within the contemplation of any orthodox Hindu family. The Hindu family is still based on patriarchal ideas. It is knit together by a sacred duty of father to son and of wife to husband. In such a condition of family life Western modes of thought clash with the ideals of an Eastern stereotyped condition of society. They tend to loosen the bonds of filial piety and the devotion of wife to husband. They have no respect for the seclusion of the zenana and the pride which veils the sacred traditions of family life from the obtrusive scrutiny of the surrounding village-folk.

In Hindu India, so sacred is the husband to his wife that she dare not mention his name in public, and so jealous is the husband of the privacy of his wife's good fame and honour that to express to him the Western greeting of hope that all is well at home is an insult resented by even the humblest villager. The portals of family life in India are closed to the foreigner as much as are the portals of the Hindu temples, for within the joint-family many families combine—husbands, sons, and wives living under a bond of sacerdotal sanction over which preside the gods and forefathers and the revered traditions of past generations. As regards the education of women in India, the Abbé Dubois wrote in 1817 that: "The immodest girls who are employed in the worship of the idols . . . are the only women taught to read, to sing, and to dance. It would be thought the mark of an irregular education if a modest woman were found capable of reading. She herself would conceal it out of shame. As to the dance, it is confined entirely to the profligate girls, who never mix in it with the men." The last Census Report, of 1913, states that there are only ten females per thousand of the population able to write or read a simple letter from a friend; the number for men is 106 per thousand.

No secular system of Western education can solve the problem of woman in India. It may implant in the son less reverence for the authority of the father and forefathers, but it has not yet weakened the devotion of the wife to the husband nor the belief of the mother that in the birth of a son she has joyously fulfilled the inscrutable dictates of nature and won the favour of the gods. It has not yet crushed the last remnant of hope in the soul of the long-suffering widow that her willing service in the household may assuage somewhat of her misery and perchance help the soul of her departed lord in its progress through the unknown. Western systems of education, if introduced into the family life of India void of all that makes that family life instinct with filial piety and womanly devotion, may result in disquietude and unrest, and in implanting in a coming generation defiance of all authority, divine or temporal. At present, although the joint-family is knit together in a sacerdotal bond of union, yet year by year there is an increase in the number of those who apply for a partition of the joint-family property on the death of the head of the family, the eldest male representative. This alone indicates a disruption of the basis on which the whole social life of India rests.

It has been urged, in defence of the ideals the past traditions of India have nurtured in the hearts of her women, that in the joint-family the influence of woman exercises a subtle spell over those who are within the inner sanctuary, where it reigns supreme. Dr. Coomaraswamy says,[1] "I cannot

[1] Op. cit. p. 2.

emphasize too strongly the fact of this influence of mothers in India, not merely over children and in household matters, but over grown-up men, to whom their word is law. One might almost say that the Native States are ruled by the queen-mothers from behind the purdah."

The reaction against some of the tendencies of Western civilization is plainly indicated in the words of the same artistic idealist where he says: "The social power of the Indian woman is already reduced, wherever industrial modes of thought have penetrated. What power remains tends to pass away from the mother and the widow to more conspicuous and self-assertive types. Another fifty years of education in India and the Indian mother will have no more hold over her grown-up sons than the European mother has now."

The ideal woman, in the thought of India, has been depicted, north and south, from the earliest ages much as she is viewed to-day. In the Mahābhārata the perfect woman is she who is gentle and views her husband as her ideal. She should rise early, serve the gods, attend to the house and sacred domestic fire, be devoted to her parents and to the parents of her husband. Such is her honour, such is her virtue. In South India, the author of the Kural, in lamenting over the death of his wife, said: "When I have lost a woman who excelled in the knowledge of the house, who was devoted to all duties of the house, who never opposed my word nor transgressed my door, who soothed me, and never

ZENANA.

To face p. 304.

slept before I slept, nor rose before I rose; woe is me! I can never again close my eyes in sleep."

In the middle of the eighth century the Tamil Nāladiyār describes the ideal wife as: "The wife is she who, although want is in the home, when relations come to feast enough to drain an ocean, gently welcomes all and shines as the goddess of the house." Again, another verse says: "The wife is she who is gentle-voiced, proud when need be, yet winning in pleasant places. She is devoted to her husband and fitly adorned for his love. She is fair to look upon and her gentle nature brings shame to the village-folk." Womanhood is worshipped, in South India, as the vitalizing force of the universe, joined half-and-half with the god S'iva, with whom united, they dance the dance of creation, life, and death.

The ideal of womanhood in India of to-day has been eloquently described in the words: "Despite the crushing weight of patriarchal authority and all its pitiable results, the Hindu home hides some very beautiful things. The faithfulness, devotion, and love of the wife and mother, the humility and willing ministry of the broken-hearted widow, the obedience and affection of the sons and daughters, even when grown up, the subdued joy and shady retirement of the zenana, the sacramental note present always and everywhere—these are things of real worth and beauty, exquisite as a bed of scented violets in an English forest glade." [1]

[1] "The Crown of Hinduism," Farquhar, p. 102.

In such a position it may be well to remember the words of Bacon, that: "It were good that men in their innovations would follow the example of Time itself, which, indeed, innovateth greatly, but quietly, and by degrees scarce to be perceived."

CHAPTER XII

PRESENT INDIAN THOUGHT

LORD MORLEY, in a memorable speech before the House of Lords, stated that in India: "We are watching a great and stupendous process, the reconstruction of a decomposed society. What we found was described as a parallel to Europe in the fifth century, and we have now, as it were, before us, in that vast congeries of people we call India, a long, slow march in uneven stages through all the centuries from the fifth to the twentieth. Stupendous indeed, and to guide that transition with sympathy, duty, and national honour, may well be called a glorious mission."

Hinduism as a caste system tends to tie down to ancestral custom the daily life, habits, and social ordinances of the people. Nevertheless, Hinduism as a creed is pliant and wide enough in its scope to admit of any vivifying influences with which it may be brought into contact. It absorbed the best of Buddhism, and emerged from those influences revived and ameliorated. As a social system Hinduism "is primarily supposed to be based on birth and hereditary occupation; but hereditary occupation no longer exists, and there is nothing in the nature of things to prevent a man, plebeian born, from rising as high in the social scale, in the European sense, as he can. Examples of this, under the benign British Government, are numerous; but at no time, perhaps, was there anything like an interdict to their rising in this sense. All castes afford authentic instances of the rise of some of their individual members, dating from the remotest times."[1]

Hinduism as a creed remains plastic to outside influences, for, as a recent Census Report states, it includes "a complex congeries of creeds and doctrines. It shelters within its portals monotheists, polytheists, and pantheists; worshippers of the gods Vishṇu and S'iva or their female counterparts . . . and a host of more or less heterodox sectaries, many of whom deny the supremacy of the Brāhmans, or at least have non-Brāhmanical religious leaders." The influence of Western civilization and thought on the educated and thinking classes was first shown by the formation of the Brāhma Samāj in 1828 by Ram Mohan Roy. This movement was a protest against gross idolatry and against the sacrificing of animals in religious functions. It was further a protest against such worn out relics of a bygone past as the burning of widows, the custom of prohibiting the remarriage of women once betrothed,

[1] Guru Prosad Sen, "Study of Hinduism," p. 162.

or married and left widowed, and against polygamy. Ram Mohan Roy, however, held firm to the Vēdas, and as a Brāhman taught that the Supreme God was the Brahman of the Vēdānta. He was succeeded by Devendranath Tagore, who, from 1841 to 1872, was the guiding light and presiding spirit of the Samāj, which afterwards continued as the Ādi, or First, Dharma Samāj. The conservative instinct of Hinduism, based as it was on the Vēdānta, was laid bare, and was first apparent in an inaugural address which Devendranath Tagore delivered before he joined the Brāhma Samāj in 1842. Here he said that English education had dispelled the darkness of ignorance and that the people no longer worshipped stocks and stones believing them to be divine. He pleaded that the God of the Vēdānta is "formless, the very essence of intelligence, omnipresent, beyond all thought or speech." Therefore, he said, "if the Vēdānta were spread far and wide, then we would never feel drawn to other religions. That is why we are thus trying to preserve our Hindu religion."[1] Devendranath Tagore uses words which have been described as "singularly reminiscent of St. Paul"[2] when he narrates his full awakening to the realization of the Infinite. Seekers after God, he says, must seek Him within their own souls, must seek Him in the universe without and in the abode of Brahma, where he exists by Himself. "By His grace," he said, "I have now come to believe that

[1] Autobiography, p. 65. [2] Ibid., Introduction, p. xv.

the Yogi who can see this Trinity of His at one and the same time, and see that while existing in Himself He exists in the hearts of us all, while existing in Himself He exists outside us all, and exists in Himself, self-contained and self-conscious, time without end, he is the true Yogi . . . he is the foremost amongst those that worship Brahma."[1]

To some it may seem that in the dreams of Devendranath Tagore were the first glimpses of the mingling of the East and West, to culminate in a "new religion for India—it may be for the whole world—a religion free from many corruptions of the past, call them idolatry or caste, or verbal inspiration or priest-craft, and firmly founded on a belief in the One God, the same in the Vēdas, the same in the Old, the same in the New Testament, the same in the Koran, the same also in the hearts of those who have no longer Vēdas or Upanishads, or any sacred books whatever between themselves and their God. The stream is small as yet, but it is a living stream."[2]

Reverence for the past traditions of India, the belief that India can work out its own spiritual regeneration, inspired the mystic sage, Devendranath Tagore, to appeal to his own people : "Where else can the children of the poor receive education except in mission schools? But is not this a crying shame? In order to spread their own religion the Christians have set at naught the waves of the deep sea, and entering India, are founding schools

[1] Op. cit. p. xvi. [2] Max Müller, "Biographical Essays," p. 83.

in every town and every village. . . . If we all combine, could we not set up schools as good as theirs or ten times better?"[1]

The flowing tide of Western influences almost seemed destined to submerge Hinduism when in 1866 Keshab Chandra Sen strove to lead the Brāhma Samāj towards a propaganda for the abolition of all distinctions of race, class, or creed. Of all the eloquent addresses of Keshab Chandra Sen, perhaps the best known is that in which he mingled Christian ideals with Eastern modes of thought in saying: "None but Jesus, none but Jesus, none but Jesus ever deserved this bright, this precious diadem, India, and Jesus shall have it. . . . Christ is a true Yogi."

Again, in a lecture in 1865, he said that "in Christ we see not only the exaltedness of humanity, but also the grandeur of which Asiatic nature is susceptible. To us Asiatics, therefore, Christ is doubly interesting, and His religion is entitled to our peculiar regard. And thus in Christ, Europe and Asia, the East and the West, may learn to find harmony and unity."

In these perfervid utterances the East and West are visioned as meeting in one common stream of thought. On the one side were arrayed the forces equipped by Western modes of thought, infused with the best of Greek, Roman, and Semitic civilizations and their views of the universe. The West had further an equipment of knowledge of ascertained facts and scientific

[1] Autobiography, p. 99.

truths. The East had dreamed its dream of life, satisfied that by its own intuitive genius it had solved all things. If this were so, then India had to fall back on its only defence, and that was the Vedic revelation. If the Vēdas were revealed by God as absolute knowledge from before all times, then why should India seek further, or why should she weary her soul? The Brāhmans of India were alone the chosen people of God. To the Brāhmans alone God had revealed all His wisdom, and in the Books of Wisdom, or Vēdas, there was knowledge that could ignore all the encroaching assaults on the dream of rest in Brahman that brooded over the land.

Many would gladly close the doors to any influences awakening unrest of thought in India, and leave the East to dream of absolute content in its own peaceful surroundings, free from struggle and strife. India, however, cannot refuse to accept the summons from the West to join in the increase and advancement of knowledge and in all efforts for the amelioration of the social and moral surroundings of mankind. The West has never sought to force any of its modes of thought regarding the universe, or religion, on India. For weal or woe India has leavened the best of its educated and intellectual thought with the best the West holds as ideals and as ascertained facts. India will inevitably mould all these factors into its own traditional aspirations towards some satisfying solutions of the why and wherefore of the universe, as well as for the improvement of its present material surroundings. Vast vested interests

The whole of the religious and social life of India was centred round the Brāhman. His influence spread from the council chambers of ruling princes to the inner sanctuary of Hindu domestic life. It is said that now: "The divine right by birth of the Brāhman is fast melting away. The monopoly of the Brāhman in administering religious sacraments and in performing religious ceremonies is being slowly but imperceptibly undermined. Even in unlettered circles his authority is being questioned."[1]

If this be so, India must replace the decaying power of the Brāhman by some authority with sanctions strong enough to uphold the religious aspirations of the educated classes and compel the moral and social regeneration of the masses. The widest spread indigenous tendency of to-day is to build up a new spiritual and social life for India on the basis of the revelation of the Vēdas and Vēdānta. This was the motive force which inspired the burning zeal of Dayananda Svāmi to cut himself adrift from the idolatry and caste restrictions of orthodox Hinduism and seek refuge in Vedic authority as the true and only salvation for India. A new life for India, inspired, on its religious side at least, by this ideal is the solution which is hoped for by over one quarter of a million of the adherents of the Arya Samāj. It is a belief which in recent years has spread throughout the educated and professional classes of the Punjāb and the United Provinces, as well

[1] Lajpat Rai, op. cit. p. 68.

as in Central India, Bombay, and Rajputana. It is a movement for a revival of Hinduism, wherein, as Sir Herbert Risley has said, "touched by reforming zeal and animated by patriotic enthusiasm, Christianity is likely to find a formidable obstacle to its spread among the educated classes."[1]

The Arya Samāj was founded by Dayananda Svāmi at Bombay in 1875 and at Lahore in 1877. Dayananda, with the cry of "Back to the Vēdas," void of idolatry, has been styled the reforming Luther of Hinduism. His father was a Brāhman, a worshipper of S'iva, learned in the Vēdas, and upholder of all the traditions and proud claims of his Brāhmanic birthright. Dayananda was born in 1842 at Morvi, in Kathiawar, Guzerat. Like all reforming saints and sages in India, his thoughts from his earliest youth seemed to have surged with unrest, disquiet, and vague hopes and aspirations.

There must be some solution for the "malady of thought" which seems at times to rage unceasingly in the mind of genius, "often akin to madness." For some such minds there is the seclusion of the monastic cell or a wandering life of unrest. For others, there are the mystic raptures of an all-satisfying love in spiritual emotions realized in devotion to a spiritual ideal. To many others, such as Buddha and Dayananda, there comes the determination to tear from out the universe the meaning of the mystery wrapped in the hearts of men, in the moan of the wind, and in the ineffable

[1] "People of India," pp. 244–5.

peace given in a communion with the heavens, with nature, and with all creation.

Dayananda set forth on his reforming mission to find if in the treasured lore of India there was not a record revealing the ways of God to man. At the age of fourteen he turned from the image of S'iva in the temple and proclaimed that it was an idol set up by man wherein there was not even a shred of divinity capable of preventing the mice from eating the holy food set before the god. At the age of nineteen he left his father's home, changed his name, so that none might know who he was or whence he came, and none of his family ever knew anything of him afterwards. From 1840 to 1875 he wandered throughout India. The language he spoke was Sanskrit, and the peace he sought was in the life of the Yogi and Sanyasi, wrapped in meditation and contemplation as taught by the Sānkhya-Yoga. Soon the news ran through the learned Brāhmanic holy places of India that one learned in the Vēdas, a speaker of Sanskrit, a Brāhman of the Brāhmans, an adept in the deepest mysteries of the Yoga, was wandering through the land denouncing the divinity of the Brāhmans, crying out against the idolatry in the temples, and preaching a common brotherhood of all men, irrespective of all caste restrictions. Dayananda's knowledge of Vedic Sanskrit and of the Vēdas was derided by the pandits of Benares. He was persecuted and stoned, and is said to have met his death by poison given to him in 1883 in Ajmere by a courtezan whose mode of life he had censured. After his

ELEPHANTA CAVE TEMPLE.

To face p. 316.

death the Arya Samāj erected, to his memory, the Dayananda Anglo-Vedic College at Lahore, an educational indigenous enterprise which was afterwards followed by the famous Gurukula, the teaching monastery of the more conservative body of the Arya Samāj, at Hardwar. The teaching institutions founded by the Samāj, with the object of diffusing knowledge and dispelling ignorance, have spread rapidly in recent years, until now, although "Christian missions maintain a large number of schools of all kinds, no single mission can claim to have as many schools for boys and girls as the Arya Samāj."[1] The Arya Samāj bases its reform of Hinduism on the infallible authority of the Vēdas as teaching a spiritual doctrine with an inspiring standard of ethics. Dayananda's faith was: "He who is called Brahm or the Most High, who is Parmātma, or the Spirit who penetrates the whole universe; who is Truth, Intelligence, and Happiness; whose nature, attributes, and characteristics are holy; who is omniscient, formless, all-pervading, unborn, infinite, almighty, just, and merciful; who is the author of the universe, sustains and dissolves it; who awards all souls the fruits of their deeds in strict accordance with the requirements of absolute justice; and who is possessed of other like attributes—even *Him* I believe to be the Lord of Creation."[2] Dayananda held that the four Vēdas were the source of all knowledge, that they are direct revelations from God. They are therefore in-

[1] "Arya Samaj," Lajpat Rai, p. 179.

[2] Op. cit. p. 82.

fallible. They can contain no error, and they form the only one and true source of all religion. All commentaries on the Vēdas, all recensions of the varied schools of Vedic teaching, are to be rejected if they do not conform to the revelation of the Vēdas. Dayananda held that there were three things which existed from all eternity: God, the soul, and Prakriti—that is, the material element of creation. God and the soul can never become one and the same. God pervades everything and pervades the soul. Therefore God and the soul are ever inseparable but distinct one from the other, the soul resting in God just as a material thing rests in space. No eternal salvation by union of the soul with God is possible. The soul may for a time gain freedom from ignorance and from the pains and sufferings of the body, but then, after enjoying such freedom for a time, it has again to assume a body. In the Census Report for the United Provinces of 1911, it is stated by Mr. Blunt that the attitude of the Arya Samāj is far more iconoclastic than eclectic to Christianity, and: "I am unable to see in its history or principles any warrant for the belief held by many missionaries that the Aryas will end by becoming Christians."

The Arya Samāj bases its faith on an infallible Vēda, as infallible as the Koran or Pentateuch. The interpretation of the true meaning of the Vedic Sanskrit, in which the Vēdas are written, presents in many cases almost insurmountable difficulties. The Arya Samāj does not assert that Dayananda's translation of the Vēdas is infallible; in fact, as Mr. Lajpat Rai acknowledges:[1] "It would take centuries of hard work and incessant care before anything like a complete and thoroughly intelligent translation of the Vēdas could be made."

Max Müller, whose life-work was devoted to the study and interpretation of the Vēda, held that: "By the most incredible interpretations Svāmi Dayananda succeeded in persuading himself and others that everything worth knowing, even the most recent inventions of modern science, were alluded to in the Vēdas. Steam-engines, railways, and steamboats all were shown to have been known, at least in their germs, to the poets of the Vēdas, for Vēda, he argued, means divine knowledge, and how could anything have been hid from that."[2]

The most daring of all Dayananda's reforms, and one which has received the most bitter denunciations from Christian missionaries, was the inculcation of the practice of Niyoga. The 47th of his Beliefs was that of Niyoga, which "is a temporary union of a person with another of the opposite sex belonging to his or her plane, for the raising of issue when marriage has failed to fulfil its legitimate purpose." It is resorted to in extreme cases, either on the death of one's consort or in protracted disease. In the Sattyārth Prakāsha of Dayananda there is a definite catechism of questions and answers on this question of Niyoga, over which the Arya Samāj is at present not united in opinion. The system is an effort to sanction temporary unions

[1] Op. cit. p. 98. [2] "Biographical Essays," p. 170.

as a recognized principle of moral law. The following quotations are from p. 113 to p. 122 of the Sattyārth Prakāsha, published at the Mufid-i-Am Press, Lahore, without date. Here it is stated that it is sinful to abstain from Niyoga connections, as abstinence cannot be practised "except in case of those who leave the world, or acquire perfect knowledge, or practice Yoga." A second marriage is impossible for Brāhmans, Kshatriyas, and Vais'yas, because the prospect of its being feasible would diminish "the natural love between man and woman," and, "if a woman marries a second time after the death of her first husband the property of the first husband will run to waste and quarrels will spring up between herself and the relatives of her deceased husband." Therefore the temporary Niyoga is made between man and woman, who "shall declare as follows in the presence of members of their family: 'we are going to enter into the Niyoga connection for the purpose of raising issue. When that purpose is fulfilled we will separate from one another.'" When a husband is unable to have children he should say, "O good wife, you should now seek another husband"; and if the wife is incapacitated through disease or otherwise she should say to her husband, "Enter into Niyoga with some widow and produce issue from her." If a wife has only female children she may be left at the end of the eleventh year, but "if she be quarrelsome then the man may leave her without delay and enter into a Niyoga connection." "Similarly, if the husband be very troublesome then the wife shall leave him and enter into the Niyoga connection with another man," but if she then has children they inherit the property of her real husband, and "as the real son is entitled to the property of his father so also is the son born of Niyoga connection."

After the Niyoga union has resulted in the birth of two children the man and woman should separate. Dayananda, however, held that the Vēdas enjoin the production of ten sons by a man and the same number by a woman in a Niyoga union, but "a widow may produce two sons for herself and two for each of four other men . . . and a widower may similarly produce two sons for himself and two for each of four widows." The Niyoga union may extend for one man with eleven women, and likewise for a woman with eleven men. It may seem to many impossible to discover any reasoned system of ethical teaching or of practical utility underlying such a reformation of sex relations by the temporary union of widows and widowers and even others. There can be no doubt that Dayananda sought to build up a new India with a virile race, and that he sought to do so on a religious basis established on Vedic authority. We are told that, "even in the Arya Samāj there is much divergence of opinion on the question. Some are thoroughly in favour of second marriages; others accept Niyoga in theory, but at the same time hold that it cannot be practised in modern conditions of life." [1]

[1] Lajpat Rai, op. cit. p. 147.

There is no doubt that Dayananda dreaded the spread of Christianity, and that he strove to set up a bulwark of defence against its inroads in an Indian monotheism and in purging Hinduism of its idolatry and caste restrictions. Religious differences, child marriage, lack of self-restraint, and neglect of an indigenous education rooted in the Vēdas he held to be fetters on Hindu India, which he believed could never be "perfectly happy" until it rose to a united ideal of patriotism.

The missionary efforts of Dayananda were to rally India against the advancing inroads of Christianity, and to seek defence for her own traditional line of thought as divinely inspired by the Vēdas. He denounced Muhammadans and Christians alike as disruptive forces amid the whole social and religious life of India. He denounced the killing of the cow, as the cow was ever held sacred by Hindus and its killing has always been a cause of bitter feuds and sanguinary contests between Hindus and all others of a different belief.

Mr. Blunt, in the Census Report of 1911, held that "the type of man to whom the Arya doctrine appeals is the type of man to whom politics appeals, viz. the educated man who desires his country's progress, not ultra conservative with the ultra conservatism of the East. . . . It is therefore not surprising that there are politicians among the Arya Samāj. But it is impossible to deduce from this that the Arya Samāj, as a whole, is a political body. From the first the

Samāj has consistently affirmed that it is not concerned with politics."

The present Lieutenant Governor of the United Provinces, Sir James Meston, stated in 1913, on a visit to the Arya Samāj Gurukula at Hardwar, that "he wanted to meet a community which had been described in official papers as a source of infinite, terrible, and unknown danger," and that he had come to form his own opinion. His opinion, after inspecting the monastery, was that the Gurukula was one of the most original experiments carried on in the whole of India. It was "one of the most wonderful, interesting, and stimulating institutions: we have a band of ascetics devoted to their duty and working in the wilderness, following the traditions of the ancient Rishis, combined with the most modern scientific methods, and working practically for nothing; and a set of students of strong physique, obedient, loyal, thoughtful, devoted, extraordinarily happy, and extraordinarily well fed."

Another movement, that of Theosophy, has recently impressed the imagination of many. Inculcating as it does a universal Brotherhood and an investigation of all religions, especially Oriental, and of the occult powers said to be latent in man, it has won a wide following. Its Central Hindu College at Benares has done much for education, while its objects appeal to many Hindus. These objects are stated to be the "pointing out to each man the sufficiency of his own faith, and urging him to deepen and spiritualize his beliefs rather than to attack the forms preferred by others." [1]

In recent years Hinduism found its most zealous champion in Rāma Krishṇa Parama Hamsa, an ascetic who lived near Calcutta and inspired many of his disciples to travel all over India and Europe teaching that all forms of Hinduism, and all religions, lead to salvation, just as all rivers merge into the ocean. His defence of primitive Hinduism has led to a wide reaction in favour of popular idolatry and temple worship. Rāma Krishṇa Parama Hamsa, as stated by Max Müller, believed that the image of the goddess Kālī, in the temple near Calcutta, was his mother and the mother of the universe: "He believed it to be living and breathing and taking food out of his hand. After the regular forms of worship he would sit there for hours, singing hymns and talking and praying to her as a child to his mother, till he lost all consciousness of the outer world." His teachings were followed by his disciple Svāmi Vivēkānanda, who attracted large audiences to his lectures in England and America. In private conversation he always maintained a quiet confidence that "Indian thought, philosophical and spiritual, must once more go over and conquer the world." To his Guru the image of Kālī was a consecrated and living image of God, to Vivēkānanda in the worship of the idol: "We are struggling to get to the thing signified, to get beyond the material to

[1] "Theosophy," Mrs. Besant, p. 69.

the spiritual; the spirit is the goal not the matter. Forms, images, bells, candles, books, churches, temples, and all holy symbols are very good, very helpful to the growing plant of spirituality, but thus far and no farther." Here the re-action against Western modes of thought becomes pronounced. There are now over fourteen millions of Brāhmans in India. It has been stated by some observers of the present condition of India, that Brāhmanism has lost its ancestral prestige and power. Brāhmanism, however, still retains its own intellectual power which in the past has never failed to overcome the efforts that have been made for its disruption. India has gained much from the West, but the Brāhman has lost much of his past social influence and sacerdotal sanctity. A Brāhman, the Rao Sahib Joshi, recently said: "In former days when the Guru, or head priest, came to one's house people used to say: 'I bow to thee, the Guru; the Guru is Brahma; the Guru is Vishṇu; the Guru is S'iva; verily, the Guru is the sublime Brahma.' This idea, this respect, the secular English education shattered to pieces, and so the income and importance of the hereditary priests dwindled down."

In the opinion of the Rao Sahib, the result is that the people lose the ideals on which their religion was based and tend to become a race of sceptics.

Western civilization in a country of many varied forms of religious conceptions and belief, has had to view its function of an educative agency solely from the secular side, irrespective of any ethical or moral training based on a religious ideal. The whole social life of India is permeated and knit together by ideals. These ideals have been slowly and laboriously evolved through the intellect and imagination of its philosophers, poets, sages, and saints. The Indian student, forced for a livelihood to undergo a secular Western education, finds that the knowledge he acquires runs counter in many respects to the record and tradition of the religion of his forefathers and to the social surroundings of his own home life. The result has been, as Sir George Clarke, the Governor of Bombay, said in a speech lately, that parental authority is weakened, ethical consideration in matters of life are ignored, and "the restraints of ancient philosophies, which have unconsciously helped to shape the lives of millions in India who had only the dimmest knowledge of them, have disappeared from his mental horizon. There is nothing to take their place. Ancient customs, some of them salutary and ennobling, have come to be regarded as obsolete. No other customs of the better sort have come to take their place."

India, under British supremacy, is now secure from internal anarchy, and freed from the dread of devastating invading hosts. She is free to progress towards the gradual betterment of her already rapidly advancing material and social progress, as well as to the full realization of her spiritual ideals. India throughout the ages—even amid the turmoil and strife of conquering hordes—

has never been bereft of the fostering care of an Aryan civilization. Being mainly an agricultural country she possesses increasing sources of productive wealth. Under normal conditions, when freed from local famine, plague, and pestilence, her wealth and resources can be applied towards her material and intellectual advancement whereby she may contribute her quota to the spiritual and temporal benefit of all mankind.

Mr. Gokhale, a Chitpāvan Brāhman, an educationalist of great distinction, some ten years ago set before India an ideal wherein love and service for India, irrespective of all sectarian differences, might form the basis of a new religion. Herein Karma, or actions, instead of being devoted to self culture, as in Buddhism, would be devoted to India. India and its progress should be the highest ideal towards which the mind and soul could aspire. The society he founded for this object was called the society of "The Servants of India." It placed no spiritual ideals before its members; religion was to centre round the devotion of all effort for the amelioration of India, and towards the building up of "a higher type of character and capacity than is generally available at present." Under such an ideal each member of the Society is to become a missionary, seeking no personal gain, engaged in no occupation save preaching the cause of India "in a religious spirit." All efforts for furthering the moral and political advancement of India are to proceed on constitutional lines, for the Society accepts "the British connexion as ordained in the inscrutable dispensation of Providence for India's good."

Educated Indians of the present generation are intellectually far in advance of the mental equipment of those who came under Western influences in the past generation, and better fitted to weave into their own modes of thought and into their social organization all that they may find suited to their racial and climatic conditions.

The present generation takes a greater pride in being Hindus, and looks forward with higher aspirations to the future of India, than the past generation could have ever hoped for. The West neither longs for, nor desires, the abandonment by India of any of the best of its beliefs or traditions. England, as an Empire, has patiently and consistently carried on the work which destiny has entrusted to her.

The study of the thought of India in the past and the study of the changes that are taking place in the present is of more than passing interest to all concerned in her administration and future welfare. The study is not merely one of philosophic questioning and doubt, but a study that will enable the future to avoid some of the mistakes of the past and to realize the truth that " the most characteristic work of our Empire is the introduction in the midst of Brāhmanism of European views of the Universe. No experiment equally interesting is now being tried on the surface of the globe. And when we consider how seldom it [is put in the power of a nation to accomplish a task so memorable, we shall learn to take an eager interest in the progress of the experiment and to check the despondency which might lead us to ask what profit accrues to ourselves for all this labour that we have undertaken under the sun." [1]

[1] "Expansion of England," p. 284.

INDEX

Index

Index

Index

Index

Index

Index

Index

Index